DATE DUE

Strange Britain

Strange Britain

Charles Walker

Brian Trodd Publishing House Limited

Published in 1989 by
Brian Trodd Publishing House Limited
27 Swinton Street, London WC1X 9NW

ISBN 1 85361 078 X

Printed in Italy

Page 1: One of the 8th century Pictish stones set along the roadside at Aberlemno, Tayside. The meaning of the symbols is not known.
Title page: The Celtic wall above Smearsett, West Yorkshire, may be the substantial remains of a prehistoric fortification. The usual local legends say that the wall was built by giants.
Right: Old Mother Shipton, the witch, curiously casting a horoscope, although there is no evidence that she knew anything at all about astrology.

Contents

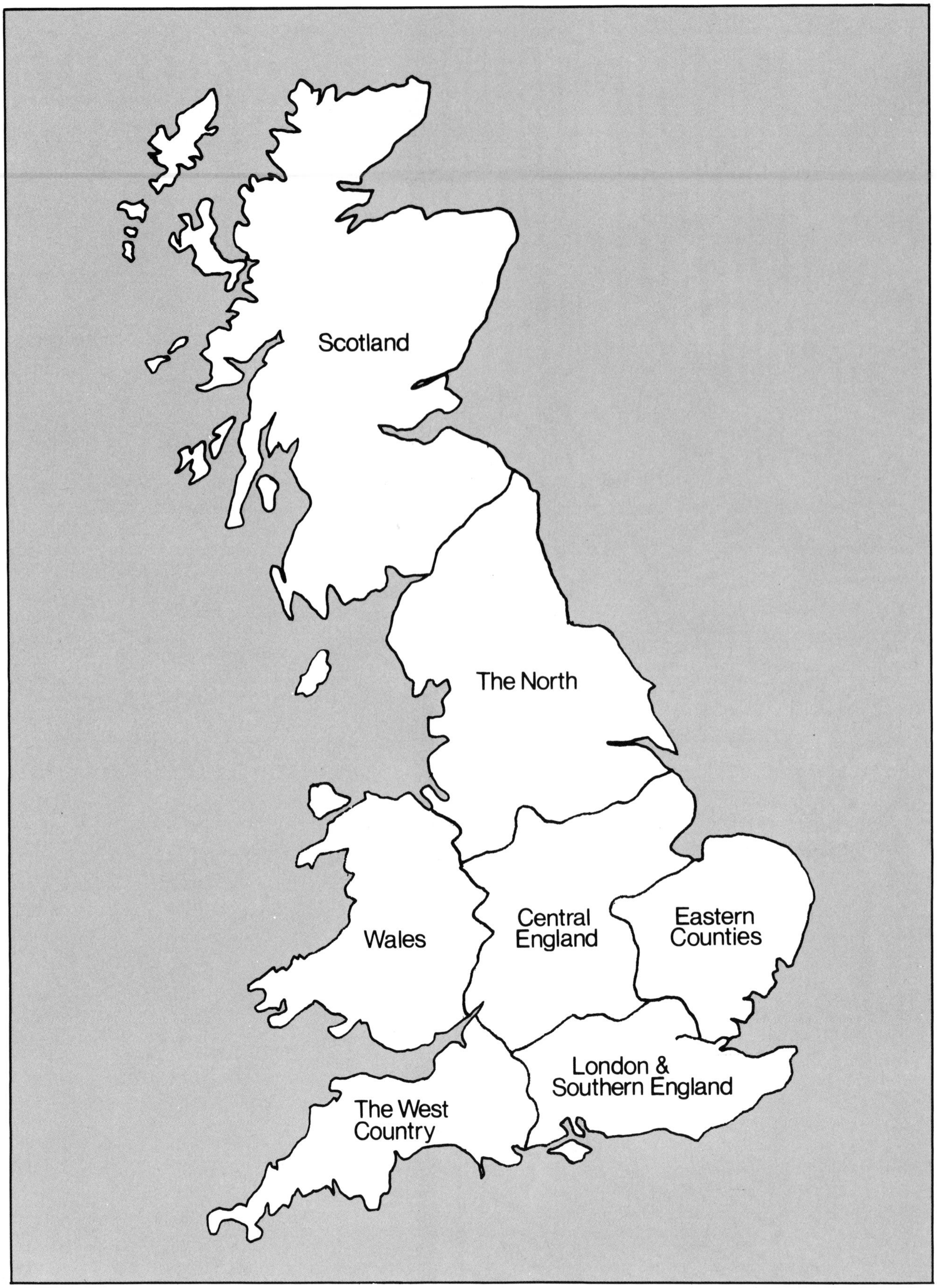

Strange Britain is divided into seven sections, as shown above.

Each section is immediately preceded by a map of the region and each entry listed within the section will be found on that map by referring to the relevant square given after the placename.

Introduction

The mysteries of Britain are both large and small. In some cases, they are so large as to be almost invisible to the human eye, and may only be seen to advantage from an aeroplane — as for example in the case of the huge hill-figures cut through turf into the chalk below, which have become more accessible only since flight became possible at the beginning of our century (figure 1). In other cases, the mysteries are so small as to be easily missed by those who have little time to stand and stare. The Christian fish symbol high on the walls of Glastonbury Abbey (figure 2) may be passed by unnoticed even by one who has gone to the place to steep himself in the more famous legends of King Arthur, or the sacred well, or the story of Joseph of Arimathaea. Even if it is not possible to study them from the air, the larger mysteries must be visited, if only to savour the atmosphere around them. Stonehenge in Wiltshire (figure 54) is a good example of such a 'must', for something of the occult power of the place may still be felt among its stones, even though much of its sacred character has been damaged in modern times by the nearby buildings, sentry posts, and the awful underpass constructed by English Heritage. The 'Carles' circle at CASTLERIGG in Cumbria is another such site, and here the mysterious forces work more freely, being less impeded by insensitive officialdom. But perhaps the most

1: The turf-cut white horse at Kilburn, on the Hambleton Hills, North Yorkshire. It is probably an 18th century recut of an older dragon figure.
3 (above): One of the standing stones at Avebury, Wiltshire (see page 32).
2 (left): A sacred fish engraved high on the wall of the ruined Abbey of Glastonbury. The design would suggest that it was incised there in the 14th century.

4: The ancient stone circle at Callanish, on the island of Lewis (see page 197).

5: The white horse of Uffington, Oxfordshire, was probably cut about 100 B.C. Above it is Uffington Castle, an Iron Age fort.

spiritually-charged of all the ancient stone circles is that at CALLANISH, on the island of Lewis, which, until comparatively modern times, was protected beneath many feet of boggy peat (figure 4) and has now been revealed as a stellar computer, on much the same lines as Stonehenge to the south. The largest of the stone circle complexes is at AVEBURY — a site which contains the vast man-made mound of Silbury Hill, the largest of such mounds in Europe (figure 51) — and though a village has been built into the middle of the stones (making use, indeed, of fragments of broken menhirs for house-building), this circle still retains that distinctive feeling of magic which proclaims it as a living wonder in our age.

The ancient circles, and the complex of stone outliers and mounds which serves them, are not the largest of the mysteries of Britain, however. By far the biggest (if it is indeed a genuine thing, and not just a figment of the human imagination) is the so-called Glastonbury Zodiac, which some authorities claim to trace in the landscape around the village of Butleigh, in a vast circle with a diameter of just over nine miles. Like the white horses which are found in the most outlandish and surprising places in Britain, such as Kilburn (figure 1), Uffington and Westbury, the Glastonbury Zodiac may be seen to advantage only from the air — though of course many attempts have been made to map out the figures traced within its vast circumference in diagrammatic form (figure 6). One wonders, indeed, how the men of ancient times saw these circles, hill-figures and earth-zodiacs which they built, for it is only occultists, and not historians, who insist that the men of old had access to a special form of flying machine. Perhaps the smallest British wonder (though it is really a Romano-British artefact) related to the stone circles and earth-zodiacs, is the Mithraic zodiac now preserved in the Museum of London (see page 69).

Although size is often one of the factors which play a part in revealing a thing as a wonder, or even as a mystery, size itself is not always important. There are other mysteries in Britain which are not as large as Stonehenge, Castlerigg, Callanish or Avebury, and are often small enough to be held in the palm of the hand, or preserved in display cases or in churches, as a part of the ornamentation. The simple truth is that the glory of Britain's history is recorded in our churches. Not only does almost every monument tell a story about some detail of British history, but, more often than not, such memorials contain symbols which reveal secret and occult notions belonging to the past rather than to the present, and are therefore mysteries to the modern mind. Such are the curious pigs on a tomb in HEREFORD Cathedral (figure 117), the lovely woman and child lying on a pillow of a lion at SCARCLIFFE (figure 136), or the curiously carved chair at SPROTBROUGH, which gave respite to criminals in a past age. The charnel case of skulls and bones in the monument to the wives of Sir Gervase at CLIFTON (figure 96) is also of a similar mysterious symbolism, even if its meaning is all too obvious. The carving reminds us that such charnel pits were once part and parcel of the British heritage, as old prints of crypts reveal (figure 7). Yet its survival in an English church is perhaps just as remarkable as the survival of the dozen or so sculptures of skeletal effigies and cadavers intended as models of those buried below, as, for example, in WORSBROUGH (figure 214) or HATFIELD.

Within the churches of Britain we find emblems of life, as well as of death. What, for example, can be more life-enhancing than the legends of the Grail, and of that armoured superman of the past, King Arthur, who has done so much to mould our image of British history and destiny? The round table of Arthur at Mayburgh (figure 170) — perhaps confused with the old circle at EAMONT BRIDGE nearby — the death-place of the King at Dozmary Pool on BODMIN MOOR (figure 32), and the secret place of Glastonbury itself, where monkish cunning claimed the King was buried (figure 39), are all well-known sites for those interested in Arthurian legends. Yet perhaps the most impressive of the esoteric collections linked with Arthurian mythology is in the church of St James, in Kilkhampton, Devon. The dedication to James, the patron saint of pilgrims, is said to arise from the fact that the village was once on the famous pilgrimage route from St David's in the far east of Wales to Compostela in Spain (see, for example, MARLOW).

In the stained glass of this lovely church we find what is undoubtedly the most impressive image in Britain of Joseph of Arimathaea (figure 9). Joseph, who holds the flowering thorn and the Holy Grail, is supposed to have

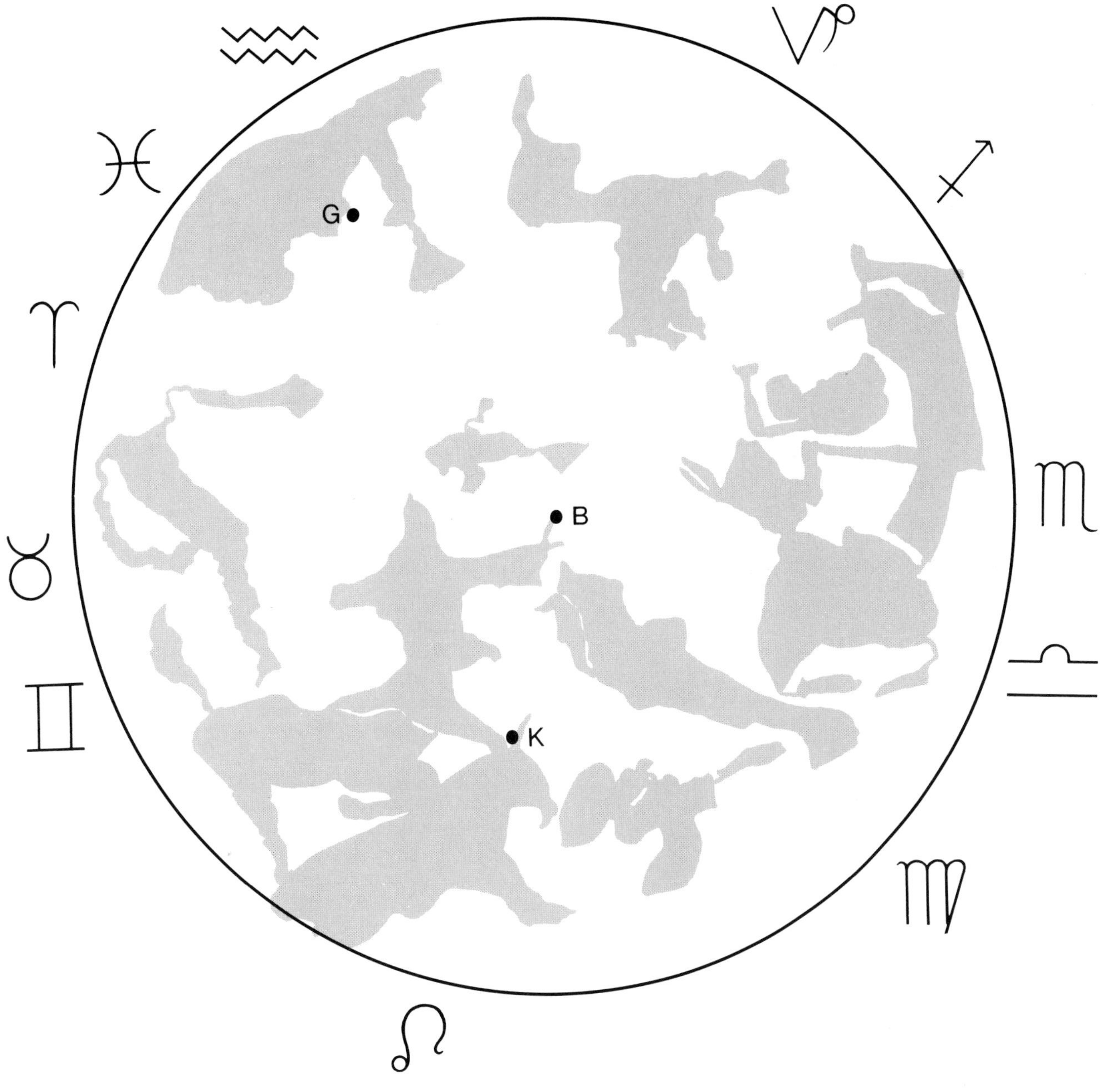

6: The constellation figures of the so-called 'Maltwood zodiac', said to be drawn into the landscape around Glastonbury. The bottom two figures are the lion of Leo (left) and the female image of Virgo holding a sheaf of corn.

7: The crypt of Ripon Cathedral, North Yorkshire, as shown in a 19th-century engraving. The crypt is no longer used as a charnel house.

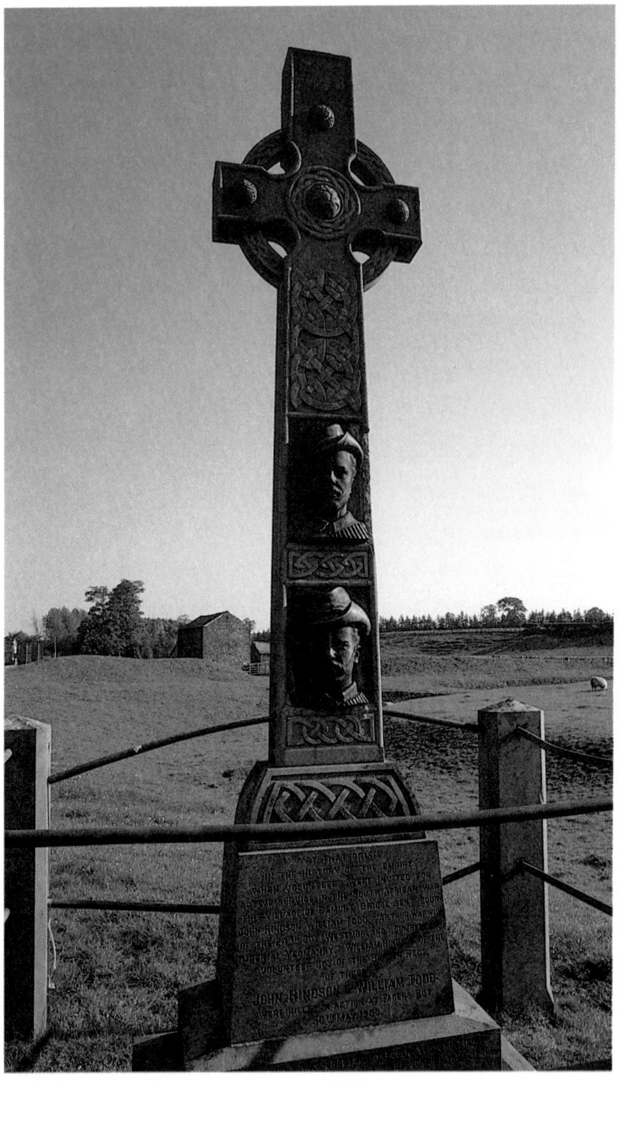

8: The memorial to South African War volunteers, to the north of 'King Arthur's Round Table' at Eamont Bridge, Cumbria (see page 153).

9 *(facing page)*: The church of St James in Kilkhampton, Devon, contains this beautiful representation of Joseph of Arimathaea, who (according to legend) planted the Holy Thorn, buried the Holy Chalice, and founded the first church, at Glastonbury.

brought the latter from Jerusalem to England and buried it under the Tor at Glastonbury. In the same stained glass of the east windows is an image of Arthur himself, in the romantic guise of a medieval knight. Among the fascinating bench-ends still in use within the church is a carving of a cup, which some take to represent a chalice and which others maintain is an image of the Holy Grail itself — as is the one carried by Joseph in the stained glass image.

Kilkhampton reminds me, perhaps more than any other church, of the way in which certain places seem to attract secret symbols, almost as though such symbols need to seek out a home where they may be preserved. Why have so many symbols of British mythology and esoteric thought found their way into one single church? It is easy to explain why so many esoteric symbols — of the ouroboros time-serpent, of the green man, of zodiacal images, and so on — should be found at Kilpeck church (figure 10) as they are the work of one man. But time and time again one finds certain places attract many mysteries from different ages and sources. This is indeed one of the mysteries of Britain itself.

The mysteries are found in the strangest of places, in sites as remote as the Hebridean islands, as accessible as the City of London, in museums, hillsides and in churches — the very places where one might expect miracles, but not mysteries. Indeed, the very number of British mysteries is almost a wonder in itself. Why have these islands been singled out as the repository for such a welter of mysterious remains? Was there something special in the British earth that the ancients should build so many stone circles, of which almost 500 still survive? Or is it true that Britain is itself a fragmented survival of the fabled continent of Atlantis, which sank beneath the waves of the Atlantic thousands of years ago? Whatever the reasons, there are so many centres in Britain where the mind is almost numbed by the weight of mythology

10: Carvings of demons from the Norman doorway of the 12th-century Kilpeck church, Hereford and Worcester.

and mystery associated with them that one is hard-pressed to visit them all in the space of one lifetime. The vastly differing histories of the countries which make up Britain have resulted in memorials and mementoes with almost regional characters. For example, the growth of witchcraft in Scotland — especially under the reign of James VI (later James I of England) — was far more pervasive than in England. This has resulted in popular witchcraft stories being linked with many Scottish villages, towns and kirks, and even in the survival of many Scottish witchcraft stones which mark places where victims of the witch-craze met their deaths. One of the most famous is the witch-stone at Spott, set into a hillside dominated by a prehistoric defensive castle which was also associated later with witch-burnings. Another is at Forres, not far from where Macbeth is supposed to have lived, while an equally well-known memorial stone is in Dornoch, marking the last place in Scotland where a witch was burned.

I doubt that there is a single stone circle or menhir in Scotland which does not have its own witchcraft story or diabolical mythology. Where curious Scottish stones are not associated with the Devil or witchcraft, then, more often than not, they are linked with the ancient giants who (as some claim) swarmed to the mountainous land from the sinking Atlantis. Such giants are supposed to have built many of the Scottish stone circles, and, since the hero Fiann was of this gigantic race, they also built the basaltic island of STAFFA (figure 13).Sir Joseph Banks, who 'discovered' the island for the modern world in 1772, wrote that it is to be 'reckoned one of the greatest natural curiosities in the world.'

There is little of the dark northern witchcraft in Wales, and the legends are mainly about heroes of battle, of song-making and of magic. More often than not, the legends and mysteries point to the delicate realm of faery, to the Celtic underworld, where dragons lived alongside

11: The south porch doorway of Kilpeck church has some of the most beautiful of all Norman carvings. This Disney-like image of a hare and hound is on the eastern end of the south wall.

12 (facing page): Near Dunning, Tayside, is this witch memorial to Maggie Wall, burned on this spot in 1657.

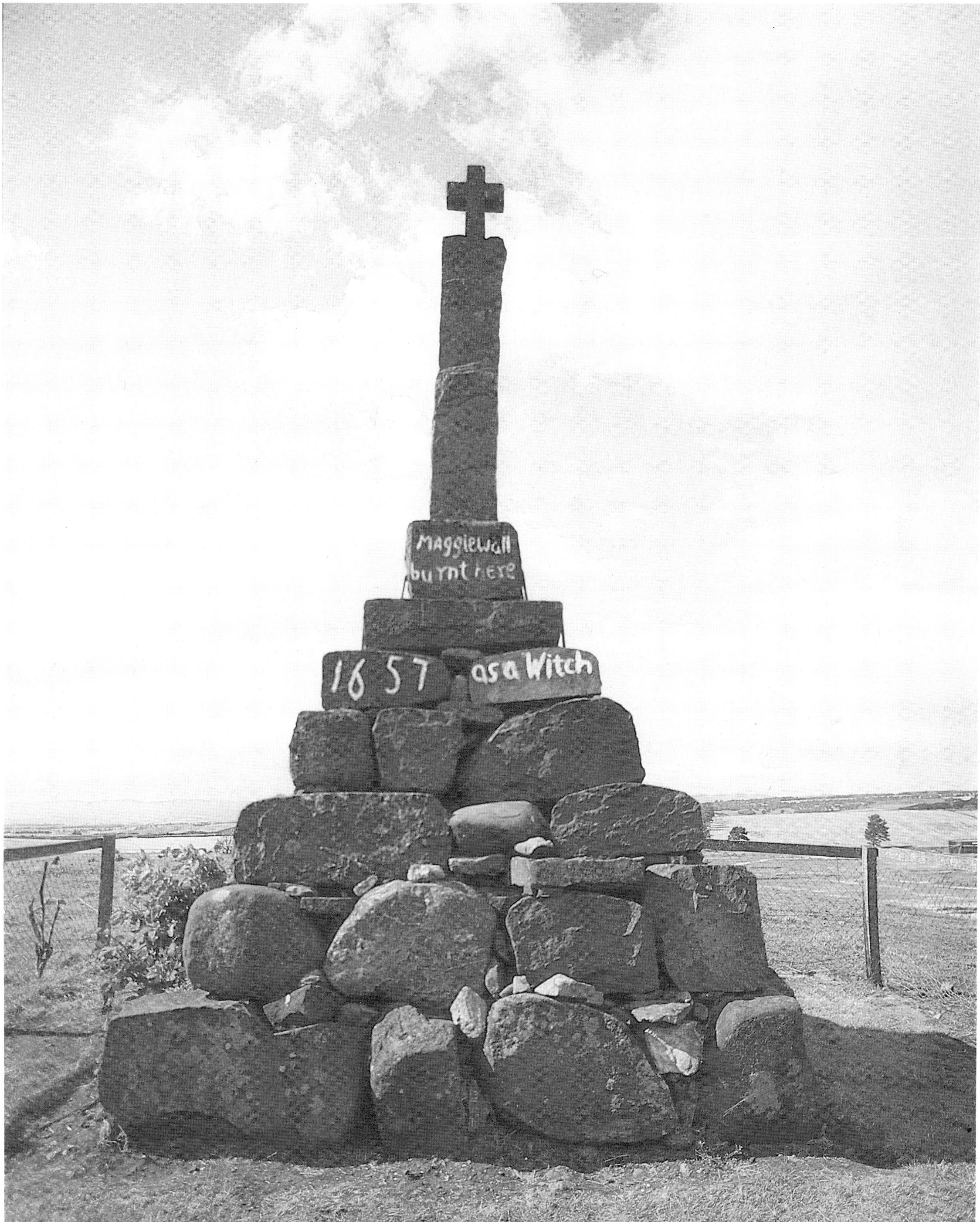
Maggiewall
burnt here
1657
as a Witch

men and sometimes had to be slaughtered in order to rescue princesses. In Wales, even today, one walks among the archetypes, and the mythological stories are impressed into the natural landscape of such wonders as PISTYLL RHAEADR (figure 87), rather than into man-made objects and buildings. Among the mysterious wonders of Wales are the chambered tombs — now so often stripped of their earth covering and revealed as so many gaunt bones of stone, petrified in some delicate balancing act, as at PENTRE IFAN (figure 86).

Stone is one thing, but in a land of water it is not surprising that Wales provides some of the finest healing wells and magical water-sites in the world. The extraordinary bathing-well at HOLYWELL, used from early medieval times as a healing well, and built into chapels and baths to serve such holy purposes, is still used for its healing power even today. The more intimate well of St Non's, near Saint David, has been used for such purposes for over a thousand years. Water is the true mystery of Wales, and there is much hidden wisdom in the story that the hill in the middle of Llyn Dywarchen actually floats, and may even fly, because Wales itself is a place as ethereal as the waters, mapped out by rivers, streams and lakes which carry their own welter of legends and myths. It is as though mythological Wales itself floats on water, and all that is most important to the land springs from underground: even the dragons of Wales were said to fight beneath a great lake, and Pistyll Rhaeadr was the watery nest of a dragon. What other country could have a lord of the land imprisoned in a waterfall because of his misdeeds in life, as in the popular tales of Swallow Falls at Bettws-y-Coed?

If one spends time studying the British mysteries, one gradually becomes aware of the extent to which the calendar plays an important part in the secrets hidden behind their forms and symbols. In modern times, expert archaeologists have revealed that the huge stone circles of Stonehenge, Avebury and Callanish were used as complex (if primitive) calendrical machines for determining the cycles of the years in terms of eclipses, sun-settings, sun-risings, and similar lunar points — all phenomena of great importance to the rituals practised by the ancients. Additionally, many of the strange and mysterious customs which have survived, in a more or less garbled form, into modern times are also linked with the symbolism of the calendar — with the zodiacal points, with the four directions of space, with the solstices and the equinoxes, and the sequence of the zodiac. For this reason, if we wish to reach a little more deeply into the mysteries of Britain, it will be as well for us to glance at one or two of the calendrical traditions. When looked at from the point of view of mythology, the British calendar is revealed as a complex thing; some of the events it marks are derived from our first Christian civilizers — those Romans who came as soldiers and stayed as monks — and some are distinctly pagan, being even older than the first recorded history of our land.

The moment one begins to relate places, architectural forms and mythologies to the calendar, one is faced with the lore of astrology, which attempts to relate man to the cosmos and to the earth (figure 14). It is the traditions attached to astrology, in regard to the pictorial imagery revealing the passing of the seasons, or the movement of the sun against the zodiacal belt, and the relationship these were believed to hold to the human being, which account for many of the secret symbols in the British Isles. It would be impossible to treat of all these mysteries from this astrological point of view, yet it will be instructive if we examine just one — the zodiacal

13: The 'cliffs' of Staffa are hexagonal columns of basalt, often believed to have been carved by giants or made by ancient magicians.

14: 18th-century melophesic figure, or representation of Man marked with the signs of the zodiac on the corresponding parts of the body.

font at HOOK NORTON (figure 119), which is one of the lesser mysteries of the British Isles.

Why should one find a figure of a horse-man archer on a font? What is the relationship between a figure of the constellation, or zodiacal sign Sagittarius, and Christianity — what has it to do with baptism, for which the font is used? In the astrological tradition there is a standard figure called 'the zodiacal man' — an image which was introduced to the west with the new astrology of the eleventh century. This figure portrays man with the twelve signs of the zodiac associated with the different parts of the body (figure 16). The rulership was intended to portray both the inner and outer forms of the connexion between the zodiac and the human body. For example, Aries the Ram had rule over the human head, but it also had rule over what went on inside the head — namely, thinking — just as the sign Leo had rule over the heart, and also over the inner activity of the heart, which was feeling. Sagittarius had rule over the thigh, but its inner activity was not as obvious as with Aries and Leo. Tradition insisted that it was the movement of the thigh which permitted man to walk as an erect being: thus, the thigh represented the inner power of movement, and by extension all movement connected with human aspiration. Since the greatest aspirations were always ideals, and linked with the wish to learn more — in medieval terms, to move out more closely to God — Sagittarius was soon linked with education and with the church, or religious life.

By this reasoning, when we find on a medieval font the image of Sagittarius, we can be sure that it is a symbolic reference to the idea that the child who is to be baptised at this font is being protected by the image, is being vouchsaved a good education, within the framework of the religious life. It is not surprising that on the same Hook Norton font we should find images of Adam and Eve next to the horse-archer, for they represent the innocence of childhood, while the horseman represents the educational guide who will protect the innocent child and teach him the way of Christ as he grows into the world, away from the Garden of Eden which is the childhood state.

The symbolism of the Hook Norton font is, indeed, a good example of how easily one may miss the hidden meaning of a symbol if one is not prepared to consider

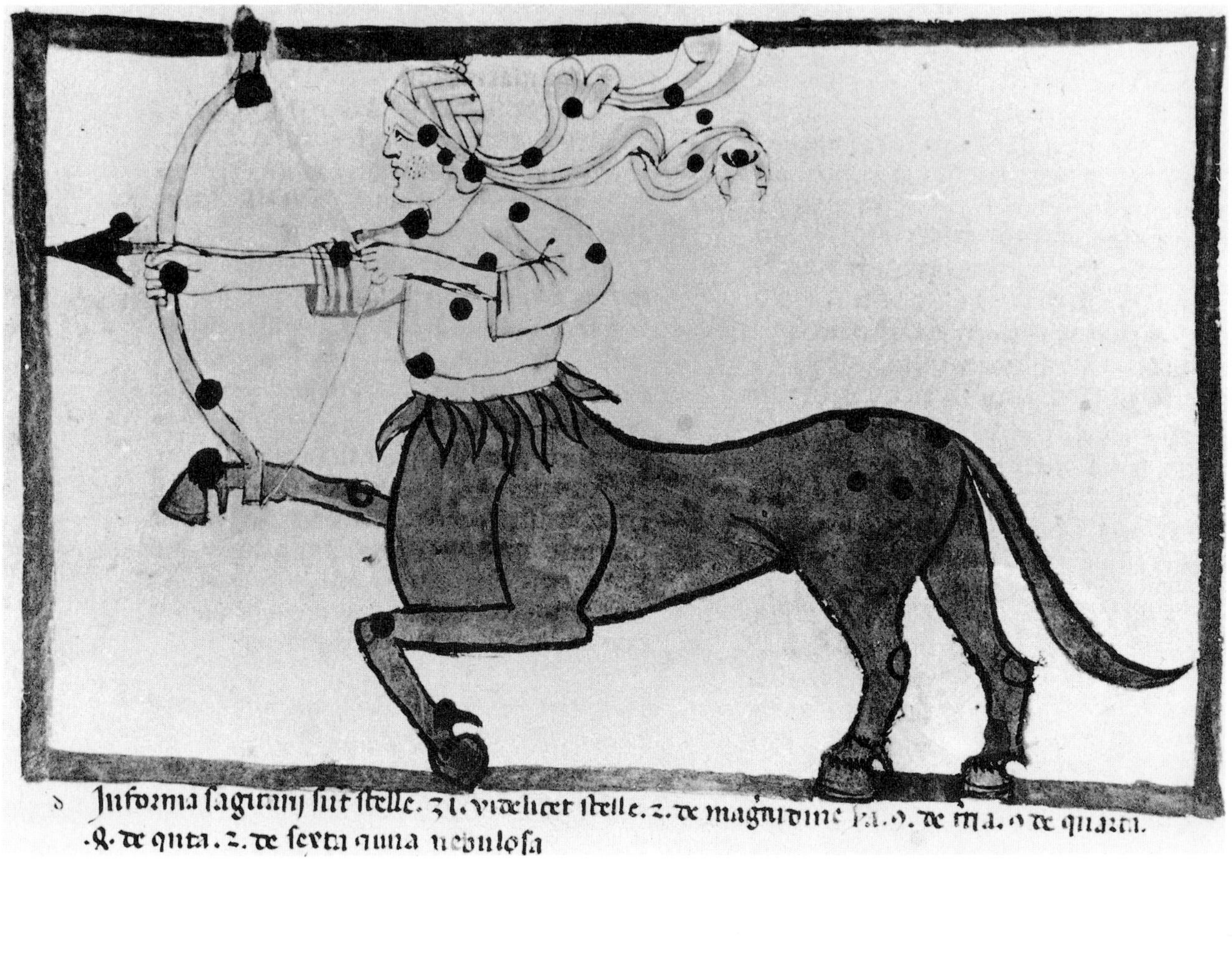

15: Sagittarius the Horseman, from a 14th-century manuscript in the British Library. The stars studding his body indicate constellation figures.

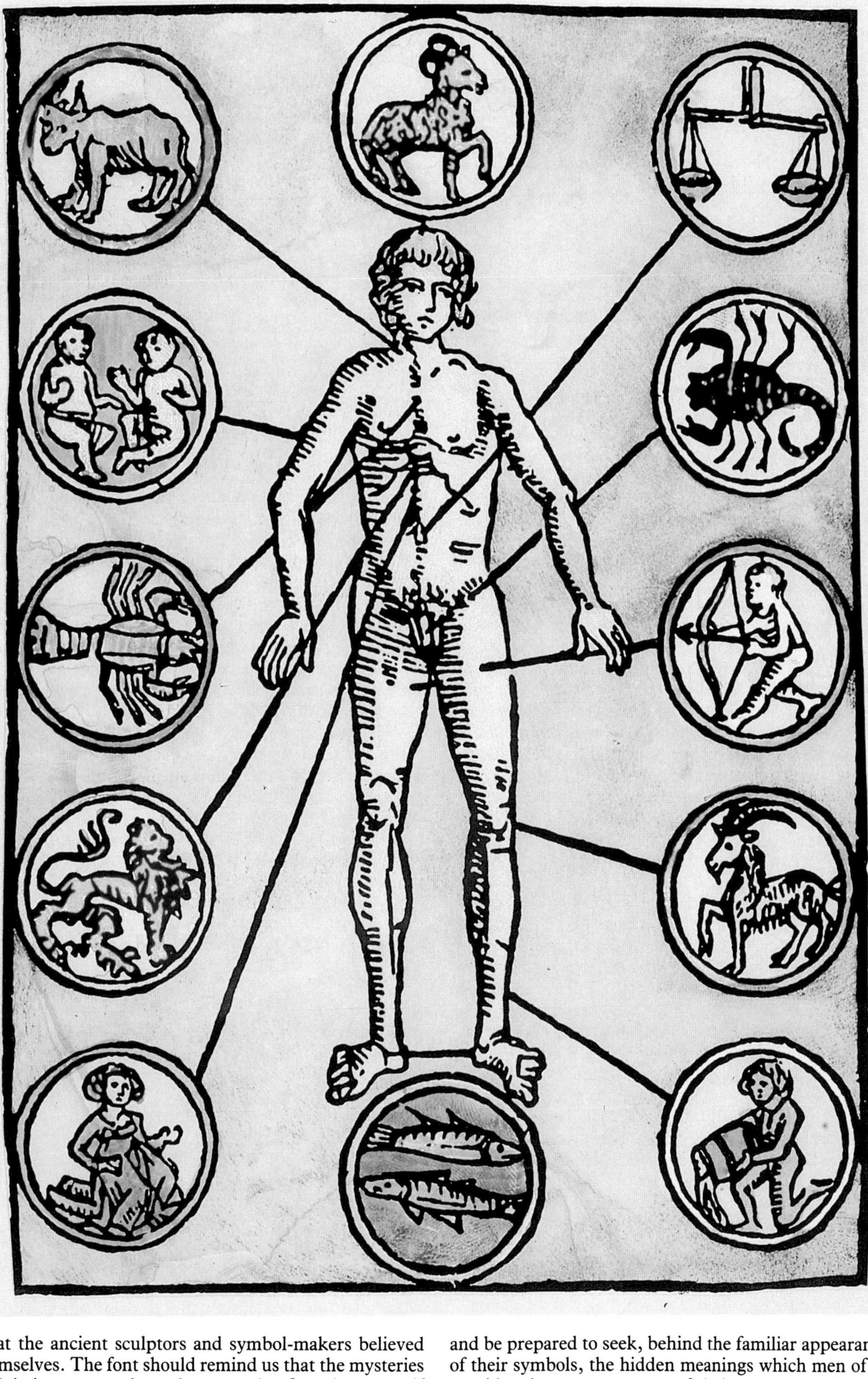

16: A medieval image showing the human being in relation to the rulership of the twelve zodiacal signs.

what the ancient sculptors and symbol-makers believed themselves. The font should remind us that the mysteries of Britain may not always be grasped at first glance, yet if one pays enough attention to them they will always speak, and reveal at least something of their inner content. To hear their voices, however, one must visit them and be prepared to seek, behind the familiar appearances of their symbols, the hidden meanings which men of old considered a necessary part of their art, and which contribute so wonderfully to make Britain such a place of mystery.

JANUARY

The word 'January' is derived from the name of the Roman god Janus, who was two-faced, and therefore provided a useful symbol for a month which begins the year (ending one period, 'looking into the past', and into the coming 'future'). In the sacred secret symbolism, Janus was one of those gods who had rule over all entrances, and over the cosmic 'entrances' of the Sun into the zodiac, by which the year was divided into four quadrants.

The night of 5/6 January used to be the old day for Christmas Eve and Christmas, and this is still reflected in the legend of the flowering of the Holy Thorn of GLASTONBURY. So widely held was the belief that this holy thorn would flower at Christmas that the legend was continued even into those trees which grew from cuttings taken from it, so that we find the same tradition attached to the Quainton Thorn, which until comparatively recently grew in the Old Rectory in that village, and which was planted from a Glastonbury thorn cutting.

The legend of Joseph of Arimathaea is told elsewhere (see page 9), but in connexion with the flowering thorn it is said that when he first arrived at Glastonbury he stuck his hawthorn staff into the ground, and much to the surprise of everyone present it burst into blossom and became a tree. Joseph interpreted this as a sign that they should settle and build their church in that place, which they promptly did. According to legend, it blossomed at 'Old' Christmas every year afterwards, keeping faith with the old date even when the new date (25 December) was adopted as the official birthday of Jesus.

From the seventh century to as late as the thirteenth, the year was reckoned as beginning from Christmas Day, but in the twelfth century some countries began the year on 25 March — this remaining in force until 1752. In the 'zodiacal calendar', January is linked with Capricorn and is especially associated with the magical gemstone called the garnet, which is said to bring about constancy, especially in matters of love.

FEBRUARY

In ancient times, the name Februata was applied to the goddess Juno, who was worshipped in ceremonies ('Februatio') held during this month — this has been associated with the purification of the feminine element in preparation for the coming Spring.

The clarification which arises from the 'Februatio' purification is perhaps reflected in the modern 'St Valentine's Day' on 14 February, when one is supposed to declare one's romances, loves or passions by sending cards or letters, unsigned. As with most British customs, the origin of this curious, and now highly commercialized, practice is found in pagan rituals. Most authorities claim that it is linked with the Roman festival of the Lupercalia, which involved somewhat sensual activities in which naked youths ran around striking women with strips of goatskin — a practice clearly linked with fertility rites. Lupercus was the Lyucaean Pan, and was so called because he protected the sheep from wolves ('wolf' in Latin is 'lupus'). Unfortunately for this theory, the Lupercalia began on the day following our own St Valentine's day. However, there was a pagan notion that the birds chose their mates on 14 February.

> 'Good morrow, friends! St Valentine is past;
> Begin these wood-birds but to couple now?'

writes Shakespeare in *A Midsummer Night's Dream* (IV, i). This choice of birds might well have been adapted as a reflection of the 'choice of human souls', for in medieval symbolism the bird was very often used as a symbol of the human soul or spirit. Records indicate that the old method of observing St Valentine's Day was involved with drawing lots for loved ones, and the making of small gifts to those drawn. Some historians claim that the day, and those rites, was originally connected with homage paid on this day to the goddess Juno, whose symbol was a peacock. The link between the pagan ideas and St Valentine is entirely accidental — St Valentine appears to have been martyred on 14 February, which day preceded the beginning of Lupercalia.

The great six-day fair which has been held in King's Lynn for 800 years, starts on St Valentine's Day. In the 'zodiacal calendar', February is associated with Aquarius, and with the magical gemstone the amethyst, which is used to protect the wearer against violent passions.

MARCH

In the ancient calendrical systems, the year began on 25 March, on the day which is now marked by that great 'beginning', the Annunciation of the Coming of Christ. This sense of 'beginning' or of 'initiation' probably explains why the month is called March, for the word appears to be derived from the Latin word Mars, the name of the god of action, the initiator.

The leek (now pursued somewhat by the daffodil in certain quarters), is the national emblem of Wales. There are several stories linking this curious emblem with St David, the patron saint of Wales, one of which tells how he went for a period of meditation to the Vale of Ewias, where the only food available to him was the meadow-leek in the fields, and the refreshing water of the River Honddhu. St David was said to be born on the 1 March, so that the ritual of 'Eating the Leek' is practised on this day by many Welshmen. For centuries this has been the Saint Day of David, as may be seen from the Welsh harp denoting the day in the Clog Calendar (figure 17 — fourth symbol from bottom in the first section to left). One explanation of the symbolic leek tells how Cadwallader persuaded the countrymen serving under his banner to distinguish themselves from their Saxon enemies by wearing a leek in their caps. This legend is confused somewhat by Shakespeare's Fluellen, who thinks that the story relates to the much later battle of Poitiers, yet refers to the Welsh 'wearing leeks in their Monmouth caps', and says impishly to Henry V, 'I do believe your majesty takes no scorn to wear the leek upon St Tavy's Day' (*Henry V*, IV.vii). It appears that in certain quarters the daffodil is beginning to usurp the leek as a symbol of Wales — perhaps, as some claim, because of certain similarities in their Welsh names. However, the symbolism of the daffodil is of a different order from that of the leek, for in ancient times it was one of the grave-flowers. Mythology tells how the flowers were white until touched by the hand of Pluto, the god of the Underworld, when they turned a golden yellow. It was this touch of death which probably explains the medieval notion that the flower of the daffodil was a sure cure for madness. In ancient times it was called the 'Lent Flower' because of its connexion with death, and presumably because of its flowering during the Lenten period.

Several of the old customs relating to March are connected with Lent, even if the connexion is not evident. Pancake Day, with its attendant races, on the first day of Lent, appears to be connected with the idea that butter

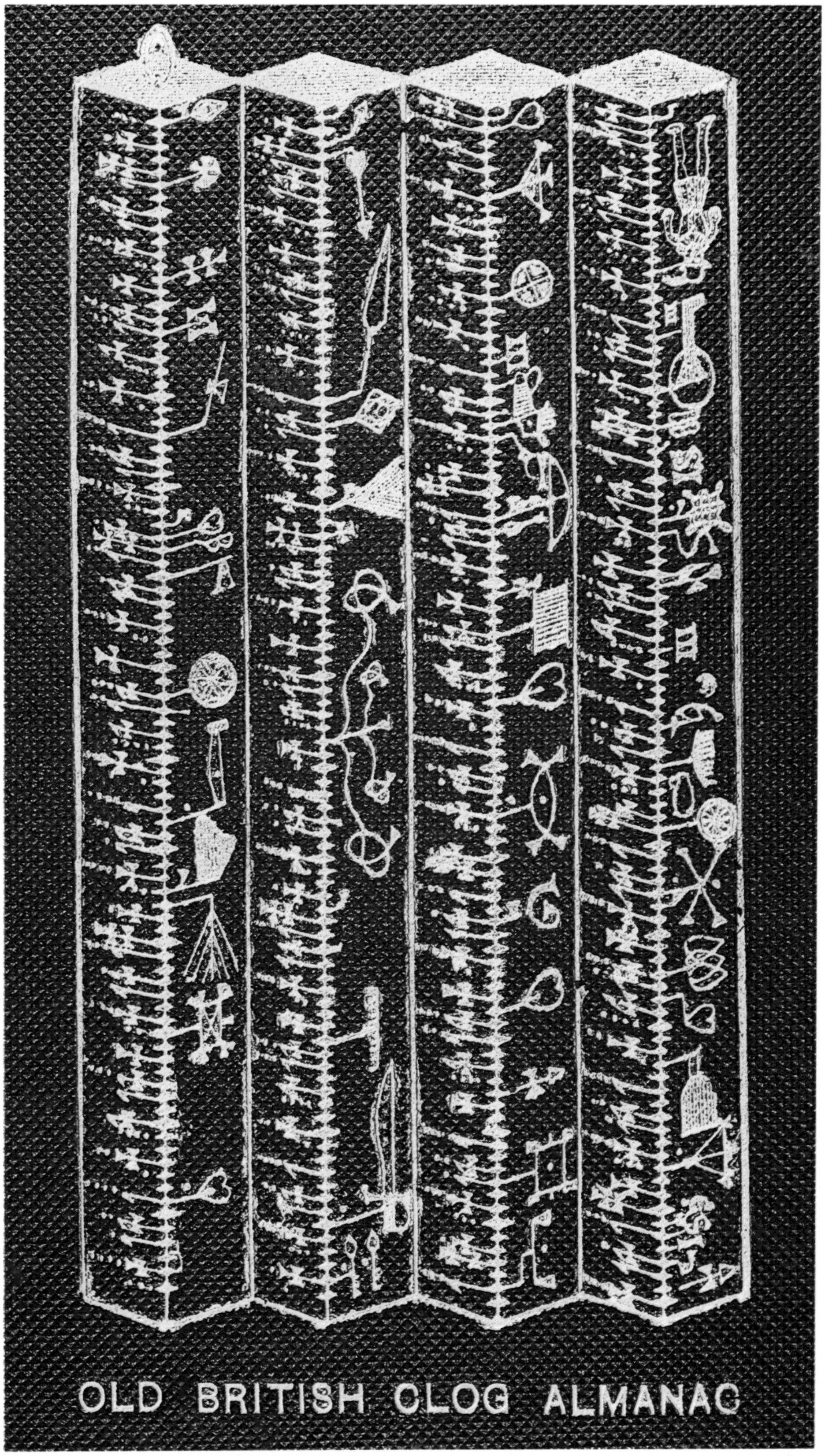

and eggs, which were forbidden food during the period of Lent, had to be used up. St Patrick, the patron saint of Ireland, has his day on 17 March — the symbolic shamrock is drawn stylistically in the first part of the clog (second symbol up) in the Clog Calendar of figure 17. Mothering Sunday falls towards the end of March — see LOUGHBOROUGH. In the 'zodiacal calendar' March is associated with the sign Pisces (see aboves) and with a number of magical gemstones, the most popular of which is the bloodstone, worn to promote courage and wisdom. In the United States the aquamarine is also associated with this month.

APRIL

The name for the fourth month of our calendar is said to be from the Latin 'aperire' which means 'to open' (hence our word 'aperture'), and is sometimes explained as referring to the opening of flowers which takes place in this month. Some specialists argue, however, that the word is from the Greek goddess Aphrodite (named 'Aphrilis') whose important festivals were celebrated in this month. In a similar vein, the Anglo-Saxons called it after their own goddess Eastre, as the Easter-Month.

The practical joking on the first day of April is a throwback to pagan rituals, and is still distinctively pagan (that is to say, anti-Christian) in that it involves the mocking of people, as well as the trifling with people's egos. A hint of the antiquity of the custom is contained in the official name for the day — 'All Fools Day' — for the 'All' does not refer to 'All the fools' but to the form 'Auld', which meant 'Old'. The custom is therefore really 'The Feast of Old Fools', which is how it is described in some medieval documents, even though it is likely that this referred to a feast held in January (the old beginning of the calendrical year). According to some, the 'Old Fools' were the Druids, which corresponds to the symbolism in which a wise man often appears in the guise of a fool.

18: A Druid with the symbols of mistletoe, a moon-shaped knife and a henged circle.

It is usual to trace these antics to the ancient feast of the Vernal Equinox (prior to the calendrical adjustments which have to a large extent divorced the calendar from cosmic phenomena). It was on that date (in ancient times) that the Sun began its new course through the zodiac, beginning with the first degree of Aries. The 'All Fools Day' pranks are not limited to Britain, of course, for there is the French equivalent, April Fish (Poisson d'Avril). Some scholars have associated this with 'Passion d'Avril', or the April Passion, relating to the fact that the Passion (Suffering) of Christ took place during this time of the year and it was then that Christ was mocked. Another explanation is linked with the notion of the 'octave', which is supposed to establish links between calendrical events. Thus eight days after 25 March falls the octave of 1 April; the Annunciation feast of 25 March (see MARCH above) was continued for eight days, and 1 April marked the end of this period, with a day of great hilarity. All these explanations scarcely disguise the fact that no convincing reason has been given for the customs practised on All Fools Day.

On Good Friday, hot cross buns are made — no doubt another Christianized form of a pagan custom. It is widely believed that bread baked on Good Friday, and marked with the sign of the cross, will never go bad or mouldy. Some indeed insist that the flour used on that day will cure certain ailments, and it is a fairly common practice for hot cross buns to be baked not for the purpose of eating but as talismans — protections against evil spirits. Historians observe that in pagan times people would buy loaves of bread at the entrance to the temple; one sort of bread favoured by the Greeks for such purposes was called 'boun' (a word related to our English 'ox'), and was marked with the representation of two horns. Is it too much to derive 'bun' from 'boun'?

19: St George and the Dragon, from an early edition of Spenser's epic poem *The Faerie Queene*.

April 23 is celebrated as St George's Day — the third spear-headed lance down in the second column of the Clog Calendar (figure 17) marks this important date for the patron saint of England. The arrow and spear above this lance denote the feast days of St Richard and St Isadore. In the 'zodiacal calendar' April is associated with Aries, and with the magical birthstone called the diamond, which is worn to promote purity and innocence. In ancient times the sapphire was associated with this month.

MAY

The name of the month almost certainly comes from Maia, the daughter of Atlas and Pleione, and hence one of the Pleiades, a group of stars which rose in May. The fifteenth day of the month was sacred to Mercury in ancient times, but the most important of the ancient festivals was the herald of May — Beltane, which marked the Spring equinox.

The ancient Beltane was held at the beginning of May, and was said to be an observance of the equinox, when the length of the day and night (nox) was the same, or equal (equi), but we may be sure that the old word 'taine' meant fire, and was perhaps linked with the Etruscan fire god who went under the name of 'Tin'. It is reasonable to assume that Bel is the Bile or Beli of the Celtic underworld, so that the entire word Beltane means 'fires to the god of the underworld' — a fitting way of describing some of the practices of the modern May Day.

Celebration of the ancient Beltane is found in many localities, but the sense of the 'sacrificial' which was part of the original pagan practices is somewhat restricted in modern times. In his *Tour of Scotland* (1771), Thomas Pennant records that on 1 May the highlanders of every village would hold their 'Bel-tein', burning a fire into a turf-cut patch of ground, into which they would pour a 'caudle' of eggs, butter, oatmeal, milk, whisky and perhaps beer. 'The rites begin with spilling some of the caudle on the ground, by way of libation; on that, every one takes a cake of oatmeal, upon which are raised nine square knobs, each dedicated to some particular being, the supposed preserver of their flocks and herds, or to some particular animal, the real destroyer of them. Each person then turns his face to the fire, breaks off a knob, and, flinging it over his shoulder, says: "This I give to thee, preserve though my horses," and so on... When the ceremony is over, they dine on the caudle.' Some historians insist that this worship of Bel is the worship of Baal, but it is certain that the Baal of the Semites, the 'Lordly God' to whom the Carthaginians sacrificed their children under the name of Moloch, is a different god from the Celtic Bel or Beli.

The maypole dancing which used to be observed more widely in the past than it is now (though it is still a living ritual in such places as Ossett) was merely a shadow of a Celtic ritual in which the religious danced around a living tree in order, as it is claimed, to raise the spirits of the tree (see also WANSTEAD PARK). The sacred pagan tree of the Scandinavians (who so left their mark on British mythology) was called Yggdrasil and was an ash tree which bound together the Heavens, the Earth and Hell. Something of this ritual lives on in the May Day practice of going out into the country at sunrise to gather wild flowers and tree branches, while the crowning of the village beauty as a May Queen almost certainly harks back to the pagan practice of the worship of Juno.

One specially sumptuous crowning of the May Queen takes place at Knutsford, but in former times virtually every village had its May Day crowning and its special veneration of maidens (a throwback to the worship of Maia, perhaps). For an interesting account of this, see HOUNSLOW, and for a story about the maypole, see LONDON — ST ANDREW UNDERSHAFT; for an interesting May Day tradition, see PADSTOW.

The famous 'Clootie Well' ritual takes place in Scotland on the first Sunday in May, when the highlanders gather at Culloden Moor to drink the waters of the wishing well near to the site of the last battle fought on British soil between English and Scottish soldiers. In the ritual, a coin is tossed into the well (as it is claimed, in recognition of the water spirit within), a drink of water is taken, and then a wish is made in secret. Once the wish has been made, it is 'sealed' in a piece of rag (a clootie, somewhat like the 'dish-clout' used in similar rituals in Yorkshire areas), and this is tied to the branch of a nearby tree, where it is left until it is in tatters.

The Furry (or 'Floral') Dance at HELSTON takes place in the first week of May, the song which marks its opening traditionally evoking the name of Robin Hood. The May festivities linked with this folk hero appear to derive from archery contests, held on almost any suitable occasion in those days when the security of the nation depended upon wood, rather than upon metal. An interesting fact is that Morris dancers used to have a Maid Marion among their numbers (as well as a fool) long before Robin Hood came on the scene and stole the show. See, however, ROBIN HOOD, page 115.

In the 'zodiacal calendar', May is associated with Taurus and with the birthstone emerald, which is worn to promote true love (May is the month of Venus, the goddess of love).

20: Venus and her children.

JUNE

The Roman name for the month (Junius) is almost certainly from the name of the Roman goddess Juno, the patron of womanhood — and it is probably because of this that June was favoured for marriage: 'Good to the man and happy to the maid' is an old Roman saying.

In Peebles during mid-June there is an echo of the Beltane festival in the crowning of the Beltane Queen outside the parish church (perhaps unmindful of the pagan origin of the festival), a ceremony which heralds a week of festive rejoicing and pageantry. It is said that the charter ordaining such a Beltane Fair in the area was granted by James VI, but there seems to be little memory of the conflagrations of the old Beltane, which were probably a fiery homage to the Sun-god. However, the original Beltane was held in May, rather than June — see MAY on page 21. In the popular imagination the great bonfire period is in NOVEMBER (page 27) rather than Beltane, but there used to be an old pagan rite of making a long chain of bonfires on the Eve of St John (23 June), which some explain as an attempt to strengthen the waning sun after Midsummer.

In a modern revival of the ancient custom, which is now practised throughout Cornwall, the first of the chain of fires is lit by a 'Lady of Flowers' who casts her sickle of 'bonfire blossoms' into the flames in order to kill the 'ill weeds' within the bunch. The Midsummer ritual most famous in modern times is the STONEHENGE Midsummer festival, made infamous in recent years by the somewhat elitist occupation of the stones. The ritual is conducted by groups claiming to represent the ancient order of Druids, who are doubtless unaware of the fact that it is extremely unlikely the Druids had anything to do with the building of Stonehenge. It is held at sunrise on Midsummer's Day in the vicinity of what has been misnamed the Altar Stone, but which was certainly not an object of veneration during the time the circle was constructed, 4,500 years ago. At the same time as the ancient Stonehenge rituals are misrepresented in Wiltshire, so in Cornwall, at ST CLEER, are those which celebrate the Eve of St John, intent on banishing witches.

In the 'zodiacal calendar', June is associated with Gemini, and with a variety of magical birthstones, the most popular of which are the pearl and the moonstone, both worn to promote purity and wealth. In ancient times the emerald was favoured as a birthstone for this month, though now it is linked with May.

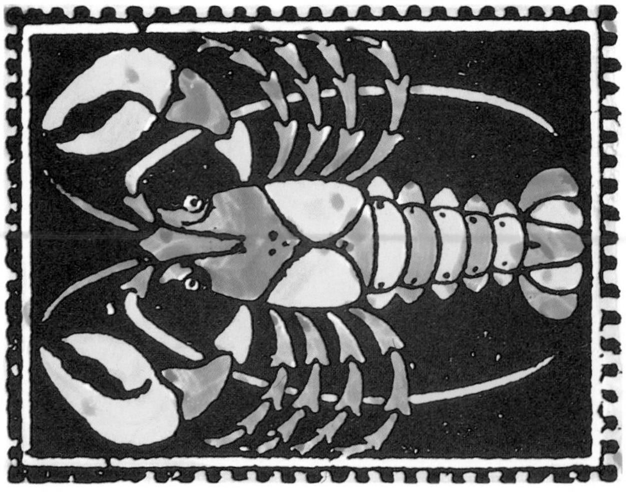

JULY

The name July is one of two month-names derived from the personal names of Roman Emperors (see also AUGUST). In the Roman calendar, which in accordance with ancient systems began in March, it was 'Quintilius' (the fifth month), but after the Roman calendrical reforms initiated by Julius Caesar, it was renamed after Caesar (by Mark Antony), born during this month.

The most popular of July saint days is St Swithin's Day (15 July), on which day (it is claimed) if rain falls, then there will be rain for 40 days thereafter. The origin of the notion is said to have been the attempt in the tenth century to relocate the body of St Swithin, formerly the ninth-century Bishop of WINCHESTER, from the external burial grounds into the Cathedral, against his expressed wishes. On the day set aside for this transfer of bones, rain fell in such a quantity that the planners had to abandon the attempt. After it had rained for the mystical 40 days, the whole idea was permanently shelved. From this supposed event, it was assumed that the saint could control the elements.

Strangest of all the customs of July is the appearance of the 'Berry Man' in South Queensferry, looking somewhat like a grape-clustered visitor from outer space, bedecked in floral headgear and an armoury of thistles and teazles. The origin of this grotesque figure has been forgotten, but records of the custom are centuries old and so one must assume some pagan origin — perhaps something of the same order as gave rise to the Green Man of medieval sculpture. For a late 'May Day' celebration held in July, see APPLETON, and for a curious bequest, see ST IVES (Cornwall).

In the 'zodiacal calendar' this month is associated with the sign Cancer and with the 'monthly labour' of scything, as may be seen on the leaden font at BROOKLAND. July's magical birthstone is the ruby, worn to cure all ills arising from love and friendship. In Britain the carnelian is also worn (following an ancient Arabian tradition), though in the classical world the onyx was favoured.

21: The Green Man (the 'Berry Man') on the Norman doorway of Kilpeck church.

AUGUST

The name of the month was chosen as a compliment to the first Roman Emperor Augustus, for whom it was supposed to be a lucky month (until this new name, it had been called simply the 'Sixth Month', as it was indeed the sixth in sequence from March which began the old calendrical year). There was a second meaning in the choice of the word, however, for the Latin 'augustus' meant approximately 'sacred and worthy of honour'. This may help to explain the significance of 'Lammas Day', which used to fall on the first day of the month and marked the time when the first fruits or 'Peter's Pence' were paid in England.

The word Lammas itself is of obscure origin, but some maintain that it is from the Old English 'hlafmaesse' or 'loaf-mass', the Mass of the Bread, or thanksgiving for the fruits of the corn. Due to calendrical changes (introduced to Britain in the seventeenth century), Lammas Day now falls on 13 August. Lammas was one of the important quarter days (when certain rents, tithes and settlements were paid on a quarterly basis), and is still so regarded in Scotland. The other days of settlement, or 'quarters', were Candlemas, Whitsuntide and Martinmas. However, the modern quarters are Lady Day, Midsummer, Michaelmas and Christmas, festivals no longer related to the stellar and zodiacal phenomena, as the ancient quarters were.

August is the month of harvesting, as reflected in the notion of the Lammas tithes, and for this reason is the month of the 'Kern Baby', a figure made from corn and carried before the reapers to the harvesting, in some places preserved for the whole of the following year. In some areas, the Kern is called the Harvest Doll, and many authorities assume that the word 'Kern' is a corruption of the Old English 'cyrnel', from which we get our modern 'kernel', relating to corn and seeds. The Kern Baby, which is a model something like a beneficent version of the witchcraft poppet or doll (see HEREFORD), is to be distinguished from the Harvest Queen, who is usually a woman dressed up in corn, or carrying a sheaf beneath her arm and a scythe in her hand, in the modern version of the pagan goddess Ceres.

The link with the past is more apparent in the Scottish name for the equivalent of the pagan Ceres, which is 'the Maiden', one of the names for the starry constellation of Virgo, which in Roman times was also called Ceres and was imagined to be a sheaf-bearing woman in the skies. From the Scottish rituals at Innerleithen we are to suppose that the Devil came to the Burgh in the third week of August, AD 737, and was confronted by St Ronan, who caught hold of the Devil's hairy hind leg with his crozier, for the ritual is now enacted in 'Cleiking the Devil'. Unfortunately, the ritual, for all its simplicity, appears not to be very ancient, for it was established by that great creator of Scottish mythology, Sir Walter Scott and his poet friend, James Hogg, in 1827. In the ceremony,

22: A witch doll of the kind used by witches in casting their spells. This one is now in the Hereford Museum.

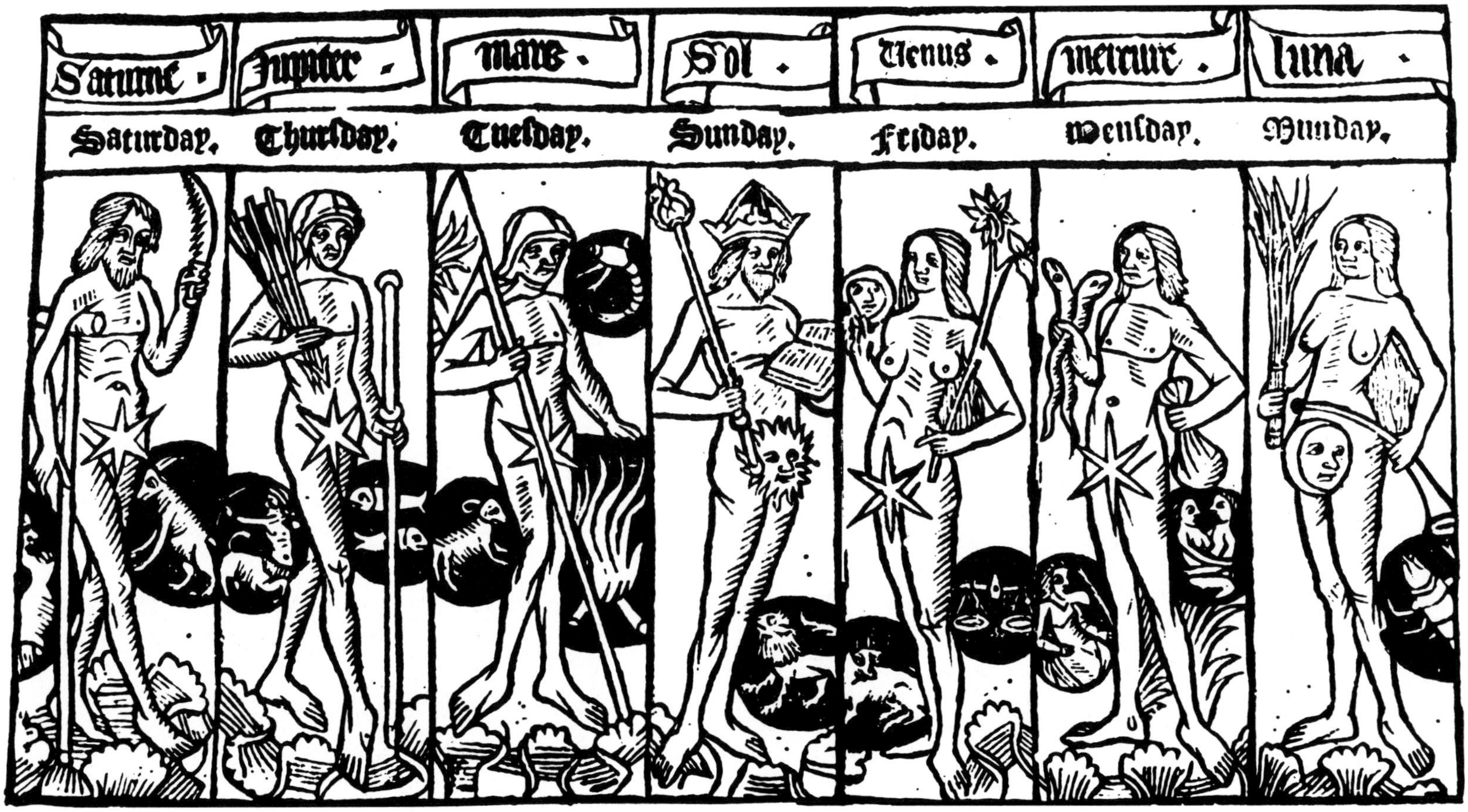

23: Personifications of the seven planets with their associated zodiacal signs and the corresponding days of the week (after a 16th-century Shepherd's Calendar).

modern or ancient, the role of the saint is played by a schoolboy (see SALISBURY), the Dux (Leader) of one of the local schools, who is furnished with a curled crozier, dressed like a monk, and instructed on how to 'cleik' or 'catch' the devil with its hook.

For a note of the August Plague Service, see EYAM, and for a ritual of horn-blowing in this month, see RIPON. In the 'zodiacal calendar' this month was associated with Leo, and with the 'monthly labour' of hay-making — see however the inset, following, which lists the 12 labours of the month as found on the zodiacal font at BROOKLAND. The month is linked in the magical tradition with the birthstones sardonyx and peridot, which was worn to foster married happiness. This may be connected with the fact that, in the horoscope, the sign Leo is directly linked with the house of creativity, love and children. In ancient times, however, the favoured birthstone was the carnelian.

The cycle of the months, expressed in the cycle of the 12 zodiacal signs, is associated in the ancient calendars with 12 specific activities related to the passage of the sun. Several examples of the relationship between zodiac signs and labours are found in medieval manuscripts, but the finest example to have survived in a church is the French thirteenth-century font at BROOKLAND, where the months are named (in French) along with the corresponding image of the zodiacal sign (also named), and a design intended to portray the corresponding labour of the month. There are one or two small errors in the font imagery, no doubt due to the ignorance of the designer in astrological matters. For example, the goat of Capricorn is confused with the Ram of Aries, and the 'animal' of Scorpio is presented as a frog, rather than a scorpion, but the general symbolism is otherwise correct. Beginning with January, which marks the beginning of the year according to the modern calendar, the font shows:

MONTH	SYMBOL	SIGN	MONTHLY LABOUR
January	Water-bearer	Aquarius	Two faced god Janus, feasting at a table
February	Two fishes	Pisces	Man in cloak, warming himself at fire
March	Ram	Aries	Man pruning a vine
April	Bull	Taurus	Female figure holding a spray of foliage
May	Two figures	Gemini	Two men with big hats, embracing
June	Crab	Cancer	Man mowing with a scythe
July	Lion	Leo	Man hay-making
August	Woman	Virgo	Man cutting corn with a sickle
September	Scales	Libra	Man threshing
October	Frog	Scorpio	Treading grapes in a vat
November	Centaur-archer	Sagittarius	Feeding swine with acorns
December	Goat-fish	Capricorn	Killing the fatted pig

24: A medieval depiction of Leo and its Occupation.

SEPTEMBER

The name of the month introduces the sequence derived entirely from the Roman calendar as 'numerical' derivations. The Latin 'septem' meant 'seven', and when the calendrical system began in March, this was the seventh month.

When Christianity was introduced to Britain, this month was called 'Halig-monath' (Holy Month) because of the number of important festivals which were celebrated. These included St Giles' Day (1 September), the nativity of the Virgin Mary (8th), the Exaltation of the Cross (14th), St Matthew's Day (21st), Holy-Rood, or Holy Cross Day (26th) and Michaelmas Day (29th). It is interesting to see that most of these are recorded in the Clog Calendar (figure 17 — the bottom third of the third part of the clog from the left) with distinctive signs: 1 September is a capital G; 8th is a heart; 14th is an arrowed cross; 21st is a square; and 29th is a pair of scales, such as St Michael uses to weigh the souls of the dead.

The ancient Gorsedd — the Cornish equivalent of the Welsh Eisteddfod — is celebrated on the first Saturday of September. The festival is entirely Celtic in spirit and begins with the sounding of the 'Horn of the Nation' four times to the four points of the compass, followed by a special prayer supported by harp music. The Grand Bard, who wears a laurel wreath, is presented with the fruits of the earth by a woman; there is a lament for those bards who have died in the preceding year, followed by the initiation of new bards, chosen for their contribution to the Celtic spirit.

On the Monday following the first Sunday of September, the famous Horn Dance takes place at ABBOTS BROMLEY, with the Hobby Horse, Maid Marion and Fool: see also the September pageant at ASHTON-UNDER-LYNE. In the 'zodiacal calendar' the month is associated with the sign Virgo, and with the magical birthstone the sapphire (sometimes the semi-precious lapis lazuli), which is worn to free oneself of magical enchantments.

OCTOBER

October was the 'Eighth Month' (Latin 'octo' means 'eight') of the ancient calendar, and was the Winmonath (Wine-month) of the Anglo Saxons, an idea which lives on in the many medieval images of the 'occupations of the months', showing men pressing the grapes as a sign of the vintage. One suspects that such a word had been imported by the Romans, however, and the alternative Anglo-Saxon 'Gerstmonath' (Barley-month) makes more sense in the British climate.

Hallowe'en is properly the 'Eve of All Hallows', held on the last day of October, and one festival or rite which is undisputably of ancient pagan origin. It is widely believed that on this night all the supernatural forces have an especial power, and many insist that it was on this night that the Druids held their greatest festival of Fire, related to the Gaelic sun-worship festival of Samhain on the first of NOVEMBER (page 00).

The numerous tales of haunting and supernatural adventures which throng this night are steeped in the pagan belief that at this time of the year the souls of the departed were free to return to the earth and seek out their beloved ones or their enemies. Whether they know it or not, those children who besmirch their faces with soot, or put on masks and pay visits in hope of gaining a few pennies, are playing the role of returning spirits. When this pagan belief was 'Christianized' by the church, it was turned from a night of returning spirits to the Vigil of All Saints, the Holy Ones, for All Hallows really means 'All Saints', the saints being the blessed dead. All Saints Day falls on 1 November.

In many rural districts of England the Hallow Evening is 'Nut Crack Night', and involves a sort of scrying of the future by means of the spirits supposedly abroad. Girls who wish to know the identity of their future husbands place three nuts in the fire, naming each one in turn; she herself is the middle nut, while the others are named after potential or real suitors. If one of the nuts explodes, then the omens for marriage (with the one named) are bad; if they burn together steadily, then the omens are good. The practice seems to be derived from Roman customs in ancient times. See also HINTON ST GEORGE.

October is perhaps a strange month for Harvest Thanksgiving, but the annual Fish Harvest Festival in Billingsgate, London, is usually held during the first Sunday of the month. It is said that the 39 different kinds of fish displayed during the ceremony represent the 39

25: Zodiac and planetary spheres with the schemes of alchemy and occult science. Print by Merian from a 1677 edition of *Janitor Pansophus*.

Articles of the Anglican faith, which were established in 1562. This Billingsgate service has a parallel in the Pearly Kings and Queens service in the Church of Lady Margaret-with-St Mary Magdalene in Walworth, which is the equivalent of a Harvest Festival held by the costermongers. The distinctive Pearlies' costumes are said to have been developed towards the beginning of the present century as a result of the import through London Docks of a number of highly-decorated Mexican costumes, the sartorial elegance and glitter of which caught the local imagination to such an extent that the local tailors had to make their own copies.

October is also the feast of St Crispian, the day made famous by the glorious speech in Shakespeare's *Henry V* (see, however, FULDA). Another day of military glory falls near to St Crispian's day: the 'Alamein Reunion' (as near to 23 October as possible) is the anniversary of the news of the Allied breakthrough under Montgomery against the Germans at Alamein in Egypt during World War II. In the 'zodiacal calendar' this month is associated with the sign Libra, and with the magical birthstone opal, though in the United States the tourmaline is also favoured. Both stones are worn to promote hope. In ancient times the aquamarine and the beryl were associated with October.

NOVEMBER

November was the 'Ninth' month (Latin 'novem' means 'nine') in the ancient calendar, which began the year in March. In the Anglo-Saxon calendar it was 'Blotmonath', which meant 'blood-month' or 'slaughter-month'. This explains why the medieval images of the 'labours of the month' (figure 26) usually depict a man feeding or skinning a pig, or some other creature, which is to be killed when the Sun enters the next sign of Capricorn.

This month opens propitiously with the great festivals of the ancient Samhain, the calendrical finale of the Gaelic year, marked cosmically by the autumn equinox, the Allantide of Cornish lore. As may be seen from the Hallowe'en of OCTOBER (page 25), the Christianized equivalent is All Saints Day, prefaced by the dark visitants of Hallowe'en. Originally this day was one of the four important festival days, when the Sun's pathway was distinctly related to the zodiac to mark one of the great quarters.

The fire-rituals of the ancient Samhain find little correspondence in the Christian rituals of All Hallows, or All Saints, the reason for this being one of economics. Originally, the dedication to All Saints (or, as it was in those days, the Feast of All Holy Martyrs — something different from All Saints) was observed on 13 May, and involved considerable pilgrimages over vast distances to Rome. In the ninth century, however, the date was moved to 1 November, on the basis that so many thousands of extra mouths were more easily fed after the harvest than in late Spring. The one significant link between the pagan cult and the Christian survives in the modern practice in which, on the evening of 1 November, which is All Souls' Eve, people visit the graves of their departed, nominally to pray for their souls or to leave candles burning in fiery vigil.

All Souls (which falls on 2 November) is the day given over in the Christian calendar to commemorating or praying for the dead in Purgatory, though in practical terms little distinction is made between those in Purgatory, Paradise or even Hell, the distinct states signified by these three 'places' being more or less forgotten in modern times. For an account of the related rites of Soulcaking, see COMBERBACH.

Mischievous Night falls in most regions on 4 November, and is inextricably linked with the quite separate bonfire rituals of the Gunpowder Plot burnings of the following day. Mischievous Night seems to have origins in pagan mythology, being one of those curious times when the Lord of Misrule was permitted a certain latitude to play pranks and to go unpunished by having the law turn a blind eye to hooliganism. It appears to be a misplaced Hallowe'en Night and not all places celebrate it (if that is the word) on 4 November — for example, Burnley had (still has, according to some) a Mischief Night on 30 April.

The Gunpowder Plot festivities, in which the image of Guy Fawkes is burnt against a background of fireworks, is one of the few pagan festivals to be supported by Act of Parliament, specifically designed to commemorate the failure of the plotters to blow up the Houses of Parliament in 1605. Some of the civic bonfires arranged on this day are of a very substantial kind, preceded by much public pomp and circumstance. The month closes with the feast day of St Andrew, patron saint of Scotland, whose distinctive symbol of the large X in the last column of the Clog Calendar (figure 17) commemorates his crucifixion upside down upon an x-shaped cross, an event which is reflected in the Coat of Arms of the city of ST ANDREWS.

In the 'zodiacal calendar' the month is associated with the sign Scorpio (see above), and with the magical birthstone topaz, which is worn to promote friendship and ensure fidelity. This is one of the few stones which has throughout history been linked with a specific month, for it was worn by those born in November even in ancient Greek and Roman times.

26: An astrological calendar from a 16th-century Shepherd's Calendar. The central image shows feminine Spring and masculine Winter; the inner concentric is concerned with the activities of the months, while the outer concentric depicts the twelve signs of the zodiac. This basic imagery is found on many medieval cathedral portals.

DECEMBER

December was the 'Tenth Month' (Latin 'decem' means 'ten') in the ancient calendar which began in March. One of the Anglo-Saxon names for the month points to the importance of the major pagan festival at this time — the Yule (Geola) which became our Christmas. Curiously enough, some specialists have claimed that our word 'jolly' is derived from this Old English word, in reference to the celebrations which took part in this Yule festival which marked the Winter Solstice.

One of the strangest customs in Britain is that practised in DEWSBURY on Christmas Eve — the tolling of the Devil's Knell on the bell of the parish church, perhaps a reminder of how December is dominated by the festival which is now called Christmas, but which has deep roots in our Nordic past.

Christmas is now celebrated on 25 December (near to the ancient Yule) in the Christian world, but this was not always the case. At one time the Birth of Christ was believed to have taken place on 6 January, and in the ancient church Christmas was celebrated on that day (see JANUARY, page 18). However, the Christian event was eventually merged with one of the pagan ceremonies of Yuletide, celebrated on 25 December, and many of the customs proper to paganism were merged with the Christian. This explains why we celebrate the day that Christ was born by burning the Yule Log, and why we festoon our houses with mistletoe, sacred to the Druids.

It is said that the practice of taking a huge mistletoe bough into YORK Minster for blessing at the high altar is a recognition of the Christianizing of the old pagan mysteries, of which the Druids were considered to be the initiates. The Druids had called mistletoe 'All Heal', and it is therefore not unreasonable for it to be linked with the Great Healer who is Christ. Some historians record that in the earlier calendar, 25 December was dedicated to Satan, to the 'heathen deities worshipped during the dynasties of the British, Saxon and Danish Kings'. It is recorded by Brand, as one of the notions of popular mythology, that the first British Christmas was celebrated in AD 521 in YORK. Before that time there is ample evidence to show that the extensive Yule Feast was observed from about 10 days prior to the Winter Solstice through to what we now call Christmas (see MAESHOWE). The Christmas tree, for all that it has been Christianized, and explained as the living tree on which Christ eventually died, was without doubt the pagan tree decorated in honour of Yule. Father Christmas also has a strange origin, for he appears to be a merging of the bearded Arch Druid of pagan lore with the patron saint of children, St Nicholas of Bari, who resurrected three children murdered by an inn-keeper, and who gave three golden dowries to three poor women.

27: Medieval Model of the Universe from Raymond Lull's *Practica Compendiosa Artis*, 1532 edition.

28: Constellation map with zodiac figures, after the design of Vale & Schenk, printed in the 18th century.

The link with children, and the 'giving of gifts', merged in the national consciousness and were superimposed over the old image of the bearded Druid in his distinctive initiate's hat. In the old Clog Calendar (figure 17), the day of Christmas is marked with what has been described as a 'drinking horn', a reminder of the practice of merry drinking; however, it is more likely that this was a sickle, a reminder of the Druidic rites.

The old belief that what is begun on Childermas Day may never find fulfilment is derived from the belief that this day (28 December) is the most melancholy in the calendar, being the anniversary of the day on which the Holy Innocents were massacred on the orders of Herod. It is said that the tradition of obliging children to read prayers in church on this day is derived from the old custom of whipping children to mark the tyranny practised on the original Innocents Day, or 'Cross Day' as it is called.

The Scottish Hogmanay, celebrated on the last day of the month with drinking, entertainment and general festivity, is a linguistic mystery. Some claim that the name is actually from a French word (aigullanneuf), said to have been used for wishing good luck to the mistletoe of the new year, and of pagan origin. The dark man who is invited into homes to 'let the New Year in' will also be derived from pagan rites connected with the Saturnine god of darkness.

The Wassail Cup, which was originally a bowl of spiced ale but is now virtually any alcoholic drink, is said to be from the Saxon drinking phrase 'Waes hael', which meant approximately 'to your health'. The practice of Wassailing was merged with that of visitations of friends to various houses where the drink flowed free, giving rise to what Milton called 'swilled insolence'.

In the 'zodiacal calendar', this month is associated with Sagittarius (page 28), and with the magical birthstone turquoise. In the United States the stone zircon is also used, but both are worn to ensure love and prosperity. Turquoise is said to indicate the state of the wearer's health according to changes in hue. In ancient times the birthstone of December was the ruby, and the tradition of wearing this stone has persisted in some rural areas.

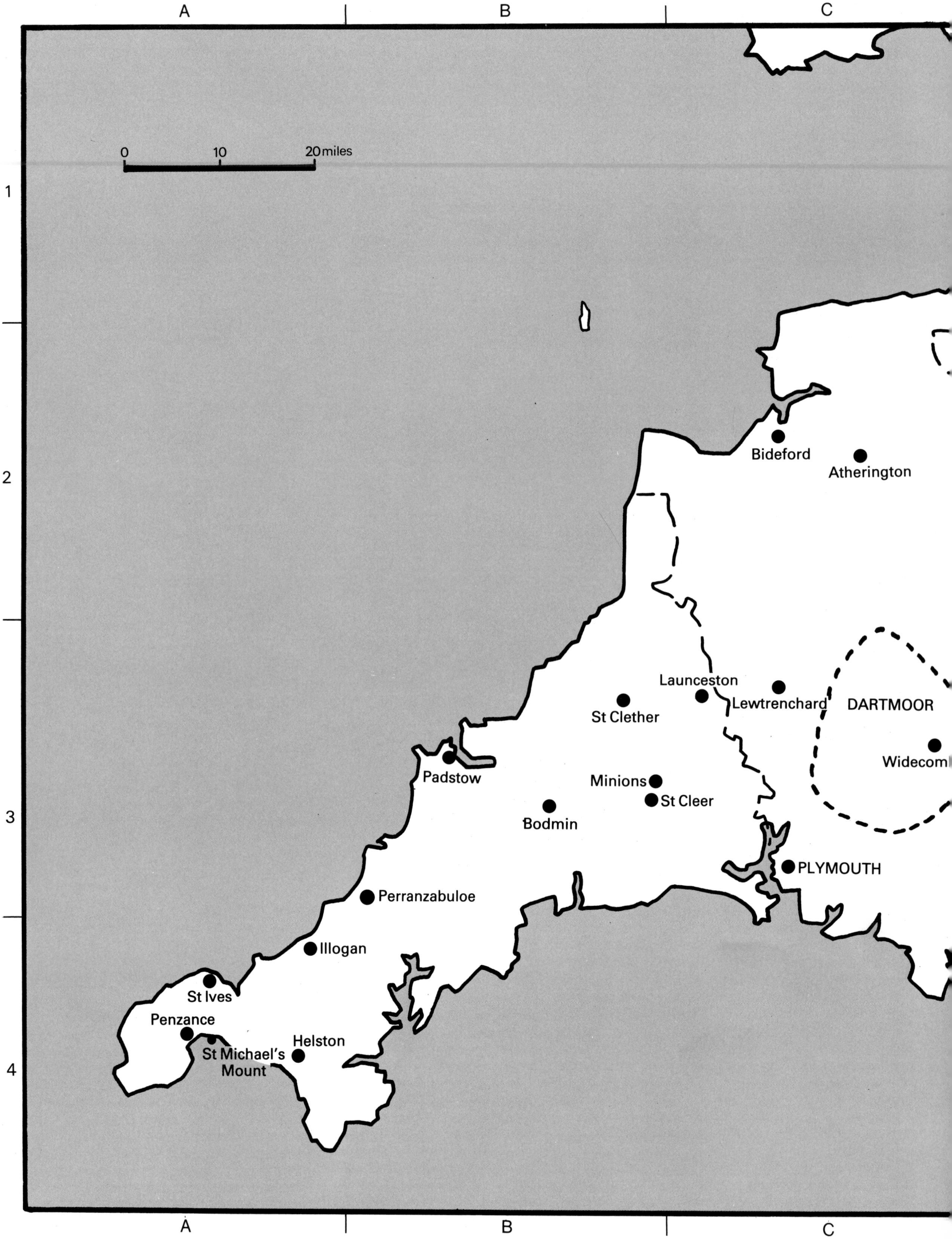

A
B
C
1
2
3
4
0
10
20 miles
Bideford
Atherington
Launceston
Lewtrenchard
DARTMOOR
St Clether
Widecom
Padstow
Minions
St Cleer
Bodmin
PLYMOUTH
Perranzabuloe
Illogan
St Ives
Penzance
St Michael's
Mount
Helston

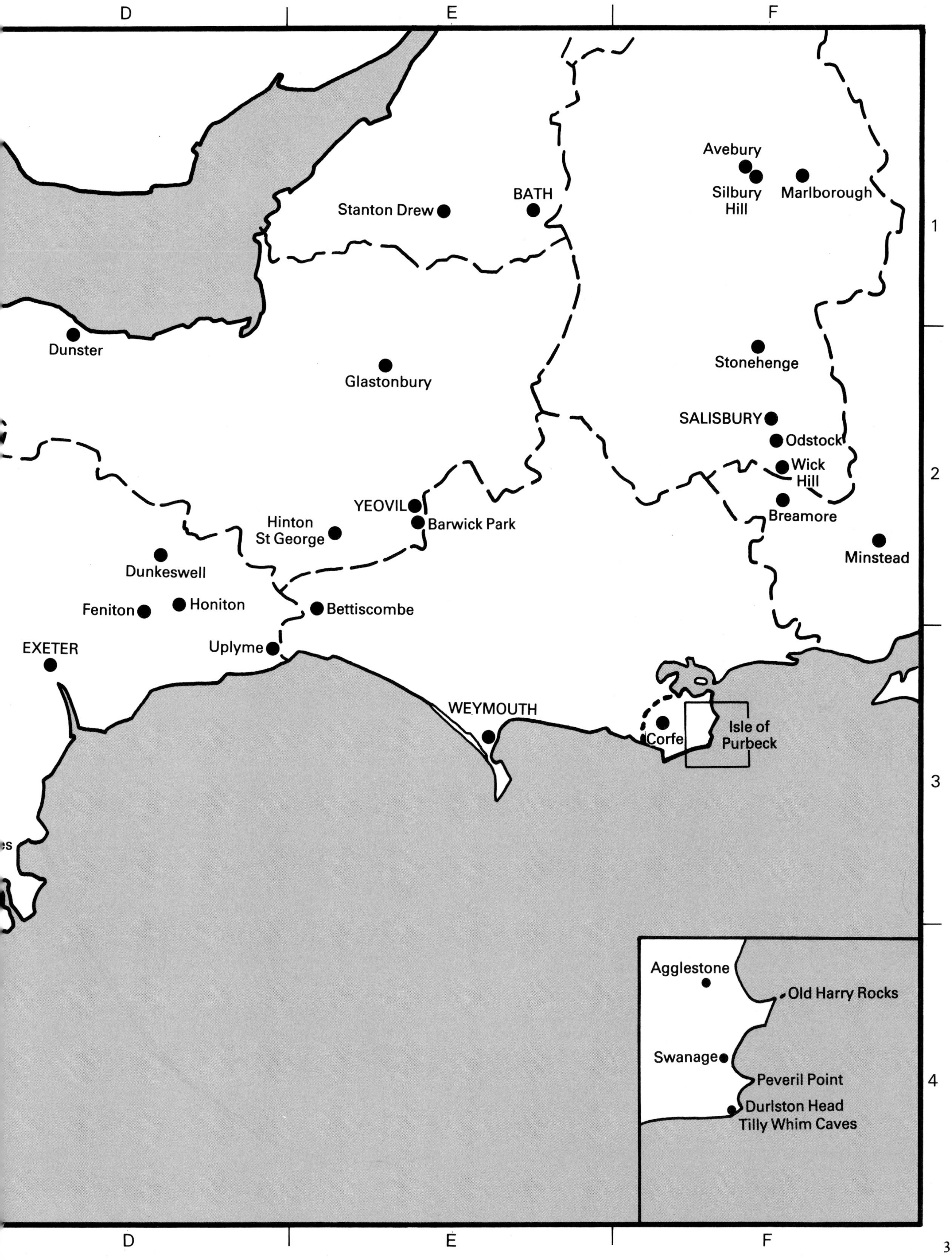
D
E
F
1
2
3
4
Avebury
Silbury Hill
Marlborough
BATH
Stanton Drew
Dunster
Glastonbury
Stonehenge
SALISBURY
Odstock
Wick Hill
Breamore
Minstead
YEOVIL
Barwick Park
Hinton St George
Dunkeswell
Feniton
Honiton
Bettiscombe
EXETER
Uplyme
WEYMOUTH
Corfe
Isle of Purbeck
Agglestone
Old Harry Rocks
Swanage
Peveril Point
Durlston Head
Tilly Whim Caves

The West Country

ATHERINGTON, Devon C2

In the parish church (north chancel aisle) is the cross-legged effigy of Sir William Champernowne, who died towards the end of the twelfth century. It is widely believed that effigies were shown cross-legged in order to indicate that the person represented had been on one of the crusades (that is, crossing their legs in a mark of respect for the Holy Cross which they protected in Jerusalem). However, this is a fallacy, though there is no record of how this misunderstanding arose. Even those effigies of the 'templar knights' in the London Temple are probably not meant to be crusading knights, and indeed it is argued by some scholars that they do not even represent templars. Another thirteenth-century cross-legged effigy in Devon is in the Parish Church at Georgeham. For a related brass, see ACTON.

AVEBURY, Wiltshire F1

The stone circles (of which the menhir in figure 29 is an inner upright) and embankments at Avebury are part of a much larger prehistoric configuration, which some trace even as far afield as STONEHENGE. Near to Avebury is the largest man-made hill in Europe — SILBURY HILL. The ceremonial monument of Avebury is itself the largest in Europe, and is usually dated to circa 2,000 BC.

29: The stone circles and embankments at Avebury are part of a much larger prehistoric configuration. The ceremonial monument at Avebury is said to be the largest in Europe and is usually dated to c.2,000 B.C.

BARWICK PARK, Somerset E2

In the grounds of Barwick House, Somerset, are a number of follies, the easterly one of which is a coned turret on a crumbling arch, which bears as a finial a statue of Hermes, the ancient messenger of the gods. The folly is said to have been built by George Messiter to give work to the unemployed in the 1830s, but the style of the buildings (as well as the idea behind them) suggest an earlier date. The eastern folly is called after Jack the Treacle Eater, who is said to have been a private messenger who would run with letters to London, and who kept fit on treacle. Other accounts speak of a murderer, hiding from justice in the grounds of Barwick House, being fed on treacle by his mother. Perhaps this curious garble of names is a mingling of the ancient Hermes, who was a messenger of the Gods, and the local pagan legends of Jan Tregeagle (see BODMIN MOOR). St Mary Magdalene church in Barwick has some very interesting bench-ends (conveniently dated 1533) with such subjects as the fox and goose, a man climbing a tree and dogs hunting rabbits — all themes derived from medieval stories.

BATH, Avon E1

The English word 'Bath' relates to the Roman baths, which were regarded by the ancients as holy waters. Magical amulets of the Roman period have been found in and around the baths by excavators. The shop-lined Pulteney Bridge (figure 30) was designed circa 1777 by Robert Adam, who lived in the nearby village of Calne. It was inspired by the old bridge in Florence, itself once a Roman city.

BETTISCOMBE, Dorset E2

The history and mythology of Britain incorporates many legends relating to human skulls. The most famous of these are the series of 'screaming skulls', of which the 'negro skull' at Bettiscombe Manor is perhaps the best-known. The story goes that should this skull be removed from the building, then terrible events will befall those within the house. Stories tell how a tenant of the manor did attempt to rid himself of the skull, by throwing it into a pond in the village, but for some days afterwards the whole house shook with screams, until the skull was returned. This skull is said to belong to a negro slave of the late eighteenth century, who was buried (against his own wishes) in the local churchyard. There is no foundation to this story, however, for forensic research has shown that it is almost certainly the skull of a Celtic woman, most probably from the nearby Pilsdon Pen Camp between Bettiscombe and Broadwindsor and therefore at least 1,500 years old. Other finds from this site, with a far less romantic and extravagant history, are preserved in Dorchester Museum.

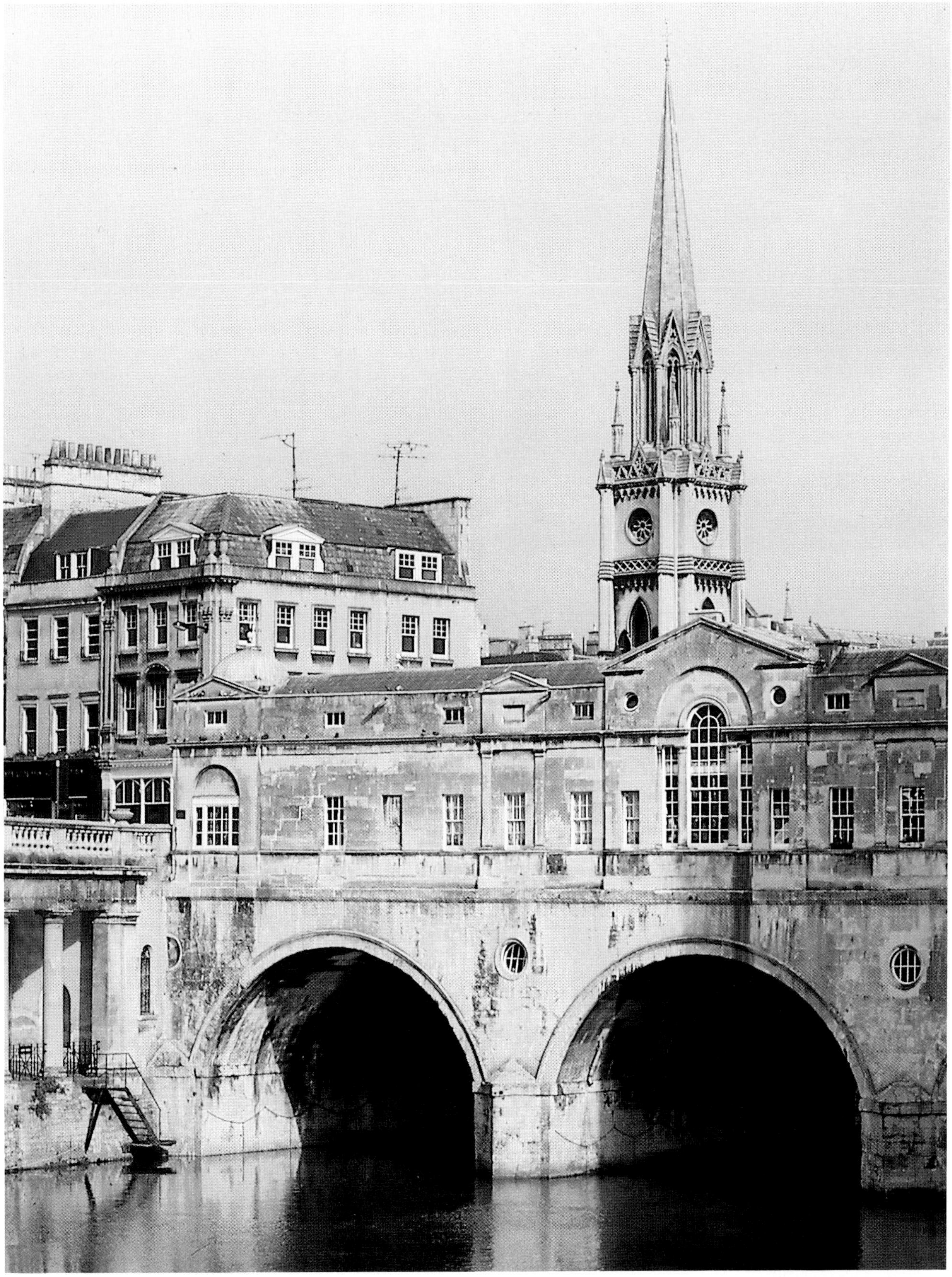

30: Bath was named Aqua Sulis by the Romans who used its healing waters (from which we get the modern name). The shop-lined Pulteney Bridge (c. 1777) in the picture was designed by Robert Adam, who lived in the nearby village of Calne.

Another 'screaming skull' is that in WARDLEY Hall.

The most famous skull is probably that of Robert the Bruce, in the Scottish National Portrait Gallery (see MELROSE). This, however, is a coloured plaster-cast, made from the royal skull of Robert when his tomb was opened in 1819.

One or two private museums and medical schools now display skulls or even whole skeletons of famous or infamous people. The partial skeleton of Mary Bateman (see LEEDS), who was executed at York and hanged in chains at Leeds, is now in the Leeds Medical School, while the entire skeleton of the giant Charles Byrne, who was the talk of the town in the late eighteenth century, was housed in the Museum of the Royal College of Surgeons in London. For the sake of emphasis, this gigantic skeleton was placed alongside the tiny form of Caroline Crachami, the 'Sicilian Dwarf' (see LONDON — HAYMARKET).

For a note of a 'charnel house' of skulls, see CLIFTON.

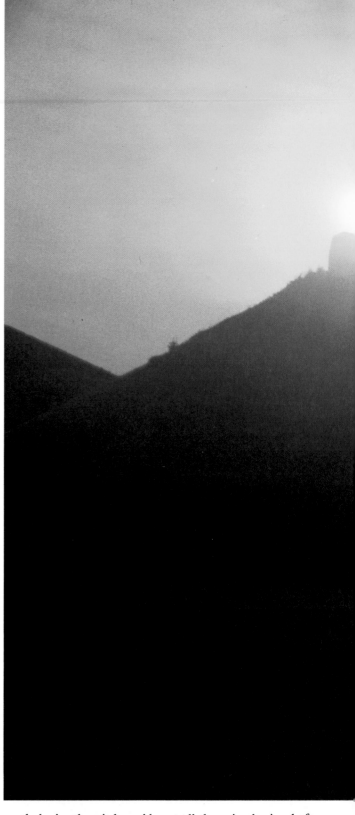

31: Behind the churchyard at Bideford is a road where a witch claims to have met the Devil in person. The first Red Indian to be converted to Christianity in Britain was baptised in St Mary's church in Bideford, in the font still within.

BIDEFORD, Devon C2

The first Red Indian to be converted in Britain, during the late sixteenth century, was baptized in St Mary's church at Bideford (figure 31). The font is still inside the church. Behind the churchyard is a road where a local witch claimed to have made a pact with the Devil in person.

32: Outcroppings on Bodmin Moor, said by occultists such as Blavatsky to be man-made and marking the places where old magical rituals or initiation ceremonies were practised. These are above the village of Minions.

BODMIN, Cornwall B3

Bodmin Moor is littered with the visible remains of primitive man in the form of stone circles (figure 32) and burial grounds, and has been the unhappy hunting ground of so many thousands of superstitious miners that one is surprised it does not have far more ghosts and

mythologies than it has. Almost all the ruined mineshaft engine-houses on the moors (figure 34) have their resident ghosts, while the long chambers within the mine shafts still have their 'kobolds', or mine-goblins, who delight in confusing the miners with acts of mimicry and the use of echoes. We learn that the name of the metal cobalt is taken from this demon's name, because the metal was considered for a long time to be useless and (because of the arsenic and sulphur with which it was found combined) harmful to health. It was therefore said to have been made by the Kobalt demon. In some Cornish mines the tin-mine demon was called a Bucca, though the same name is also used for a wind-goblin

34: One of the many derelict tin mine engine-houses on the Cornish moors. Almost every one of them is believed to have a resident ghost.

33: The ruins of Corfe Castle, Dorset. There was a castle on this spot long before William the Conqueror came to Britain.

which could foretell shipwrecks, and which was popular with the wreckers. It may be just a question of shaft acoustics magnifying underground waterfalls, but inexplicable and often deafening noises were frequently reported in the days when the tin-mine shafts were still worked. Most famous was that called 'Roaring Shaft' in the complex of mines on Goonzion Down: the noise was described as being akin to 'a battery of stamps falling regularly with thuds and reverberated through the ground'. Such noises were probably natural in origin, but they served only to feed the dark images of spirits and demons in the minds of those who worked in those hellish corridors to mine copper, silver and gold. The mining took on its modern face (now recorded only by the gaunt and beautiful engine-houses on the Moors) relatively late, for it was not until 1837 that the main copper ore beneath Caradon was discovered. This explains why most of the mythologies wear a modern face. We are told of wife-auctions among the miners. In Camelford one reject wife was auctioned for 'half a crown' (12½ new pence), which was then the equivalent of a week's wages. A better male chauvinist tale is told of Bodmin, where a used wife was sold for 'sixpence' (less than a day's wage), and the thick rope with which she had been pulled to market was thrown in for free to the lucky buyer. See also MINIONS.

CORFE, Dorset F3

The spectacular hill castle at Corfe has seen most of the calms and upsets of British history, for there was a castle commanding this site long before William the Conqueror came to these lands. Indeed, it was the presence of this castle which appears to have given rise to the notion that Purbeck was an island (see ISLE OF PURBECK). Corfe achieved historic infamy when Prince Edward's stepmother Elfrida invited him to stay in the castle for a hunting trip and, whilst he was still in his stirrups, had him knifed to death. Legends tell that she then hid the body in a well near to the Castle, but that during the night a mysterious ray of light began to glow over the well's head and revealed the body by supernatural means; the well was afterwards called St Edward's Fountain. Other stories recount that when she tried to follow his funeral party to his reburial at Shaftesbury, she was miraculously prevented from doing so. The founding of the Abbey is said to be her response to this miracle.

The castle fared like many others during the interlude following the Conquest, and by the time King John owned it the walls were strengthened and the rooms transformed into a huge royal prison. It quickly gained a justified reputation for the starvation of prisoners in its deep dungeons, which were used as little more than oubliettes. Princess Eleanor was incarcerated within its walls for almost forty years, and it was during this time (1212) that a 'wizard', Peter of Pomfret, prophesied that on the following Ascension Day the bad King would lose his throne. The King's response was to have this prophet dragged behind horses from the Castle to Wareham, then back for good measure, prior to having him drawn and quartered — that most ghastly of all medieval deaths. As it happened, the wizard was proved wrong, for John lived another four years in which he had time to witness with his seal the famous Magna Carta.

If Corfe's historic reputation began with an evil woman, then it came to an end with a very brave one. In the absence of her husband, Lady Bankes held Corfe Castle for a long time against Cromwell's troops. Part of the local mythology insists that in 1643, when the Parliamentarians ran out of shot, they melted down the lead roofs of Lulworth Castle and the local church, and used the sanctified organ pipes as receptacles for powder and shot. Lady Bankes' spirited defence of the castle was cut short by betrayal, when one of her own officers led the Parliamentarians back to Corfe from Weymouth. The castle is in ruins, but the keen-eyed gargoyles of Corfe parish church look down into a prosperous village, in which past traditions have not been entirely lost.

The craft guild of The Marblers and Stonecutters of Purbeck still present the Lord of the Manor with a pound of peppercorns, probably in lieu of rent. In modern times a headless white ghost has been seen by different people (the last time in 1976) hovering by the castle gates.

DARTMOOR, Devon C3

Dartmoor is infamous for the so-called 'Whist Hounds', the 'Hounds of Hell', said to be a pack of spectral dogs which haunt the locality and inspired Sir Arthur Conan Doyle to write *The Hound of the Baskervilles* . The Whist Hounds are associated with the demonic Wild Hunt, which has the devil as the night huntsman; in particular, legends tell how the pack chases benighted travellers to the edge of Dewerstone Rock on Dartmoor to drive them

over the edge to their doom. The notion of 'spectral' or 'ghostly' dogs, whether single or in packs, is found throughout the British Isles even today, and may be demoted versions of the ancient 'Ride of the Valkyries' of Norse mythology. The tendency to introduce historical personages as an outer guise for the forgotten gods may be seen in the fact that some locals claim the Whist Hounds are led by none other than Sir Francis Drake. In the north of England the hell hounds are sometimes called 'Gabriel Hounds', but the name has nothing to do with the Archangel of the Annunciation for the word comes from the ancient term 'gabbara', which was the equivalent of a 'dead body'. In Cornwall the Whist Hounds are called Dandy Dogs. Whatever their names, it is widely believed that when the baying of the hounds is heard then disaster bodes for the one who is listening, and those who see them, with their slavering jaws and red-coal eyes, is bound for a sudden death. Ralph Whitlock's *In Search of Lost Gods* suggests that the prevalence of black-dog ghosts might be a result of the ancient practice by which dogs were sacrificed and buried under the doorposts or walls of new buildings, that their spirits or souls might act as guardians of the place. Very many stories are told of black-dog hauntings, but the 'spectral hound' weather-vane on the parish church at Bungay must be unique. The demon hound of East Anglia is called Black Shuck — but see BUNGAY.

35: Dunster Castle, founded in 1070 and continually inhabited ever since, mainly by the Luttrell family. It is linked with the legends of a local giant, and with ghost stories.

DUNKESWELL, Devon D2

In the parish church is a Norman font which includes a carving of an elephant, said to be the earliest representation of this animal in English sculptured art. It was, however, a favourite subject of painters — especially those who illustrated the 'bestiaries', or zoological books, of the medieval period. As noted in the entry on COVENTRY, in those days it was believed that elephants had no knees, so that the cunning ivory hunter needed only to cause the elephants to lie down in order to render them helpless (once down, they could not climb to their feet again). Since they could not lie down, elephants were supposed to sleep by leaning their heads against tree trunks. With this in mind, the ivory-hunter would cut almost through the trunk of the tree, near to the base, so that when an elephant leaned against it the tree would fall over and with it the elephant, which would then be an easy victim for the hunter, who would cut off its tusks at his leisure.

DUNSTER, Somerset D2

The medieval castle at Dunster (figure 35) has had its kings and aristocracy, its legends, its underground passageways and ghosts. Originally dating from Norman times, it was modified several times and has been the home of the Luttrell family since the late fourteenth century. The castle was besieged by King Stephen in 1138, by the Royalists in 1642, and by the Parliamentarians in 1645 — while, under better circumstances, Charles II stayed here and no doubt enjoyed studying the leather embossed panels in the banqueting hall which depict the story of Antony and Cleopatra. It is said that the acorns carved on the pillars and tying posts of the stables at Dunster were intended to symbolize the escape of Charles to BOSCOBEL after the battle of Worcester.

As with all medieval castles, ghost stories have wrapped themselves around the walls, yet one comparatively recent find has lent some support to the notion of foul deeds in the past; during restorations in 1869, the seven-foot high skeleton of a man was found buried upright in the wall of the guardhouse. The skeleton was chained, with iron grips around its neck, wrists and ankles, suggesting that he had been imprisoned in a walled-up oubliette and left to die. Inside the castle is what is called the 'Spirits Room', in which William Prynne was incarcerated for seditious libel in 1650. It is said that during the eight months of his imprisonment he was taken out of the room only twice — once to be branded, and once to have his thumbs cut off.

FENITON, Devon D2

In the church of St Andrew at Feniton is an unusual fifteenth-century effigy of a 'cadaver', a life-sized human body in the last stages of emaciation, partly covered by a shroud. It is thought that this particular example represented a member of the local Malherbe family. For another striking 'cadaver', see WORSBROUGH.

GLASTONBURY, Somerset E2

Among the most fascinating aspects of the development of the Glastonbury mythology is the little-known activity of the archaeologist Frederick Bligh Bond in 'researching' the location and extent of lost chapels within the site of Glastonbury Abbey by means of clairvoyant techniques. By 1907 Bond and his friends (working mainly in Bristol) had developed a method of communicating by automatic writing with disincarnate entities (which we might for the sake of convenience call 'spirits') who provided them with detailed information about the siting and measurements of two chapels, the lost Edgar and Loretto Chapels, which had once formed an important part of the Glastonbury complex but had been lost to history, save in one or two marginal notes. The period during which the automatic scripts were produced lasted for about four years, from 1907. By November 1907, a disincarnate being calling himself 'William the Monk' drew, in response to questions put to him, several small plans of the original Abbey (figures 37) along with details of the lost Edgar Chapel as it had been built by the Abbot Beere, naming the chapel Capella St Edgar (see figure 36). In a later communication the spirit-monks admitted that they wanted the living to know about the Abbey — 'the times are now ripe for the glory to return and the curse is departing'.

36/37: Two examples of the automatic writings produced by 'spirits' in communication with the archaeologist Frederick Bligh Bond.

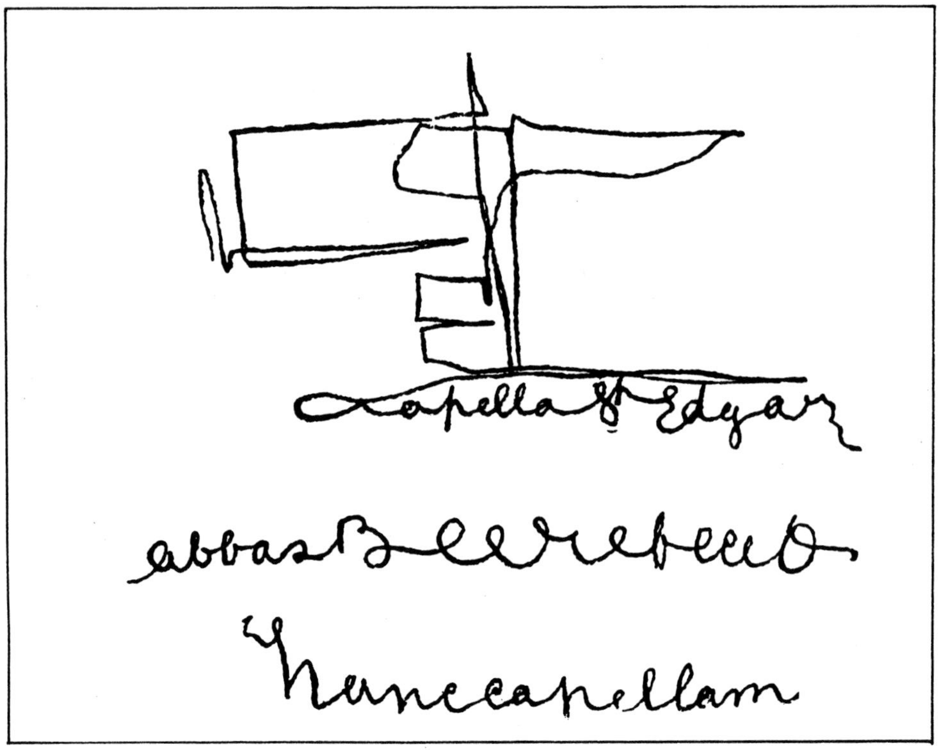

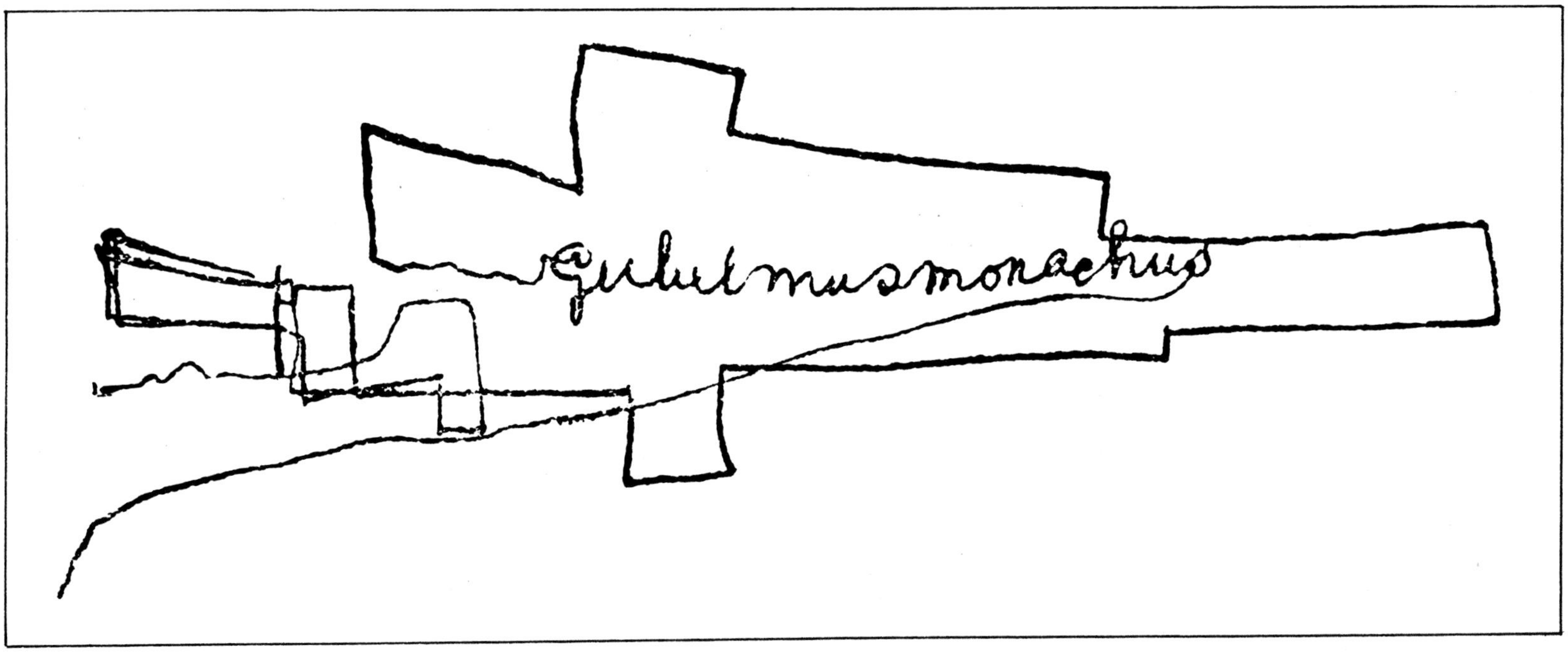

When Bond sought to find out more about the monk who was the main communicator in this matter, the spirit admitted 'Yn 1533 obitus' (I died in 1533). In his remarkable book which deals with these scripts and their influence upon the archaeological survey of Glastonbury, *The Gate of Remembrance* (1918), Bond published a table in which he compared the written notes derived from the spirit-monks alongside the then-known data, and the results of these findings. Even in those cases where no known record of architectural features had been preserved, the indications given by the monks were exact. An example is the script for 16 June, 1908, which mentions 'he who followed made new schemes for a certaine roofe in golde and crimson'. Nothing was known or recorded of such a scheme at that time. Subsequent digs showed that the script was accurate, for the arch-mouldings discovered later were painted in red and black, and retained traces of gold leaf. By a similar method of automatic responses to questions, another chapel, the Loretto, which had been mentioned by some early travellers, was also discovered. A later script admitted that 'our Abbey was a message in ye stones. In ye foundations and ye distances be a mystery...in ye floor of ye Mary Chappel was ye Zodiac, that all might see and understand the mystery.'

Was this perhaps the zodiac to which the Elizabethan magus John Dee referred in his sixteenth-century diaries, one wonders? Zodiacs were found in several continental churches, abbeys and cathedrals, but most of them have

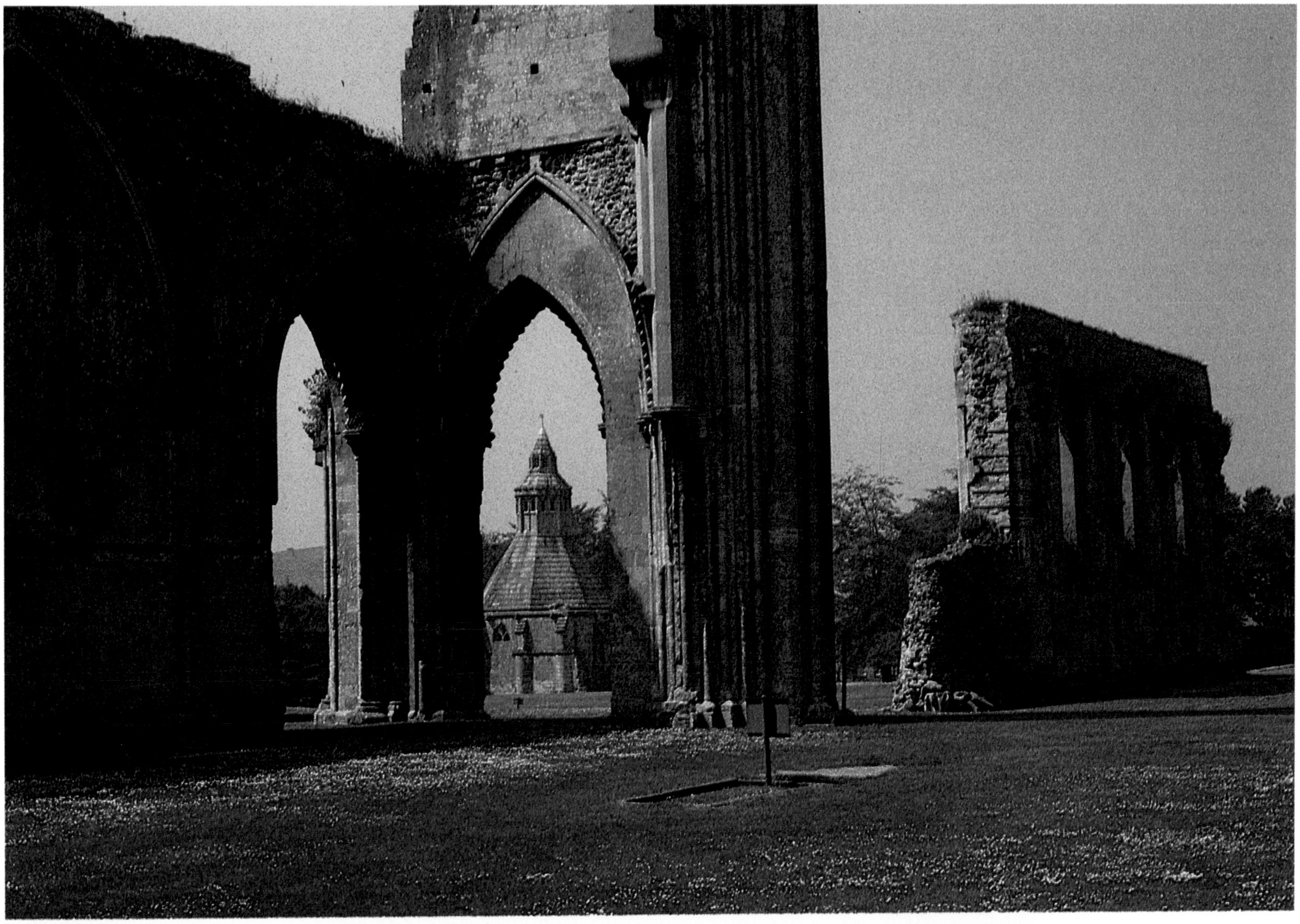

38: The ruined remains of Glastonbury Abbey.

39: Glastonbury Tor, with the ruined church of St Michael burning in the sunset. Some believe that Joseph of Arimathaea buried the Holy Chalice beneath the Tor.

40: Albrecht Durer's map of 1515, according to the calculations of Heinfogel and Stabius. The constellation figures are distinguished in tones of grey.

been lost from British churches. A badly-defaced series of zodiacal images is found in the Becket Chapel in Canterbury Cathedral, and a few zodiacal images survive on Norman doorways and fonts, but on the whole the art of the astrological secrets to which the monks refer has been lost. William of Malmesbury, writing in the twelfth century of this Mary Chapel, admits, 'In the pavement may be seen on every side stones designedly inlaid in triangles and squares, and figured with lead, under which, if I believe some sacred enigma to be contained, I do no injustice to religion.' The mystery of the Mary Chapel zodiac and its 'sacred enigma' is now lost, and was only resurrected as an idea by the automatic writing. Sometimes the automatic script of the spirit-monks is charged with great beauty and insight, at other times it throws some light on the nature of the world beyond, as for example that given on 4 December, 1916: 'The material world is the screen between the complex fabric of the simple weaving. The essential facts are eternal which (? move) in a circle, and to them that know the circle, somewhat will pass into all times, only see but little at a time. The centre is the point on which all revolves, and ye, revolving, are conscious of the influence, but cannot know the radius...'

HELSTON, Cornwall — A4

The 'Furry Dance' at Helston, celebrated in the first week of May, is said to have been the 'Floral Dance', held to welcome the spring. Couples dance to popular and traditional tunes (sometimes played on the horn-pipe) in and out of houses through the village, among scenes of much jolly banter and play. Traditionally the dance was heralded by 'troublesome rogues' who 'go round the streets with drums, or other noisy instruments, disturbing their sober neighbours; if they find any person at work, make him ride on a pole, carried on men's shoulders, to the river, over which he is to leap in a wide place, if he can; if he cannot, he must leap in, for leap he must, or pay money.'

HINTON ST GEORGE, Somerset — E2

On the last Thursday of October the inhabitants of Hinton St George have a sort of preview of Hallowe'en (see OCTOBER, page 25), which is called Punkie Night and is clearly linked with the Gaelic fires of the

Samhain. The village children beg from door to door for candles which they light and place in their lanterns made from mangel-wurzels, called 'punkies'. As with the goblin heads of Hallowe'en, the punkies are often carved into grotesque faces, and are sometimes carried on sticks over which float sheets to simulate the appearance of ghosts. So armed, the children march around the village singing 'It's Punkie Night tonight'.

ILLOGAN, Cornwall A4

The early days of the railroad have entered into a confused mythology in which schoolchildren learn that the first steam engine was invented by George Stephenson, although this is not so. Historians usually claim that the first steam locomotive was built in Paris by the Frenchman Cugnot, the idea being put into a working model by him as early as 1763. It was not until 1784 that William Symington made a working model driven by steam and that (working independently) William Murdock constructed a similar model. The great inventor Richard Trevithick, who was born in Illogan, Cornwall, in 1771, had been Murdock's pupil in engineering; he invented a high-pressure engine based on that of his teacher, which appears to have run as early as 1802. This was the first steam engine ever to draw passengers. It was this invention which led George Stephenson to construct his locomotive *Blucher*, which ran some distance on a trackway on 25 July, 1814. It was Stephenson who designed the first railway (running on lines, in 1825) to carry goods and passengers. Before this, however, there are records of other locomotives being in use; one invented by Blenkinsop and Murray, which went into service in June 1812, worked for over 20 years. The first railway train (in those days called a 'steam horse') to run at any considerable speed was Stephenson's *Rocket*, in 1829. There is a window in Westminster Abbey which commemorates Trethivick, who died penniless in Dartford.

ISLE OF PURBECK, Dorset F3

What a strange history there is in the marble on which this island floats! It is an entirely fictitious island, so-called from the days in which the only satisfactory land-pass into the area was by way of CORFE, which for millennia has been guarded by forts and castles. The visible chalk which extrudes in stacks towards the Needles of the Isle of Wight, with the famous Old Harry Rocks on the mainland side, fronts the veins of marble in the land beyond. Old Harry, like his stack wife who was lost to the sea in an 1896 storm, is an interloper, chiselled by the waves in comparatively recent times in an area where the most complete section of dinosaur tracks was found. These are now in the Natural History Museum in London.

This interloping Old Harry is named after the Devil himself, as though he belonged to a pagan tradition, but the Devil who threw the Agglestone near Studland did so in Christian times, for he was said to be throwing it in jealousy at the marvellous Norman church, and missed his aim. The 400-ton Agglestone is made of sandstone and is perched as though reluctantly on the softer eroded stone below. For all the stories of its demonic origin, some of the locals are pagan in attitude and swear that a dance around its bulk will improve fertility. Even

41: The 'Old Harry Rocks' (named after the Devil) near Swanage, Dorset, beyond Ballards Down. This natural formation, with its outlying stack, figured in the novels of Thomas Hardy at a time when 'Old Harry' had a wife, since thrown down by the sea.

stranger creatures than the Devil have trodden this island of Purbeck, as the Mammalian Bed near Durlston Head has revealed. Here have been found the remains of the world's earliest mammals, as well as the warm-water-loving crocodiles, which are a mute testimony to there once being decent weather conditions in this country.

Durlston Head has a 50-ton stone globe of the world, and the benches around have been marked with useful astronomical data, this display of largesse being from the unstinting pockets of George Burt. Those who have a cynical frame of mind consider that part of the inscription to this globe, 'He Made the Stars Also' refers to Burt, but it is of course a quotation from the Bible, a mention of God who made the Earth. Not that Burt was incapable, for he was one of the great Swanage men and the one who cleared all the ground to the curiously named Tilly Whim Caves, which are man-made interiors in the Purbeck Stone. Tilly Whim means something like 'The man with the stone-lifting windlass', and needs no explanation in this context of cave-making. The thin vein of Purbeck marble itself is seen as outcroppings at Peveril Point.

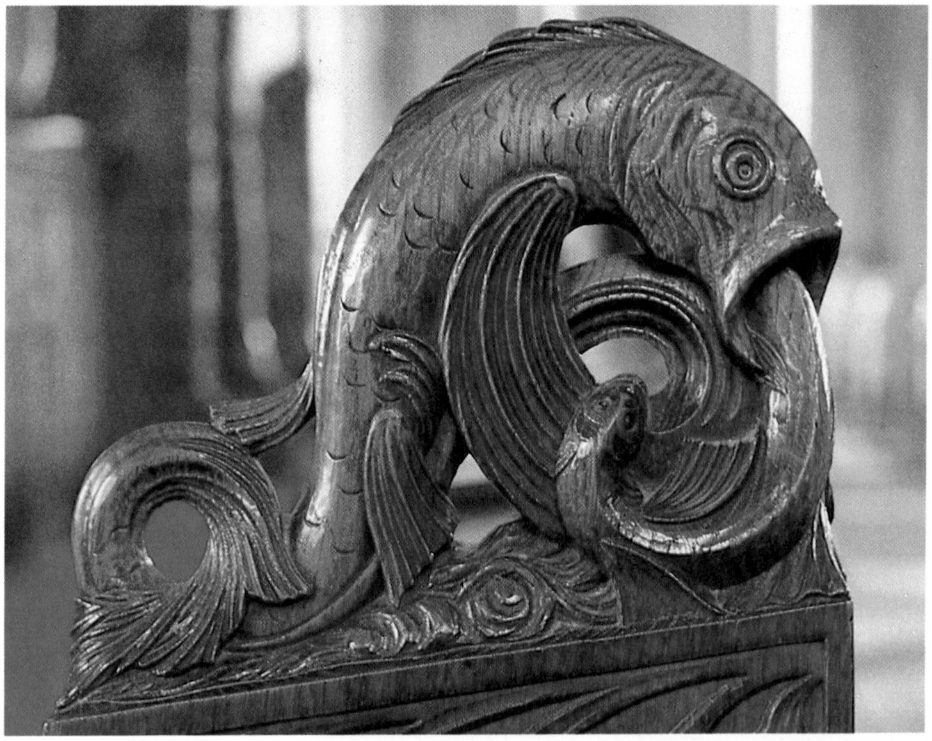

42 *(above)*: A bench end in the form of an exotic fish, inside the church of St Mary Magdalene, Launceston. The carving is from the 19th century.

LAUNCESTON, Cornwall C3

Launceston Castle looks less grim in modern times (figure 42) than it did in the sixteenth century, when it was one of the most important centres of the Cornish rebellions and riots against Edward VI. The rebellions arose mainly from an understandable, yet vain, attempt to preserve the Cornish independence and language, and reached their peak of violence when Parliament passed an Act in 1549 insisting on the use of English prayer books even in Cornish churches. Many of the Cornish 'rebels' were hung in public, then drawn and quartered on Launceston Green, where now only trees and tourists are found. Cornish men from all the main cities and towns, such as Launceston, marched on Exeter, but the King brought in a small army of mercenaries from the Continent, who gained a grisly reputation for cruelty in the way they put down the rebellion.

The last pocket of rebellion, under the command of Humphry Arundell, was fought at Sampford Courtenay, but his followers were put down and he was thrown into the deep dungeons of the Castle, eventually to be hanged on the Green. The prayer book rebellion is still part of

43 *(right)*: St George and the Dragon (probably 14th-century) on the stonework facade of St Mary Magdalene, Launceston.

Cornish history and mythology, and among the many stories and legends connected with it is that of Nicholas Boyer. Boyer was recognised by all Cornishmen as one of the leading rebels, and was elected mayor of Bodmin. In this official capacity he had supper with the hated King's Provost Marshal, who requested that while they dined the mayor's workers should erect gallows for the 'business' which was to come. After the expansive meal, the Provost Marshal and his men went to inspect the newly-made gallows, and persuaded Nicholas Boyer to mount the scaffold. As soon as he was near the rope, the Provost Marshal had him hanged as a rebel.

LEWTRENCHARD, Devon C3

Lewtrenchard House is said to be haunted by a White Lady whom many assert to be the spirit of Mrs W.D. Gould, who died there in the nineteenth century, seated in a chair. Before certain modern alterations were made, there was a corridor running the whole length of the upper storey of the house, and the ghost was often seen walking along this at night-time. The ghost does not restrict itself to the house, however, for as the Reverend Baring-Gould writes of the spectre: 'On the confines of this property, called Orchard, is a deep gloomy valley, through which trickles a rill of dark water, under the shadow of the thick fir plantations which clothe the sides of the glen. It goes by the name of the Black Valley, and the Bratton-Clovelly road plunges down into it, crosses a little bridge, and scrambles by the opposite side through the gloom of the overhanging trees... On the side of the road is an old mineshaft, long abandoned. It is confidently asserted by Lew and Bratton people that, on dark nights, Madame Gould is to be seen, dressed all in white, standing by the side of the stream, in a phosphorescent light streaming from her face and her clothes; and that she stoops and takes up handfuls of water, which she allows to trickle down in sparkling drops through her fingers. Sometimes she combs her long brown floating hair with a silver comb; and many a Bratton man, returning from the market, has seen her and been nearly frightened out of his wits. Not many years ago, a man of that village had his leg broken by falling over a hedge, in his attempt to escape from the apparition, as it issued from the old mining-shaft and made towards him'. A local man who knew the Gould family, and had lately returned from living in America, was riding home from Tavistock through the Lew Valley when he saw a seated lady, looking up to the moon. He recognized her immediately and took off his hat before wishing her a good night. She bowed in return, and waved her hand, so that he noticed in particular the sparkle of her diamond rings. On returning home he greeted his aged parents and told them that he had seen Madame Gould sitting on a plough 'with frost on the ground, looking at the moon'. Their serious reply was, 'Madame was buried three days ago in Lew Church'.

MINIONS, Cornwall B3

This small village on Bodmin Moor is pressed in on all sides by myths, some of them recorded in bizarre natural stones such as the precarious balancing act of the legend-crossed Devil's Cheesewring (figure 44), the half-natural stones raised by prehistoric men in a series of interlinked circles (figure 32), and the ruined man-built stones of the old mine-shaft engine houses (figure 34). Life was always hard on this weather-beaten moor, and its young sons rarely found fame. It is said that when mining for copper beneath these moors was at its height (more accurately, at its greatest depth) the average life of a miner was 21 years.

Those who managed to wrest an education for themselves gained almost glory for the little they knew, and two of the locals became famous — one rightly so, the other with more questionable ability. John Arnold of Bodmin had learned to make watches from his father, and achieved fame in this trade in London. In 1764 he made the smallest working watch in the world, which was set in a golden ring and given to George III. Daniel Gumb is more famous nowadays, mainly because of the tourist industry which seems to have a special rule over this part of Britain. Nowadays one is directed to Daniel Gumb's unusual 'house' close to the Cheesewring quarry above Minions, but there is no real evidence that Daniel and his large family lived in this cave, or that he built it. The area was widely settled in prehistoric times, and it was probably in existence then. One is invited to inspect the 'Pythagoras theorem' which Daniel Gumb carved on these rude walls, as a sample of his genius — but there is no genius in this theorem, which could have been copied from any child's textbook on geometry. Daniel Gumb is said to have been born in Linkinhorne, and to have been a stonecutter, whose great love was philosophy, mathematics and astronomy, the study of which subjects he pursued in this lonely shelter. It would be difficult to track down the origin of this myth, but one gets the impression that he may have impressed the locals with some rare ability to read and write — and that may have been the extent of his wisdom. Great myths often grow from the smallest of truths.

The strange balancing act of the Devil's Cheesewring on Bodmin Moor.

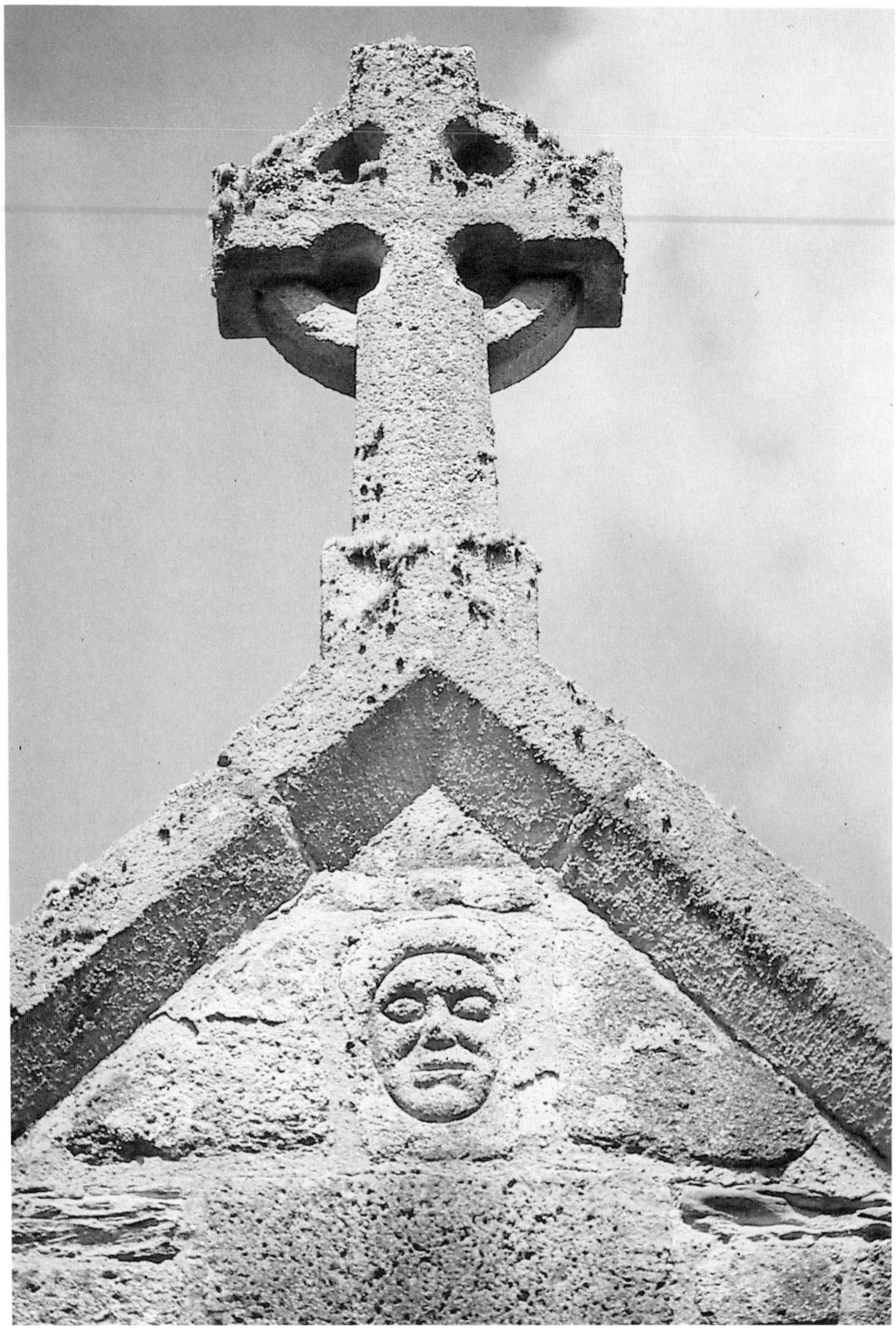

45: The 'seeing eye' of God in the stonework of the church of St Piran, Perranzabuloe.

ODSTOCK, Wiltshire F2

The Odstock Curse is said to have originated in 1801, when a gypsy was hanged in Salisbury and buried in the churchyard at Odstock. The travellers sought to visit his grave, but the Rector refused them permission (because, it is said, they were rowdy and drunken). The result was that the Queen of the Gypsies laid a curse on any person who should lock the church doors in the future. It is said that afterwards the churchwardens (and indeed the parish constable) suffered violent or early deaths.

PADSTOW, Cornwall B3

On May Day, the Padstow Hobby Horse is paraded through the town. The 'horse' is explained by a curious history relating to the siege of Calais (1346) when, in the absence of Padstow men during this fracas, French ships turned up and began to attack the little harbour. For some unexplained reason, a strange and somewhat fearsome model of a horse was taken to the harbour mouth in the hope that this would scare away the French. The French sailors are supposed to have fled from what they took to be the devil in disguise.

PERRANZABULOE, Cornwall B3

Above the porch of St Piran, Perranzabuloe, a head has been let into the stonework (figure 45), perhaps intended as the seeing eyes of God, and reminiscent of the 'Eye of God' in NEWCHURCH-IN-PENDLE, which was designed specifically to ward off the evil-working of witches. The Perranzabuloe amuletic stone is more of a mystery.

ST CLEER, Cornwall B3

The 'Banishing of the Witches' is practised on 23 June each year at St Cleer, in a ceremony involving the casting of herbs and flowers on to a bonfire in such a way as to avert the power of witchcraft for the coming year. The fire into which the herbs and flowers are thrown is built upon a hill, and crowned sometimes with an effigy of a witch, often in her traditional garb. Into the blaze is thrown an oak sickle, said to represent the human sacrifice of former times, but perhaps indeed a symbol of the Druidic rites which had adopted the sickle form as a central symbol because of its connexion with the moon. This reminds us that the symbols adopted for the Russian Communist flag (the sickle, the hammer and the star) were all ancient esoteric symbols, the one representing the Druidic initiation methods, the hammer representing the Scandinavian esoteric lore, and the star being directly from the Egyptian lore. The rationale behind the symbolism — that the sickle represents the labour of the land, and the hammer productive factory work — is scarcely relevant, for all heraldic devices emerge from unconscious rather than conscious thinking.

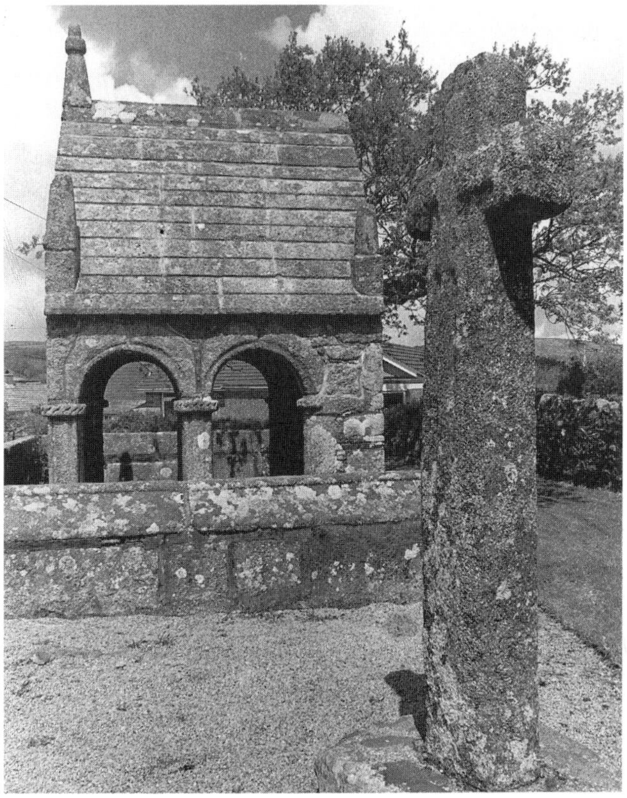

46 (right): The Holy Well and Cross at St Cleer, Cornwall.

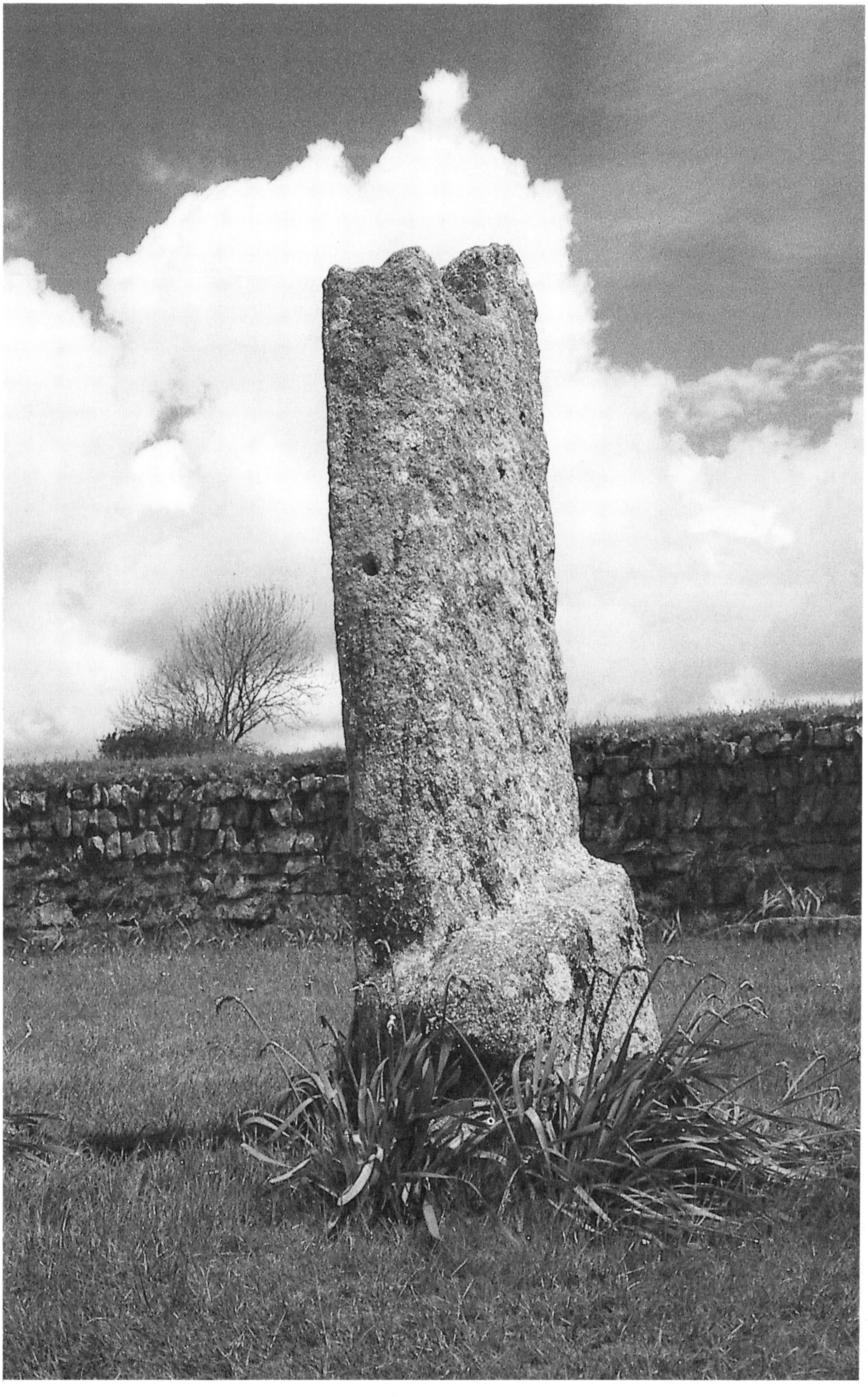

47: An incised menhir called the Doniert Stone, near St Cleer, is said to have been raised in ancient times in memory of a local king.

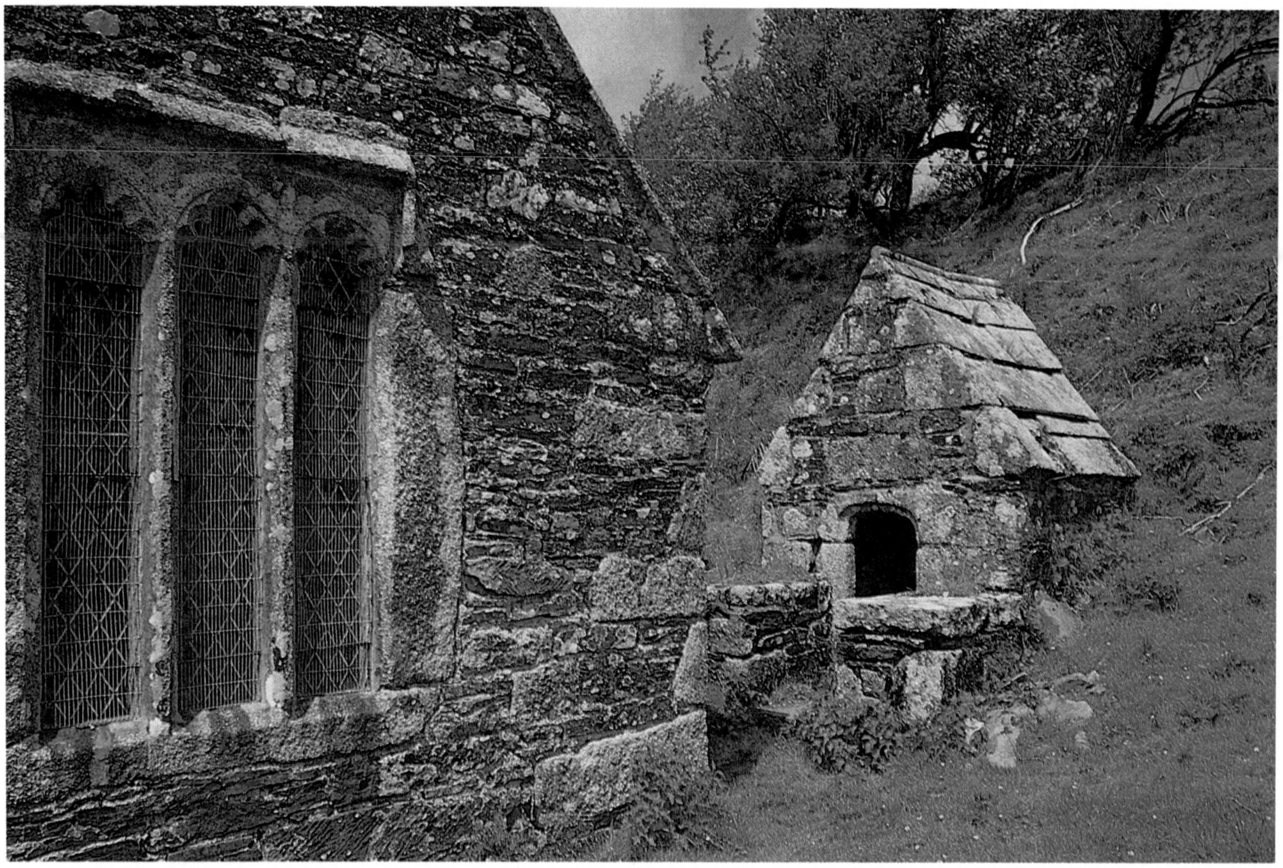

48: The well of St Clether in Cornwall.

49: The engraving which links St Clether with the Bretons' St Cleder.

ST CLETHER'S WELL, Cornwall B3

The holy well at St Clether (figure 48) is probably the finest of the chapel-wells in Britain, designed to allow waters from the sacred well to flow under the chapel altar, where (it is said) the body of the saint was once placed. The water of the pagan well was thus sanctified by contact with the Christian saint, and made even more powerful as a healing force. The engraving in figure 49 is preserved inside the chapel, and links the historical St Clether (or St Clederus) with the St Cleder of Brittany.

ST IVES, Cornwall A4

The feast day of the patron saint of Cornish St Ives, the saintly Ia, falls on the first Monday of February. This Ia is said to have crossed the Irish Sea on a leaf, in order to escape her pagan tormentors. Some of the more materialistically minded regard this miraculous 'leaf' as being something like a coracle, ignoring the fact that an escape across such waters in a coracle is just about as miraculous as on an open leaf. The St Ives Feast Day is celebrated with a sort of mass football-cum-rugger game (somewhat like the JEDBURGH Candlemas Ba'), though officially at least it is restricted to children and in recent years has been played on the beach. The game lasts for one and a half hours, starting at 10.30. Whomsoever has the ball in his or her possession at the stroke of midday is given a small prize.

The 'Knill Steeple' on Worvas Hill is a 50-foot high triangle of granite erected according to the will of John Knill as his mausoleum, though fate directed that he be buried in Ilford. Another clause in the will has been fulfilled, however, for every quinquennial on 25 July (St James's Day) two widows over the age of 64 and 10 girls below the age of 10, all dressed in white, dance around the monument to the sound of a fiddle, after which they are rewarded by a small bequest provided for by John Knill.

ST MICHAEL'S MOUNT, Cornwall A4

The mount of St Michael (who is the archangel of the sun), with its fairy-tale castle (figure 50), may be reached only by boat before low tide, after which a causeway is revealed, making it possible to walk across to the island from the mainland. Although given to the National Trust, the castle is the 'embattled home' of the St Aubyn family, who purchased it in 1567.

50: St Michael's Mount, in Mount's Bay opposite Marazion, was once a monastery but is now a private home.

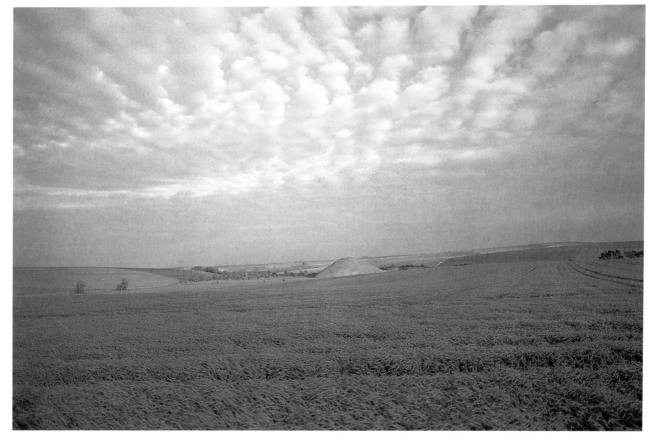

SALISBURY, Wiltshire F2

On the north side of the nave of Salisbury Cathedral is a small statue said to be the 'Boy Bishop' effigy. Whatever it does represent, the mythology of the Boy Bishop appears to be genuine enough. It seems that, during the medieval period, the choirboys in the cathedral were permitted to elect from among their numbers a representative 'bishop', for the period of 22 days from the feast of St Nicholas (the original Father Christmas, and patron saint of children) to Holy Innocents Day, or Childermas, which occurred on 28 December. It is said that during this time the Boy Bishop would perform some of the duties of the genuine Bishop, save for acts of Holy Office. It is claimed that the Boy Bishop whose effigy is in the Cathedral died in office, and was thus buried with all the honours associated with the rank of Bishop. There are sixteenth-century records showing that the pupils of St Paul's School would go to St Paul's Cathedral in London to hear the 'Childe-Bishop' sermon, delivered there on Childermas Day.

51: Near to Avebury is the largest man-made hill in Europe, although the purpose of Silbury Hill is unknown. The mound is 130 feet high and covers an area of over five acres, with a flat top almost 100 feet in diameter.

SILBURY HILL, Wiltshire F1

More of a cone than a hill (figure 51), and entirely built by human hands in prehistoric times, Silbury Hill is clearly part of the AVEBURY complex of stone circles and embankments, the larger part of which is visible from its summit. No-one knows why it was built, though some occultists suggest that it was a sighting point for stellar phenomena, much like the circles of stones below. It remains one of the most tantalizing mysteries in the British landscape.

STANTON DREW, Avon E1

To the east of the village of Stanton Drew are a number of prehistoric stone circles said to be about 4,000 years old, suggesting that this area was comparable to AVEBURY as an important religious centre; the architectural historian Pevsner says that it is the 'most important prehistoric monument in Somerset'. The largest of the circles has a diameter of 360 feet, and probably was marked by over 30 stones, averaging about six feet in height, most of which are still intact. On the eastern side is an avenue (of which only eight stones now remain) leading to the river Chew. This is joined by another avenue, which has its focal point in a smaller circle approximately 100 feet in diameter, with eight stones. The third circle consists of 12 stones, with a diameter of 140 feet, but this is some 700 feet away from the other circles. There is the indication of a ley line, for an imaginary line drawn from the south-west circle, to cut through the Great Circle, cuts an outlying stone (now fallen and called Hauteville's Quoit) on the north side of the Chew. About a mile to the NW are two related megalithic stones.

Alongside the church of St Mary is the Cove, which appears to be the poor remains of a chamber tomb consisting of three large stones, one of which has now fallen. As with the majority of other large pagan religious complexes, a number of myths and legends have developed around the circles of Stanton Drew, the most popular of which accounts for the local name given to the complex — 'The Devil's Wedding'. It seems that a wedding party held its revels among the stones one Saturday evening and, as Sunday approached, the piper (being a religious man) refused to play beyond midnight. As silence fell, another piper appeared (the Devil in disguise) and offered to break the Sabbath law. As he played, the guests were compelled to dance, and the faster he played, the faster they had to dance. When the first light of sunrise lit up the ancient stones, the members of the wedding party had all turned to stone, thus adding to the numbers of pagan uprights at Stanton Drew.

STONEHENGE, Wiltshire F2

Without doubt, the ancient circle of Stonehenge on Salisbury Plain (figure 54) is the most enigmatic of all the mysteries bequeathed us by the ancients, and it is not surprising that some people believe the stones to have been carried from distant places by magical means.

It has been recognized from very early times that Stonehenge was built to mark calendrical periods — the ancient Roman author Diodorus Siculus wrote of the Sun God visiting the circle once every 19 years. Within a day or so, the 19-year period does measure a cycle of considerable importance to Stonehenge for it measures a period-return of the moon's node to a solar point. The movement of the nodes of the moon is in a gradual circling of the ecliptic (which of course marks the movement of the sun), in contrary direction to the planets. This 'lunar node cycle' is 18 years and seven months. In three of these nodal revolutions, which take a sequence of 56 years, the moon completes a circuit of eclipses and then begins the same sequence again. The cycle describes a complete relationship between sun and moon. The arrangement of uprights at Stonehenge is designed (among other things) to mark this periodicity of 18 years and seven months, which Diodorus Siculus rounded-up to 19 years.

Some authors — most notably Professor Gerald Hawkins of Boston University, who followed outline plans drawn up by earlier investigators — have treated the arrangement of stones as though it were a complex graphic computer of critical solar and lunar positions. In his *Stonehenge Decoded*, Hawkins claimed that 10 of the alignments of the circle point to significant positions of the sun, within an accuracy of under one degree, while a different set of 14 alignments point to extreme positions of the moon. Further, he claims that when the winter moon rises over the horizon above the Heel Stone, then an eclipse of sun or moon will follow. The eclipse of sun and moon is one of the most obvious pointers to the 19-year cycle of Diodorus Siculus, for the lunar node is actually the point where the path of the moon crosses the path of the sun (the ecliptic).

Hawkins' own conclusions have been subjected to a battery of criticism, yet there may be little doubt that in some mysterious way the circle of stones was raised as a ritual centre, its stones marking out significant solar-lunar positions, the most important of which was linked with the '19-year' cycle.

Cotsworth of ACOMB recognized at the end of the last century that for the stone circle to measure precisely the full range of amplitude for sunrise and sunsets at the Winter Solstice, another stone (long removed) should have marked the direction of sunset at the south-western end of the axis line which marked the period of the Yuletide (Christmas) festival. A fallen stone, now dramatically and quite erroneously called the 'Slaughter Stone', once stood erect, and, through the resultant aperture it formed with a nearby stone, the sun could be seen to set on the shortest day.

Cotsworth proposed that this fallen stone formerly stood erect in line with the vertical Friar's Heel stone, to align the amplitude of the Summer Solstice. Cotsworth's propositions appear to confirm Sir Norman Lockyer's view that, 'Not only does the sun rise on June 21st, at one end of the axis or line which divides the circle of Stonehenge, but it also appears to set at the other end of this same axis at the time of the shortest day (21 December)' — see figure 52. Cotsworth derived much pleasure from the fact that this orientation appears to have been echoed in the arrangement of the central tower of YORK Minster. He took the matter of orientation a step forward, however, by pointing to the two vertical stones which had not attracted the attention of earlier writers, and had therefore not been explained, even though they fell on the winter sunrise and summer sunset axis. After a careful examination of these orientations, he was convinced that these marked the ancient Druidical festivals of Beltane (see MAY, page 21) and Hallowe'en (see NOVEMBER, page 27), so important in the ancient rites.

52 (left): The plan drawn by Cotsworth to demonstrate his propositions concerning the orientation of Stonehenge.
53 (below): This 19th-century lithograph shows the tidy result of a proposed reconstruction of Stonehenge.

TOTNES, Devon D3

The bad late winter which descended upon Britain in February 1855 was responsible for one of the most inexplicable tales in English demonology. In the shallow bed of snow which fell on 9 February was a trace of strange footprints which zigzagged and curved in a regular progression through the countryside for almost 100 miles between Totnes and Littleham. Drawings of the prints made at the time would suggest something like the hooves of a donkey (though one naturalist considered they must have been made by a kangaroo). Yet they were set out quite unlike the motion of a quadruped, and in any case the prints went over haystacks and walls, even over roofs, as well as through a pipe with only a 6-inch aperture. When a Dawlish farmer called out his dogs to scent the trail into the undergrowth, the dogs howled and refused to take the scent. Inevitably, the widespread reports of this strange phenomenon led to the notion that the cloven-hooved devil had pranced through Devon.

UPLYME, Devon D3

There is a ghostly legend attached to the name of 'The Black Dog Inn' at Uplyme. The story tells how a local man, tired of being haunted by the ghost of a black dog, chased it into his attic and struck at it with a pole. The dog escaped through the thatching, but the pole disturbed some old beams and a treasure of ancient coins fell to the floor. With the money, the man bought the inn, which he renamed after his ghostly intruder. Like so many of the spectral hounds which are said to haunt the British landscape, the black dog has been seen running at dusk in the neighbourhood, even in modern times.

WICK HILL, Wiltshire F3

On an octagonal-topped pedestal at Wick Hill (half a mile NW of Bremhill) sits a curious statue of Maud Heath, erected at the expense of the Marquess of Lansdowne and the eccentric poet William Bowles. From this 'aerial height' (as the inscription puts it) Maud looks towards the village of Kellaways. Maud Heath of Langley Burrell was a pedlar of the fifteenth century who amassed sufficient money to change the region for those who followed her own trade. It seems that she never forgot the unpleasant trek between Bremhill and Chippenham, which in those days involved walking through mud and slime, and so in her will of 1474 she directed that her considerable properties be used to build a walkway raised above the flood-level, between Wick Hill and Chippenham, to make the journey easier. Maud Heath's Causeway still exists and runs for just over four miles, at one stretch supported on a 'bridge' of 64 segmental arches. The start of the arches, at Kellaways, is marked by a pillar with a ball on top, erected to her memory in 1698.

WIDECOMBE, Devon C3

What is probably the worst storm ever to hit the British landscape has been turned by the local Devonians into the legend of a diabolical visitation of the Satanic Majesty. The 'natural' event of the storm itself took place in October 1638, and records of its events centre upon the service which was being held in Widecombe parish church by the Reverend Lyde. It was as though the sun withdrew from the skies, leaving the inside of the church so dark that people could not distinguish each other, but then every detail was picked out in the sudden eerie light of lightning flashes. A huge ball of fire burst through the stained glass windows and streaked down the nave, followed by explosions sufficient to literally make parts of

the tower fall to the earth. Several people were killed, personal clothing was set on fire, and over sixty people were injured. A dog (what was a dog doing in the service?) was picked up in a whirlwind and thrown through the door, and then, just as abruptly as it had started, the storm finished, leaving calm. It was some time afterwards that the legends began to grow. It seems that one of the congregation, Jan Reynolds by name, had made a pact with the Devil that if Reynolds ever fell asleep during the church service, then the Devil might take his soul. This Jan was one of those who died in the Widecombe church storm, and some say that he was not killed but was carried off on the back of the Devil's horse, and whisked out of the church. It seems a high price to pay for falling asleep in church!

54: Stonehenge, looking towards the west at sunset early in June. Completed c.2,200 B.C., the various elements of standing stones, earthworks, Aubrey holes and avenues were not constructed together. It is a ritual centre and stellar computer.

A
B
C
BUCKINGHAMSHIRE
Bisham
Wanst
1
Aldworth
R. Thames
GREATER
LONDON
Hounslow
BERKSHIRE
Hampton
Court
Chertsey
Basingstoke
SURREY
Chaldon
West Clandon
Guildford
Dorking
2
Abinger
Frensham
HAMPSHIRE
Winchester
Horsham
WEST SUSSEX
3
Lewes
Arundel
Chichester
Lyminster
Brighton
PORTSMOUTH
ISLE OF WIGHT
4
A
B
C

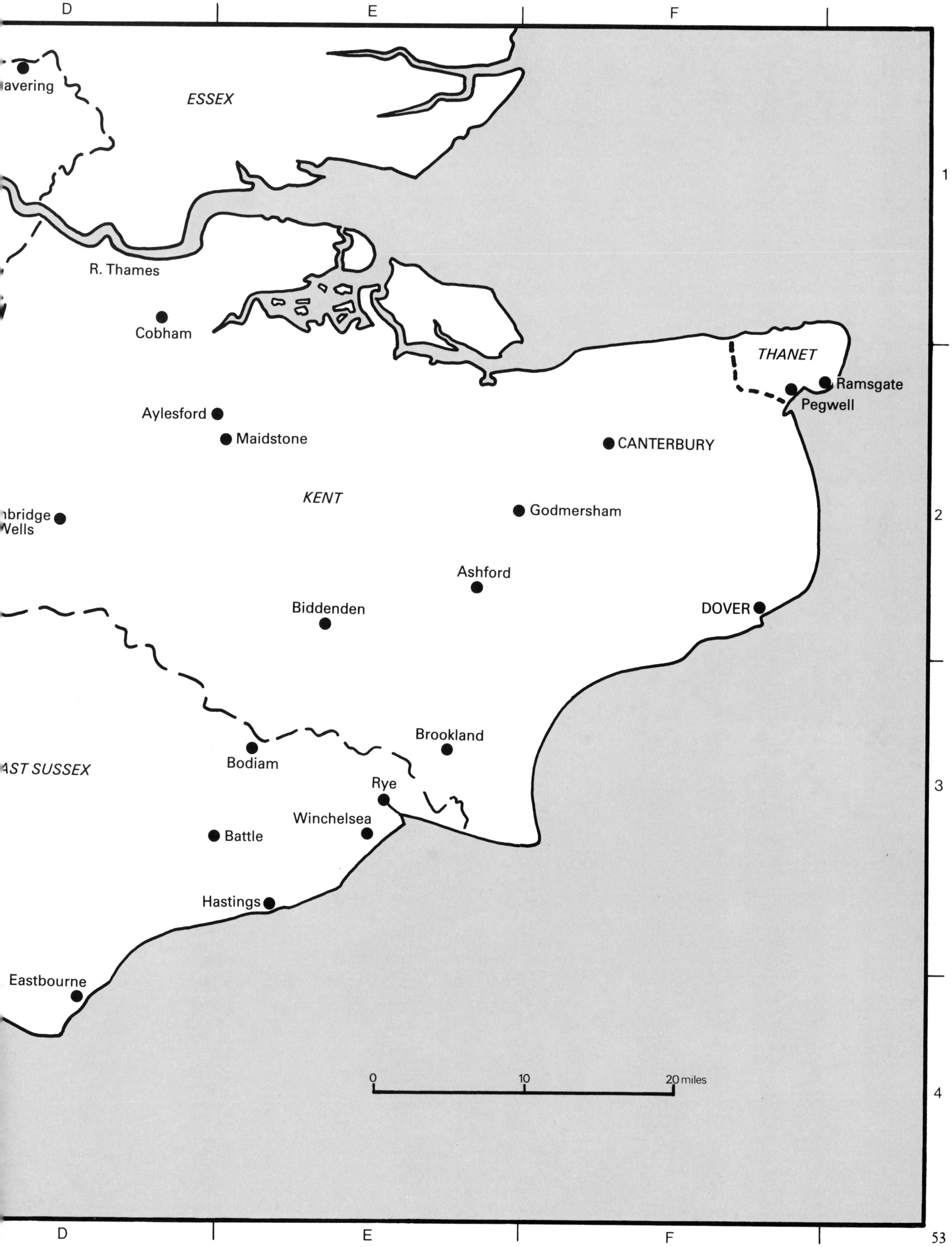
D
E
F
avering
ESSEX
1
R. Thames
Cobham
THANET
Ramsgate
Pegwell
Aylesford
Maidstone
CANTERBURY
KENT
Godmersham
nbridge
Wells
2
Ashford
Biddenden
DOVER
Brookland
Bodiam
AST SUSSEX
3
Rye
Winchelsea
Battle
Hastings
Eastbourne
0
10
20 miles
4
D
E
F

ABINGER HAMMER

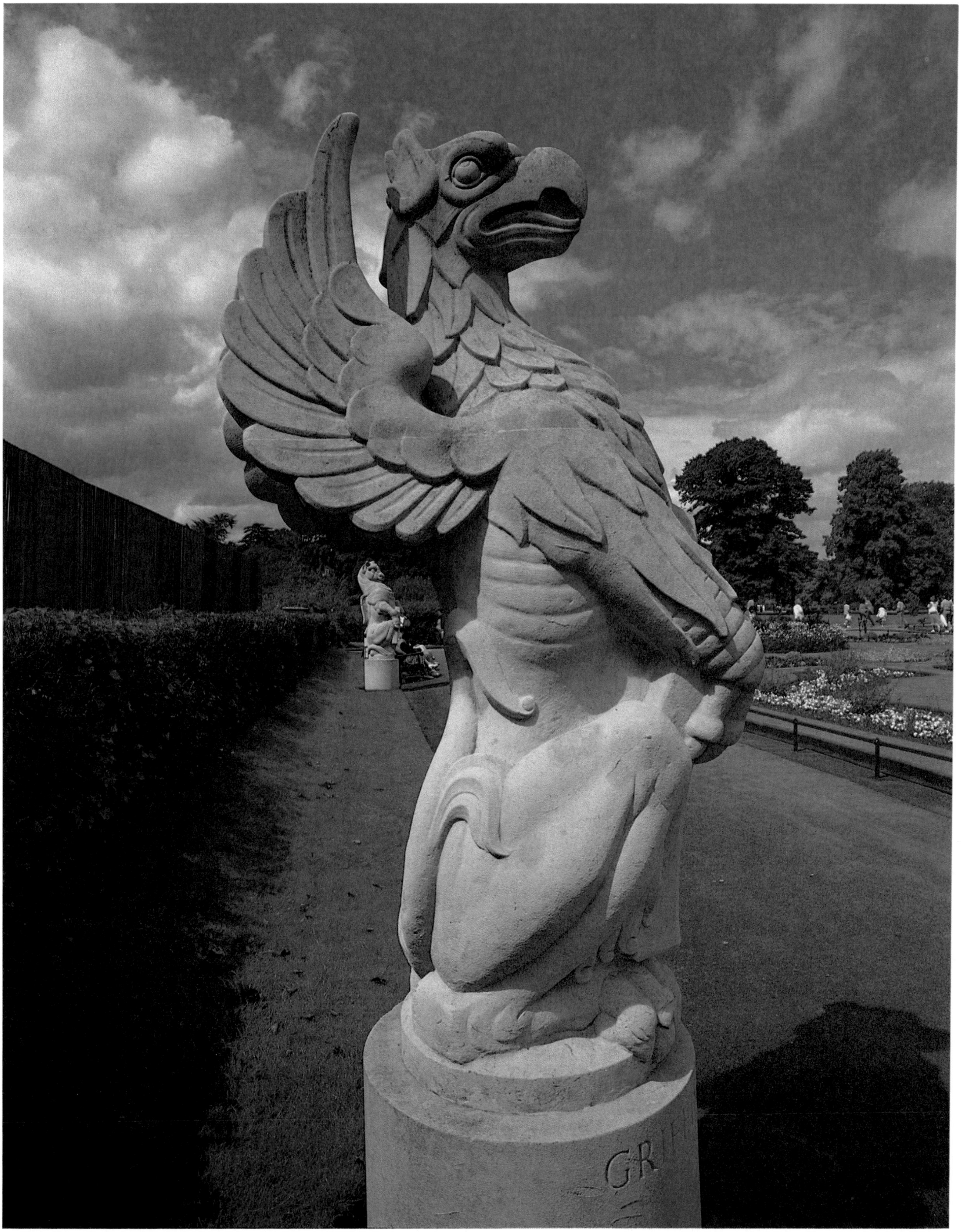
GR

so that the ten 'King and Queen's Beasts' now in place are copies and reconstructions made in the present century to the designs of E.E. Dorling by the craftsman George Wilson.

The building of the gatehouse made it necessary to remove two of the original ten, so that one greyhound and one unicorn were omitted from the modern sequence. Each of these 'beasts' is heraldic, and were related to the line of Henry VIII — for example, the yale was one of the supporters of the Beaufort family, from whom Henry was descended, while the dragon was the famous 'Welsh Dragon' (see WINCHESTER) which had been adopted by Henry VII as one of his shield supporters. The bull is the black bull of the house of Clarence, while the unicorn was the principle heraldic support of Queen Jane. The full array of beasts may be seen with greater ease in Kew Gardens, where life-size reproductions stand in front of the glasshouse behind the ornamental pond (figure 62)

HASTINGS, East Sussex E3

In the solid rock beneath Hastings Castle (figure 65) is what has been called an 'Ear of Dionysius', which is a whispering post allegedly designed to enable gaolers to listen to the speech of those imprisoned in nearby cells. The original Ear of Dionysius was a bell-shaped chamber connected by a narrow passageway to the palace of the tyrant King Dionysius of Syracuse, who was anxious to overhear what was being said in his underground prisons. The example at Hastings Castle has a listening post shaped like an ear, and is claimed by some to be of a pre-Roman design. However, the Hastings ear is not connected by any narrow passageway to any other part of the prison, and the fact that it is possible to hear sounds in nearby 'cells' of the underground chambers is almost certainly connected with the natural acoustics of the chamber, rather than with anything in the nature of the

63 & 64: A greyhound and (facing page) a lion and a dragon, some of the Queen's Beasts on the moat bridge of Hampton Court Palace.

65: Hastings Castle was the first to be built by the Normans, work on it beginning as early as 1066. Fierce storms swept away a great part of it in 1287 and the importance of Hastings was reduced shortly afterwards by the silting-up of the harbour.

ear itself. In fact, it is probable that the 'ear' was nothing more than a natural formation, which has been amended a little by human activity to more closely resemble the form of an ear.

A most interesting interlude in the history of animal-forgeries was the 'Hastings Pygmy Bison', which was recorded as being in the collection of a dealer named Murray in Hastings in the early part of the nineteenth century. This bison was said to be only seven or eight inches high, yet a perfect replica of the huge American bison. An engraving of the two, for the purposes of dramatic comparison, was reproduced in the *Magazine of Natural History* in 1829. The leading authority on such animal fakes, Peter Dance, records that it was made from the skins of a pug-dog and a young bear, with the horns having being carved from a buffalo.

HAVERING, Greater London D1

There is a story that during the consecration of St John's Church at Havering, in Essex, King Edward the Confessor gave a golden ring as a gift of alms to an old pilgrim who was present at the ritual. It later transpired that the pilgrim had been St John himself, who had come to earth in disguise to witness the dedication of the church in his name. Before John left the earth, he returned the ring to King Edward with the advice that he should dispose of his personal belongings as within half a year Edward would be in Heaven with him, where he would obtain his rewards for a good life. This legendary 'Confessor's Ring' appears in the coat of arms of the Borough of Romford, in which Havering is situated.

LONDON

London has a secret life of symbols which belong to the many strata of history still preserved within the compass of a few miles of buildings and streets which have been burned, bombed, razed and constantly rebuilt, over a known period of 2,000 years.

In particular, the City of London itself is filled with fascinating ancient symbols. Many of these are secret, being derived from the occult, hermetic or astrological traditions, and some of them are intended to denote hidden meanings, or to point in direct symbolism to the functions practised within the walls which they decorate. Those interested in myths and symbols are unlikely to find a more interesting Sunday stroll than from the northern end of Blackfriars Bridge, along Queen Victoria Street, as far east as the end of Lombard Street.

Almost at the beginning of Blackfriars, which marks approximately the beginning of the old city, in

Blackfriars Lane itself, is the old Apothecaries Hall, reconstructed after its destruction during the Great Fire of 1666, with three external coats of arms which are among the most hermetic of all such heraldic devices, supported by the secret and fabulous animal the unicorn (figure 66). The golden Apollo standing over the dragon in this 'arms' is itself a reference to the healing power of the Sun, which can drive back the 'Old Serpent' which is the Devil and illness, and which promotes the growth of those plants used by the apothecary herbalists of old. The moon-symbolism — for the unicorn is the most obvious of all lunar symbols, with its single horn in reference to the crescent moon — is representative of the moon force which, according to the occult tradition, gives plants their individual forms. The three coats of arms may be seen on the facade of the Apothecaries Hall, and inside the beautiful courtyard. Fifty yards south down the Lane, into Queen Victoria Street, one is confronted by the ancient dragon bearers of the city arms (figure 67) raised above the name-plate for the nearby railway station.

Further east, along Victoria Street, is the ship-symbol on the bell tower of Cole Abbey Presbyterian Church. In Cannon Street there is the most lovely zodiacal clock in Britain, over the front door of Bracken House (figure 68). In Mincing Lane, behind the extraordinary modern

66: Detail of coat of arms with unicorn supports on the external facade of the Apothecaries Hall in Blackfriars Lane, City of London.

67: The coat of arms with wyvern/dragon supporters is found throughout the City of London.

Lloyds Building, is Plantation House, which is decorated with many symbols derived from the occult tradition, including a most beautiful series of elephants with castles upon their backs (figure 70). A short walk east is Leadenhall Market, with its many superb dragons in cast iron, worked into the girder system supporting the roof of this lovely Victorian building.

Lombard Street, near the end of the old city limits, has the most crowded population of hermetic symbols in Britain, for here we find the personal insignia alongside a proliferation of bank signs which were designed and adopted in the days when families had secret symbols to denote their scions or activities, or links with the ancient guilds. The Golden Grasshopper, the Cat and the Fiddle, the Crown and Anchor, the Rampant Bull, the Phoenix, are all on display in this most remarkable of streets, while off the street, in George Yard, we find a statue of Neptune, the sea-god of the ancients. On the passage wall leading into the same yard are images of the moon-goddess Phoebus, and of the constellation Ursa Major, which points to the still point of the turning stellar world — a symbol for that wisdom which is needed to control finance in a hectic world.

At the top end of Lombard Street is the almost-hidden church of St Mary Woolnoth, founded in Saxon times, and first mentioned in the twelfth century. Near the entrance, delightful images of children's heads peer out of the darkness as one descends to take the tube from Bank Station, which was built beneath the church.

In the space of less than half a mile through the City

68: The most beautiful zodiacal clock in Britain is at Bracken House, Cannon Street, until 1988 the offices of the *Financial Times*.

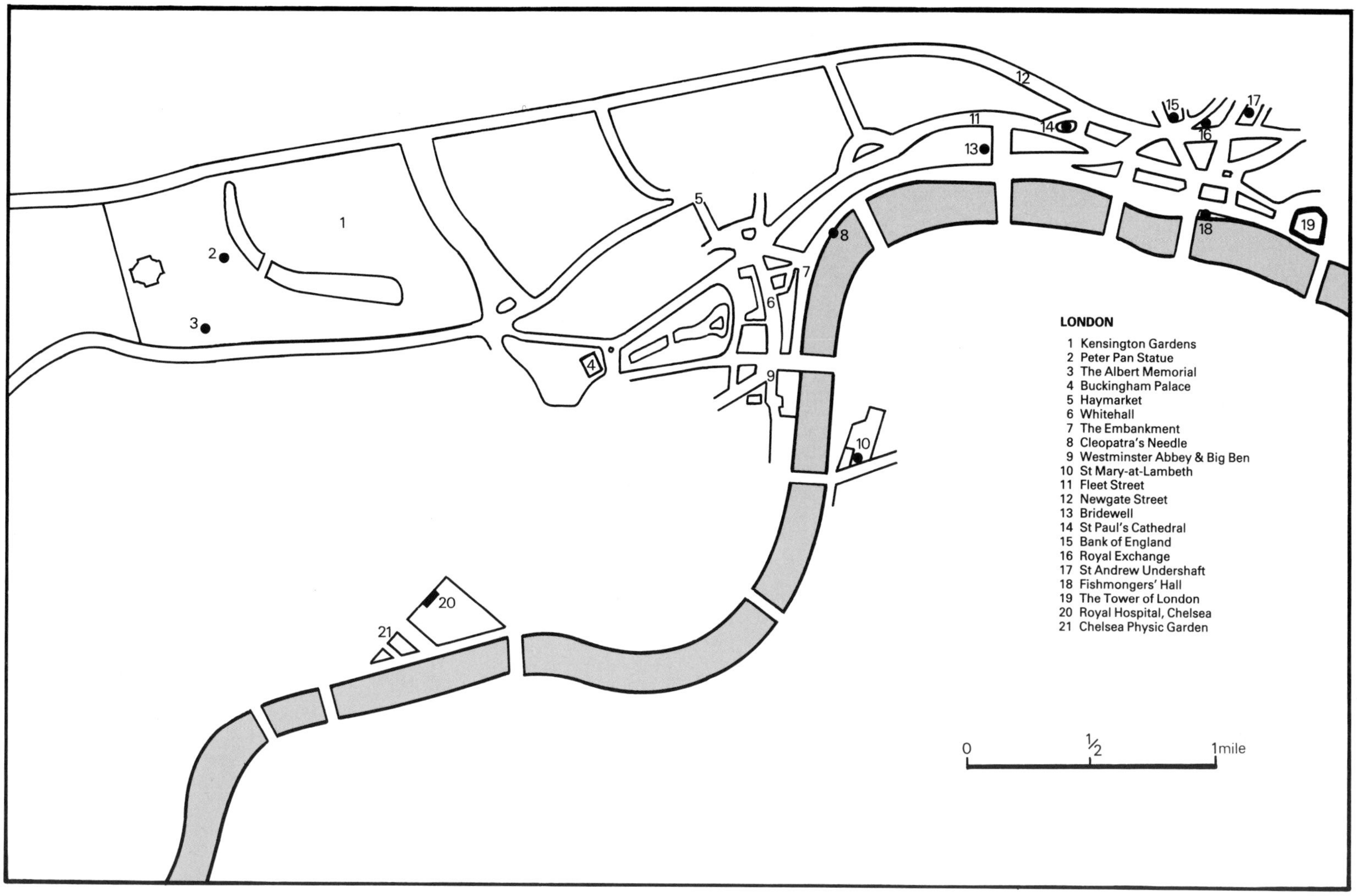

69: The carving of Mithras, now in the Museum of London, was excavated during redevelopment of a site in Queen Victoria Street in 1954. The remains of a temple dedicated to Mithras are preserved on the site, now occupied by Bucklersbury House.

of London, along the route indicated above, it is possible to count no fewer than 350 symbols linked with the esoteric or secret tradition.

If the City is a square mile of secret symbols, then within the Museum of London itself (in the Barbican) is a square foot of stone which contains what is probably the most esoteric symbolism in Britain — a Roman carving intended to serve the eastern cult of Mithras (figure 69). This portrays Mithras killing the celestial bull (the same bull which is found in a living posture on the Bank of Scotland in Lombard Street), its genitals attacked by the scorpion (the same zodiacal scorpion as on the Sun Alliance building in nearby Cheapside), which points to the ancient warfare between the celestial bull of Taurus and the opposing sign of Scorpio. Around this bull-killing, intended to symbolize how the annual solar powers of the blood-sacrifice of the cosmic bull replenish the earth forces, are the 12 symbols for the zodiacal signs, which, while carved almost 2,000 years ago, are more or less in a form that we would recognise today.

70 (above): An elephant with a castle, on the Mincing Lane facade of Plantation House.
71 (above right): The Albert Memorial in Kensington Gardens.

LONDON — ALBERT MEMORIAL

The Albert Memorial in Kensington Gardens was designed by Sir George Gilbert Scott, and finished in 1872, to commemorate the Prince Consort, beloved husband of Queen Victoria. The life-size effigy of the Prince portrays him in life, reading a copy of the catalogue of the Great Exhibition of 1851, which he participated in organizing. The figure itself is almost dwarfed by the complex symbolism of spires, pinnacles, bas reliefs and symbolic groups (figure 71) — for example the 'four Empires' of Britain, in which the Middle Eastern Empire of Egypt and the Suez Canal is represented by a group of figures gathered around a sphinx and a camel (figure 72). The complexity of the design may actually hide its inner meaning, for in effect it is nothing more than a vast ciborium, or design intended to be placed over an altar — thereby symbolically raising the Prince Consort to the status of a God. A similar approach to the deification of the Prince is found in an earlier group opposite the Town Hall in Manchester, designed by Thomas Worthington in 1864.

LONDON — BANK OF ENGLAND

The reason why the Bank of England is called 'The Old Lady of Threadneedle Street' is uncertain. According to some, the name was bestowed in the eighteenth century after a cartoon by Gillray showed 'The Old Lady of Threadneedle Street in Danger', when the bank suspended payments in 1797.

LONDON — BRIDEWELL

Originally in this place in Blackfriars there was a holy well, famous for its healing properties and dedicated to St Bride (usually taken to be the equivalent of St Bridget — but see BRIDESTONES). Because of its healing powers, a royal palace in the vicinity was turned into a hospital. After the Reformation, in the early sixteenth century, this Bridewell hospital became a House of Correction for vagrants and law-breaking apprentices, who were put to the tedious and tiring job of pounding hemp.

LONDON — EMBANKMENT

Cleopatra's Needle (figure 73) has nothing to do with Cleopatra. It takes its name from the fact that it was unearthed from the sand outside Alexandria, which had been associated with this Queen. However, it was far older than Cleopatra, and the hieroglyphics upon it tell us that it was erected by Thothmes III in what we now call the Eighteenth Dynasty. It came to London in 1878.

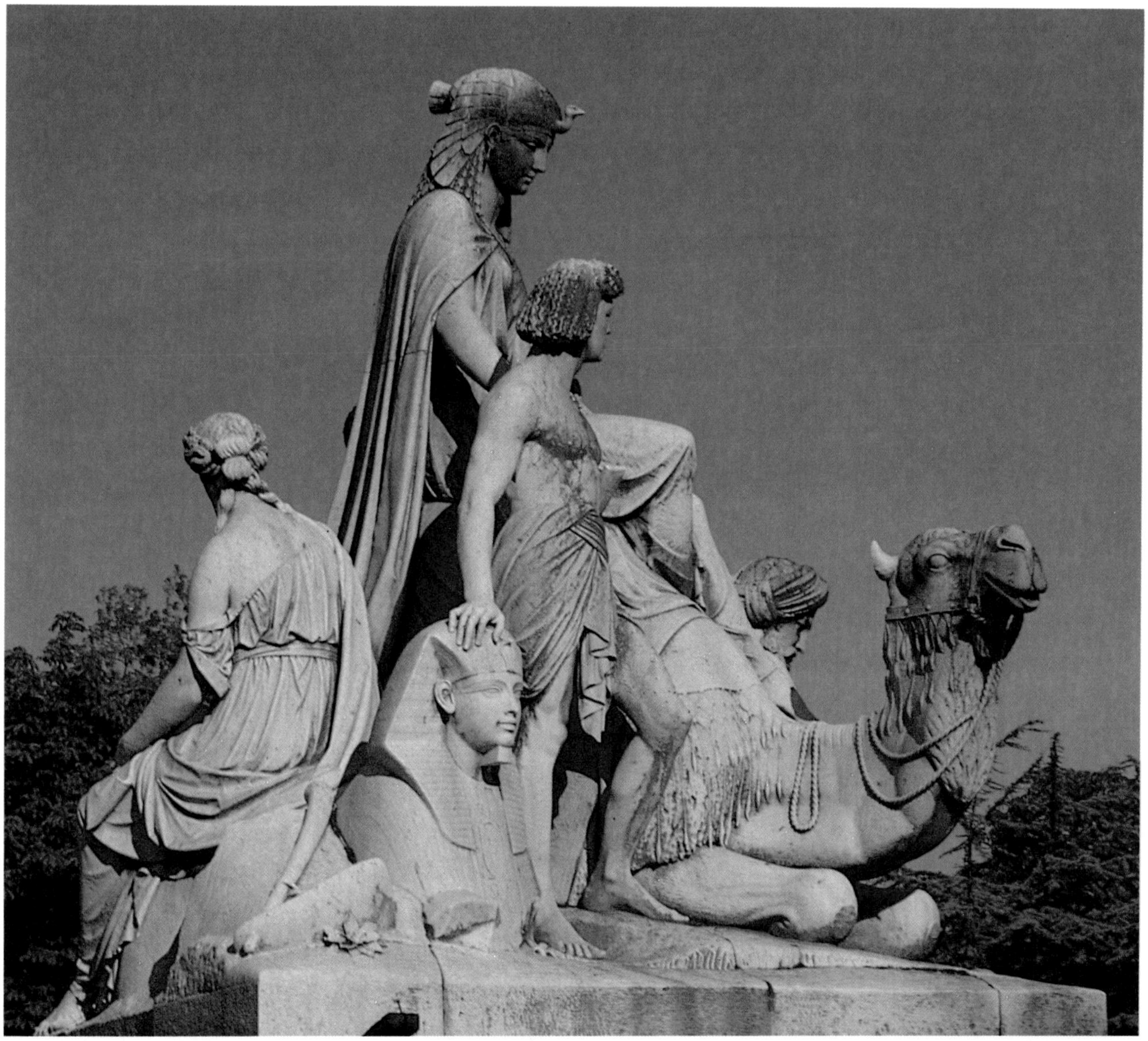

72 (*left*): The detailed symbolism of the Albert Memorial expresses much of the romanticised history of England. This corner statuary represents the Empire in the Middle East.
73 (*below, left*): The Egyptian obelisk now called 'Cleopatra's Needle' was set up on the Embankment in 1878. It was originally at Heliopolis, northeast of Cairo.
74 (*below*): The Egyptian sphinxes which guard the Needle are Victorian additions.

75: Detail of a wooden carving on the front of a mock-Tudor inn at the western end of Fleet Street. The monk is helping himself to wine or spirits.

LONDON — CHELSEA

The great Italian artist Bernini (1598-1680) sculpted a most impressive bust of Charles I after a painting (specially commissioned in 1637) of the King from three points of view. This painting, by Sir Anthony van Dyck, who was the chief painter to the King, is now preserved in Windsor Castle. It is said that when the sculpture was first delivered to Charles, he was sitting in the garden of his Chelsea Palace. He ordered the bust to be unwrapped, but just after this had been done a hawk swooped overhead with a dead bird in its beak and a drop of blood fell on to the throat of the bust. This was naturally taken as an evil presage, though at that time few suspected that the King would be beheaded in public. For another statue of Charles with an equally interesting history, see WHITEHALL.

LONDON — FISHMONGERS' HALL

In Fishmongers' Hall is a statue of Sir William Walworth, the Lord Mayor, carrying a dagger. It is said that the original weapon was that which he used to kill the rebel Wat Tyler on 15 June, 1381, in Smithfield. There is a story that this was the dagger which Richard II added to the Arms of the City of London (figure 67) to commemorate the slaying. However, this is not the case, for there was a 'dagger' in the Arms long before 1381 — though it was not really a knife but a sword, said in fact to be the sword of St Paul, who was the patron saint of London.

LONDON — FLEET STREET

The so-called 'griffin' which is recognized as the 'Beast' of the City of London, and stands at the western end of Fleet Street, is really a dragon. The true griffin is an eagle in the top half, and a lion in the bottom half. This 'Beast' is one of the supporters of the shield of the City of London and, as Wilfrid Scott-Giles points out, had an unnatural origin. It seems that originally the City shield was supported by lions but, by the sixteenth century, over the shield in the city seal was a helmet with a curious fan-shaped crest. This was later interpreted as being the wing of a monster, and it was this misinterpretation which prompted the designers at a later stage to adopt a winged dragon as a supporter for the City shield. Thus, as Scott-Giles confirms, the City dragons have no heraldic ancestry. For other mention of the London dragon, see BATTLE.

LONDON — HAYMARKET

A curious tale is told about the 'Irish Giant' Charles Byrne, who used to exhibit himself for financial reward in the Haymarket from 1782, as 'the most extraordinary production of the human species ever beheld since the days of Goliath'. He died at the age of 22, in the following year, and was obsessed with the idea that after he died his body would fall into the hands of surgeons anxious to preserve his remarkable skeleton. In order to avoid this fate, he ordered that after his death fishermen should be paid to place lead weight upon his corpse and sink it in the middle of the Irish Sea. Upon his death, the famous surgeon John Hunter paid far more for possession of the corpse than Byrne had offered for his sea-burial. How this pecuniary affair was arranged is a matter of dispute, but the end-product was that the skeleton of the giant achieved the infamy which the living Byrne had feared. Until it was destroyed in the bombing during the Second World War, it was displayed in its full glory of almost 7 feet 8 inches in the Museum of the Royal College of Surgeons, London. Hunter had not been alone in seeking the interesting skeleton, for according to C.J.S. Thompson, 'The whole tribe of surgeons put in a claim for the poor departed Irishman, and surrounded his house, just as harpooners would an enormous whale.' As if to add insult to injury, the Byrne skeleton was placed next to the diminutive figure of the dwarf Caroline Crachami, who was just under 1 foot 8 inches high. The same 'body-snatching' attitude towards the dwarf was as evident as towards the giant; apparently the newly-dead body was stolen immediately after her death in 1824, and when found it was donated by her father to the Royal College of Surgeons, who voted him a pacifier of £10.

HIGHGATE, London

Halfway up Highgate Hill is a stone model of a cat (figure 76), said to mark the spot where Dick Whittington and his cat stopped while leaving London, but were persuaded back by the sound of church bells. While the story of this 'return', and indeed the whole account of the role played by the cat in the story of Dick's becoming Lord Mayor of London, is almost certainly fictitious, there was indeed a Richard Whittington who was first a sheriff and then Lord Mayor of London several times between 1397 and 1419. In 1416 he was elected Member of Parliament for London (see also PAUNTLEY).

76: The memorial to Dick Whittington's cat on Highgate Hill, just north of Archway underground station.

77 (*below*): Drawing after a stone relief in Bullhead Court, Newgate Street, depicting the giant William Evans with the dwarf Jeffrey Hudson.
78 (*bottom*): The statue of Peter Pan in Kensington Gardens.

HOUNSLOW, Greater London

An interesting article in *The Morning Post* for 2 May, 1791, records a more countrified view of Hounslow than is possible today. 'According to annual and superstitious custom, a number of persons went into the fields and bathed their faces with the dew on the grass, under the idea that it would render them beautiful. I remember, too, that in walking that same morning between Hounslow and Brentford, I was met by two distinct parties of girls, with garlands of flowers, who begged money of me, saying, "Pray, sir, remember the Garland."'

LONDON — KENSINGTON GARDENS

If the ALBERT MEMORIAL in Kensington Gardens marks the extreme attempt to deify a man and to almost bury him (and his spirit) under a welter of symbolic marble, then the other extraordinary monument in the same Gardens is a most simple memorial to a writer and reveals the very essence of his spirit. The Peter Pan statue (figure 78) is one of the most delightful memorials in the world — almost a reminder of the one to Perrault, another fairy-tale teller, in the Tuileries Garden, Paris. The Kensington statue is intended as a memorial to Sir J.M. Barrie, creator of the character Peter Pan, the boy who would not grow up. Peter is represented playing a flute, a reminder that it was no accident when Barrie chose a name to echo that of the Greek Pan, the God of Nature. Peter stands on an organic column which is alive with the fairies and animals of Peter Pan's world. Barrie died in 1937; he wrote *Peter Pan* in 1904, and *Peter Pan in Kensington Gardens* in 1906. He was fortunate in having the artist Arthur Rackham to illustrate these books, which gained almost immediate universal fame.

LONDON — NEWGATE STREET

Over the entrance to Bullhead Court in Newgate Street there is a stone relief which is said to represent 'The King's Porter and Dwarf' (figure 77). The giant of the pair is William Evans, who lived in the early seventeenth century and was porter to Charles I; this 'giant' was said to be 7 feet 4 inches tall. His companion the dwarf was one 'Jeffrey' who was only 3 feet 9 inches high. The pair would sometimes entertain companies in the way of giants and dwarfs, with the former carrying the latter around in his pocket, 'first to the wonder then to the laughter of the beholders'. For an account of another British giant, see HALE.

LONDON — ROYAL EXCHANGE

In the Royal Exchange is a wall-painting by the fresco-artist Ernest Normand, which shows King John with his barons at Runnymede, witnessing the Royal Seal being fixed to the Magna Carta. Normand was an artist obsessed with the idea of representing only historically accurate pictures, and one of the purposes behind this fresco was to correct the popular error that King John signed the Magna Carta. To acknowledge his Royal assent, King John was required merely to touch the document, the Seal being impressed upon it as record of his assent: it is indeed argued that King John could not write.

LONDON — ST ANDREW UNDERSHAFT

The church of St Andrew Undershaft derives its name from the maypole shaft which, until 1517, was set up each Mayday outside the church. In the north-eastern corner of the church is a fascinating memorial to John Stow, the first historian of London, who died in 1605. There is a strange tradition in which the Lord Mayor of London, at a special church service, annually renews the goose-quill pen in the right hand of the effigy.

LONDON — ST MARY-AT-LAMBETH

The lovely church of St Mary-at-Lambeth, with its fourteenth-century steeple, is next door to Lambeth Palace, on the south side of Lambeth Bridge. By 1972 the church which had once served the Lambeth region, and had been the place of worship of some of the most famous English men, was no longer in use; it had been decon-

79: Detail of a skull and hydra on the tomb of the Tradescants, dating to c.1662. The design is a mystery, though it was carved at the request of John Tradescant's widow.

secrated, had fallen into disrepair, and had inevitably become the object of vandalism. Two years later, mainly through the indefatigable efforts of Rosemary Nicholson, it was rescued from further decay. The Tradescant Trust was formed, and the church was eventually refurbished and turned into a fascinating Museum of Garden History.

The churchyard still houses many interesting tombs of famous men, including those of the esotericist and collector Elias Ashmole, and the infamous Captain of the mutinous *Bounty*, William Bligh, who used to live at Farningham in Kent. However, by far the most interesting tomb is that of the Tradescant family itself, which offers one of the most puzzling and mysterious of symbols in any English churchyard. The south side of the tomb bears the Tradescant shield of arms, while the west portrays civilization in decay, in a proliferation of broken columns, buildings and upheaved pyramids. On the east side is the symbol of nature, in the form of growing trees, a crocodile, shells, and so on — doubtless a reference to the Tradescants' passion for nature, for gardening and for collecting strange things.

It is not surprising that this 'natural paradise' — albeit populated by crocodiles — should be found on the east of the tomb, as tradition always insisted that the biblical Paradise was to the East, as in the medieval *mappa mundi* in HEREFORD Cathedral. The most puzzling aspect of the tomb design, however, is on the north face: this shows a skull and a hydra (figure 79), the fabulous many-headed monster of the Lernan swamps, which Hercules finally killed, even though each time he cut off one head another one grew in its place. The hydra is a curious symbol to find on a tomb as the monster is normally used as a symbol of natural disorder, or rebellion, or of contagion. When, in 1691, the medallist Luder was commissioned to design a medal to commemorate the recent suppression of the Irish rebellion, he chose to depict Hercules killing the Hydra — the hero symbolizing the English general or army, while the monster symbolized the rebellious Irish.

It is likely that Hester Tradescant (the widow of John Tradescant), who commissioned the design of the tomb, had heard from Elias Ashmole, or one of his astrological friends, of the celestial symbolism of the Hydra. In the southern skies there is the constellation 'Hydra', which is usually depicted as a single-headed water-snake, and which seems to have little connexion with the Hercules myth. In one of the most famous of astrological poems, the 'Poeticon Astronomicon', which came into print as early as 1488, this Hydra is confused with the dragon of Hesperides, whose task it is to guard the sacred apple tree (Hydra being confused with the mythology of the constellation Draco). This image, which shows the Hydra resting its head among the magic apples on the tree in the Garden of the Hesperides, was well known to astrologers, and perhaps it is this symbolism which is hinted at in the tomb carving. The many-headed Hydra probably symbolizes the many interests of the

80: St Paul's Cathedral, the masterpiece of Sir Christopher Wren. It was built between 1675 and 1710.

Tradescants, the reference to the paradisial garden being especially fitting as both father and son of the last Tradescants were royal gardeners. Additionally, the reference to the symbolic apples sought by heroic treasure hunters was often adopted as a symbol of secret knowledge, or of spiritual power. When the classical mythology was translated into Christian terms, the golden apples of the Hesperides were transformed into the 'apple' of temptation, which brought about the fall of man in another Garden, due to the enticement of another hydra-like creature.

The symbol of the skull on the Tradescant tomb is probably intended as the standard image of the death of the body, while the many-headed monster is a symbol of spiritual redemption, of the Tradescants' guardian role over nature as gardeners, as well as of their interest in secret things. The Tradescants themselves are linked with the 'secrets' and the 'fruit' which the dragons guard.

LONDON — ST PAUL'S

In Walcott's *Memorials of Westminster* we find a story about the clock of St Paul's allegedly striking thirteen. It seems that the soldier John Hatfield was court-martialled for falling asleep on duty while guarding Winsor Terrace. In his defence he claimed that he could not have been asleep as he had heard St Paul's clock strike thirteen. His claim was supported by several witnesses. For another unlikely 'striking clock' story, see WESTMINSTER.

A statue of Queen Anne stands in front of St Paul's (figure 81). She was well known before her death as a lover of brandy, and since a 'gin shop' used to stand at the south-western corner of the church-yard, a wit wrote the doggerel:

Brandy Nan, Brandy Nan, left in the lurch,
Her face to the gin-shops, her back to the church.

In St Paul's is the monument to the great English poet John Donne, who was at one time Dean of the Cathedral. This monument reflects the poet's well-known obsession with death and portrays him wholly covered in his death-shroud, with only his bearded face peering into the darkness of the cathedral interior. Carved by Nicholas Stone in 1631, the year Donne died, it is said that the poet actually posed for the preliminary drawings wrapped in a shroud (see also HATFIELD). The monument had a strange destiny, for it appears to have been the only one to completely survive the Great Fire of 1666, which

81: St Paul's Cathedral stands 360 feet high and the lantern alone weighs 850 tons.

destroyed the Old St Paul's. It was therefore one of the few figured tombs to be re-erected in the new Cathedral designed by Sir Christopher Wren and completed in 1710.

LONDON — WESTMINSTER

It is recorded that Edward IV's coronation in Westminster was postponed for a day when it was realized that, as originally planned, it would fall on Childermas. This is 'Holy Innocents Day', which falls in the modern calendar on 28 December. It is said to be the most unlucky of all days in the Christian world and commemorates the slaughter of the 'innocents' on the orders of Herod, who was anxious to kill the prophesied King of the Jews. The day is one of the evil 'Egyptian Days', and is regarded as being unfortunate for almost every enterprise, from setting sail, or starting out on a voyage to even walking out of doors. There are indications that at one time there was a ritual enactment of the murder of the innocents in the whipping of children on the morning of Childermas, as Gregory of Tours put it, 'that the memories of Herod's murder of the innocents might stick the closer'.

In modern times it is often mistakenly believed that the clock on the four faces of St Stephen's Tower (the clock tower of the Houses of Parliament) is called 'Big Ben'.

However, Big Ben is actually the thirteen-ton bell which chimes in that tower. It is named after Sir Benjamin Hall, who was Chief Commissioner of Works in 1856 when the newly-cast bell was installed. On the morning of 14 March, 1861, Big Ben struck repeatedly, and many of the locals assumed this was intended to mark the passing of a member of the royal family. These irregularities continued throughout the day, until a mechanical fault was traced. However, on the following day Queen Victoria's mother was declared to be on the point of dying, and by the next morning was dead.

LONDON — WHITEHALL

The full-size equestrian bronze of King Charles I which looks down Whitehall was modelled and cast by Le Sueur in 1639. After Charles had been executed, the statue was removed and sold to a brazier with the expressed understanding that it be melted down. The brazier buried the statue, and then made a nice profit selling mementoes allegedly made from the melted bronze. After the restoration of the Monarchy, he dug up the figure and it was soon remounted (1674) in its present position.

LYMINSTER, West Sussex B3

One of the two ancient tombstones in Lyminster church is said to be that of the man or knight who killed the local dragon. There is no foundation for this tale, as the 'sword' which decorates the top of the tombstone is actually a cross, and the 'ribs' of the dragon upon which it lies are nothing more than standard zig-zag patterns, quite common to the later medieval symbolism. The dragon of Lyminster may be just as imaginative, though the story is well entrenched in local legend; it was said to have made its nest in the 'Knucker Hole', from whence it would proceed at times to ravage the surrounding countryside. The traditional hero finally managed to kill it by means of a stratagem, and it is this knight who is supposed to be immortalized by the standard Christian symbolism on the stone. The 'Knucker Hole', which is one of a series of pools alongside the public footpath which leads to Arundel, was probably the 'Nicor Hole', for the word Nicor was Anglo-Saxon for 'serpent'.

MINSTEAD, Hampshire *page 31* F2

North-west of Minstead is the Rufus Stone, said to mark the place where William II (nicknamed Rufus) was killed by an arrow in 1100. Some historians who believe it was not an accidental death have proposed a theory that it was one of the last 'ritual slayings' of a king, or perhaps an assassination planned on the orders of William's brother, who came to the throne as a result of the death. These writers maintain that the disastrous flood of the preceding year was interpreted by the priests as demanding a royal sacrifice, and towards this end, on the May Day of 1100, William's nephew was 'accidentally' shot in the New Forest. However, this sacrifice proved insufficient, so on the following 'holy day of Lammas' (see AUGUST) the King himself had to die. For reasons which are hard to grasp now, the actual sacrifice was delayed for one day, but it would appear that the 'death' of the King was known on Lammas Day (that is, on the day before the actual killing) as far abroad as France.

PEGWELL, Kent F2

An astonished-looking monster-headed prow of a Viking ship looks towards the new hovercraft terminal at Pegwell Bay, no doubt as surprised by what goes on today as when the infamous marauders Hengist and Horsa landed here in the fifth century. The longship was sailed from Denmark to Pegwell in 1949, to commemorate the arrival of the Saxons who so moulded the history and mythology of our country. The Saxons brought with them their pagan gods, which were later introduced into a sort of genial English demonology and a complex tanglewood of mythological tales, of which the story of Beowulf, the slayer of Grendel and other monsters, has survived. Hengist was traditionally the founder of Kent, and many of the name-places of old Saxon stomping grounds (their earliest thefts) of Kent, Sussex and Wessex are derived from their method of naming the localities they took over from those who had previously (or currently) owned them. Hastings was from the followers of Haesta ('the violent one'), reminding us of our schoolboy Latin, 'hasta, a spear', while the followers of Raeda ('the red one') gave us Reading. More difficult to grasp (though well recorded) is the derivation of the name Nottingham from its founders, the family Snotr, 'the Wise ones'. Perhaps the only query one may raise of the monstrous Viking longship is, why Pegwell? The earliest historian of the subject, the Reverend Bede, tells us that Hengist and Horsa came to Kent in AD 449 at the request of Vortigern, and landed at Ebbsfleet. What is this Ebbsfleet now? All that remains of Ebbsfleet, above Pegwell Bay, is a copy of a Saxon cross, some 18 feet high, covered with crumbling reliefs. Tradition has it that the cross marked the place where Hengist and Horsa arrived, and where, over a century later, Augustine was received by King Ethelbert of Kent under the 'Ebbsfleet oak'. It is said that the monks truly believed themselves to be the first Christians in Britain, yet when they arrived at Canterbury they found there an old Roman church dedicated to Saint Martin, perhaps the first of the stone churches built in England. The monks should have known better — had not the legends told of the coming of Joseph of Arimathaea to Glastonbury, and was not the Queen who stood at the side of Ethelbert already a Christian before they arrived?

PORTSMOUTH, Hampshire A3

The coat of arms of Portsmouth contains a 'star and lunar crescent' which is swathed in mythology and mystery. This same device is found in the twelfth century pavement of the Becket Chapel of CANTERBURY Cathedral, which also incorporates several secret symbols. This is a symbol around which occultists have woven a rich set of associations, claiming that it is derived from ancient Babylonian sources. However, it is likely to be linked with (if not actually derived from) the badge of King Richard I, which was said to be a 'sun over two anchors', the anchors becoming the crescent moon. At any event, it was Richard I who granted the coat of arms to Portsmouth City, which includes a six-rayed flaming star over a crescent moon. This is often linked with the abiding Islamic symbol, which has a five-rayed star over a crescent moon. However, it is likely that the star was originally a sun (or a 'sunburst'), for there are many references to the sun in the badges of Richard I and his successors Edward III (see GLOUCESTER) and

Richard II. After this last King, it was generally presented in the form of a star, and it was suggested that it represents one particular star which is called even in modern times 'Cor Leonis' (Latin for 'the Heart of the Lion') which is set literally in the heart of the heavenly constellation of the Lion. Perhaps this is why the name 'Richard the Lionheart' was used of Richard I. The star and crescent was not adopted by the Mohammedans until the fifteenth century, after the Turks had captured the city of Constantinople (now Istanbul) from the Christians. Legends tell that it had come to that city after being saved from destruction by an attacking enemy by its patron goddess, who caused the Moon to shine with special brilliance on that night. Since this was not adopted until the fifteenth century, it is clearly a popular misconception which claims that the badge used by Richard I (a star over a crescent) symbolizes the superiority of the Crusader (the Star of Bethlehem) over the Turk (the Crescent), since in his day the crescent was not yet a symbol of the Turk. In addition, as we have seen, it was unlikely that the star was really a star at all. The only element of truth in this mythology is that Richard I was a crusader, and that he did bestow the symbol on the arms of cities which were concerned in some outstanding way with the deeds of the Crusades. For example, the star and crescent appears in the arms of Dartmouth and Portsmouth because the crusading ships of Britain are said to have set sail for the Levant from these ports.

82: The white horse of Uffington is typical of those found throughout the country.

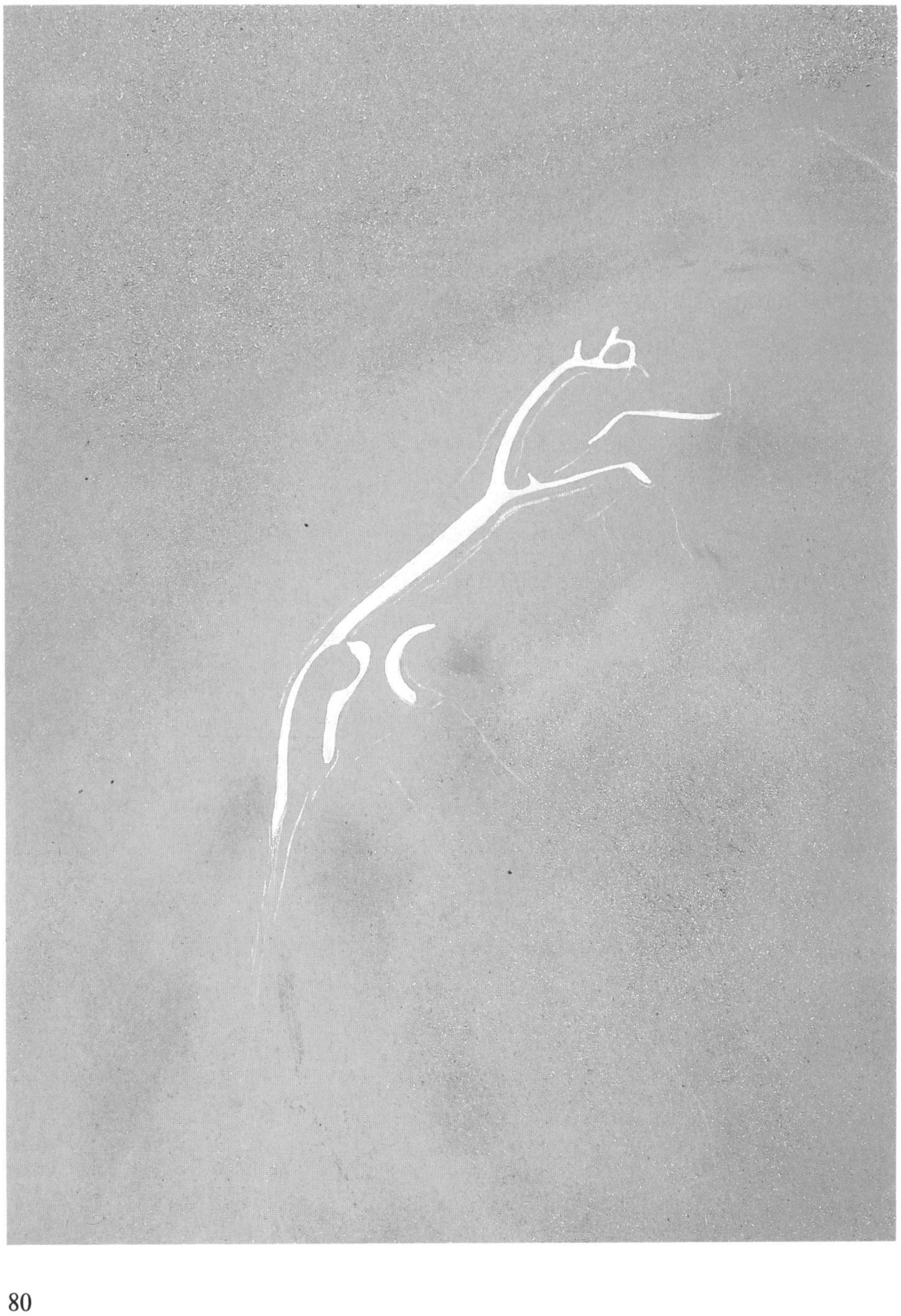

RAMSGATE, Kent F2

The white horse which prances on the coat of arms of Ramsgate tells a most ancient story which probably links up with some of the turf-cut horses in other parts of England — see for example those of Uffington and Westbury. The horse as an emblem came over to England with the Saxon invaders, and it seems (contrary to what our school-book histories tell us) that the two names Hengist and Horsa both meant simply 'horse', and probably refer to the horses on the banners of two successive invasion parties. 'The White Horse was the ensign of the invaders,' writes the specialist Dr Donaldson. 'The Frisians called it their Haengist, and the Anglians their Horsa'. In his most entertaining book *The Romance of Heraldry*, Wilfrid Scott-Giles suggests that the chieftain of this horse-bearing invasion party was believed to have been descended from the Nordic god Odin. This in turn might suggest that the origin of the white horses of England was the magical horse Sleipner, which was the faithful steed of Odin. We see, therefore, that not only did Odin's ravens enter into British mythology (see LERWICK) but also his favourite horse. Scott-Giles records that the horse was held in some importance by the Saxons, and that their neighing prior to a battle was taken as a presage of the eventual outcome of the fight. Whatever the origin of this magical white horse, we do know that it was introduced to England by the Saxons, and that it is this same horse which is found on the coat of arms of the County of Kent, and on several of the towns within its domain, including Ramsgate, Bromley and Lewisham.

THANET, Kent F2

The medieval historian Bede records that when St Augustine and his monks first came to convert King Ethelbert, meeting him in Thanet in AD 596, they carried a banner bearing a silver cross. This legend is commemorated in the coat of arms later constructed for Augustine, which shows a silver cross with his archbishop's cross and a silver lily, an ancient symbol of the Virgin. What is important to the development of British mythology (and history) is the fact that St Augustine found many parts of Britain already Christianized — sure evidence that the very earliest streams of missionaries had reached the land with the Roman armies (see therefore GLASTONBURY).

WANSTEAD PARK, London D1

When Sir Isaac Newton erected one of the earliest giant telescopes in Wanstead Park, its vertical support was made from the last maypole which had stood permanently in London, in the Strand, near to Somerset House. This had been removed in 1718, by which time it was already something of an anachronism as one of the puritanical Acts of Parliament in 1644 had ordered that all maypoles be destroyed. Thus effectively ended one of the ancient pagan customs (or 'heathenish vanities', as the Puritans called them) of the Druidic ceremonies of

83: Among the remarkable medieval sculptural details to be found in Winchelsea church is this large-eared, grinning monstrous face.

Beltane, held on 1 May, which had continued from prehistoric times in the enormously popular guise of morris-dancing, hobby-horses, masquerades, and the like — see MAY (page 21).

WEST CLANDON, Surrey B2

In the south porch of the church of St Peter and St Paul in West Clandon is a carved panel showing a dragon and a curious reptile fighting. Some historians have linked this with a local legend about a dragon which lived in the nearby Send Marsh and was despatched by a soldier and his dog. The only problem is that, in the panel, the dragon is not confronted by a soldier, nor is the creature attacking it a dog! There is a good-quality scratch sundial in the south side of the chancel.

WINCHELSEA, East Sussex E3

Among the remarkable medieval sculptural details in Winchelsea Church is a hunchback (probably intended as a support for a statue) and a large-eared grinning monstrous face (figure 83).

WINCHESTER, Hampshire A2

According to ancient legends, King Arthur's father, who was named Uther, saw two golden dragons in the sky and took them as an omen that he and his son would one day become kings of Britain. Later he had two images of these dragons constructed and, after dedicating one to the church at Winchester, carried the other into battle, mounted on his standard. This has been suggested as the origin of his full title 'Uther Pendragon' (Uther Dragon-head). However, historians of heraldry point out that the dragon was brought to Britain long before Arthur's day — by the Romans, who had themselves taken it from the Dacians whom they conquered under the Emperor Trajan in the second century. It was adopted by the Roman cohorts, and remained a symbol of authority in Britain until the Romans departed. Perhaps this dragon was adopted (as a symbol of continuing authority) by those Britons who partly clung to the Roman traditions when they warred against the invading Saxons. It is likely that the part-mythical Arthur took to himself a title equivalent to the departed Roman generals (his Welsh name was 'yr amherawdyr', which meant 'Imperator', one of the titles of the Roman Emperors), and had upon his banner the golden dragon. It was only the later chroniclers, anxious to point to the Christianity of their hero, who record that his shield bore the Cross and an image of the Virgin. The county of Somerset, which has long claimed to be the area where Arthur lived, fought and died, adopted the emblem of the red dragon holding a blue mace; one wonders to what extent they realized the antiquity of this dragon. As Wilfrid Scott-Giles says, 'If the British dragon may be identified with the Roman cohort standard, it follows that "y ddraig goch", the red dragon which is still the badge of Wales, is a descendant of the emblem of Imperial Rome.'

BLESS·YE·THE·LORD.
O·YE·DRAGONS

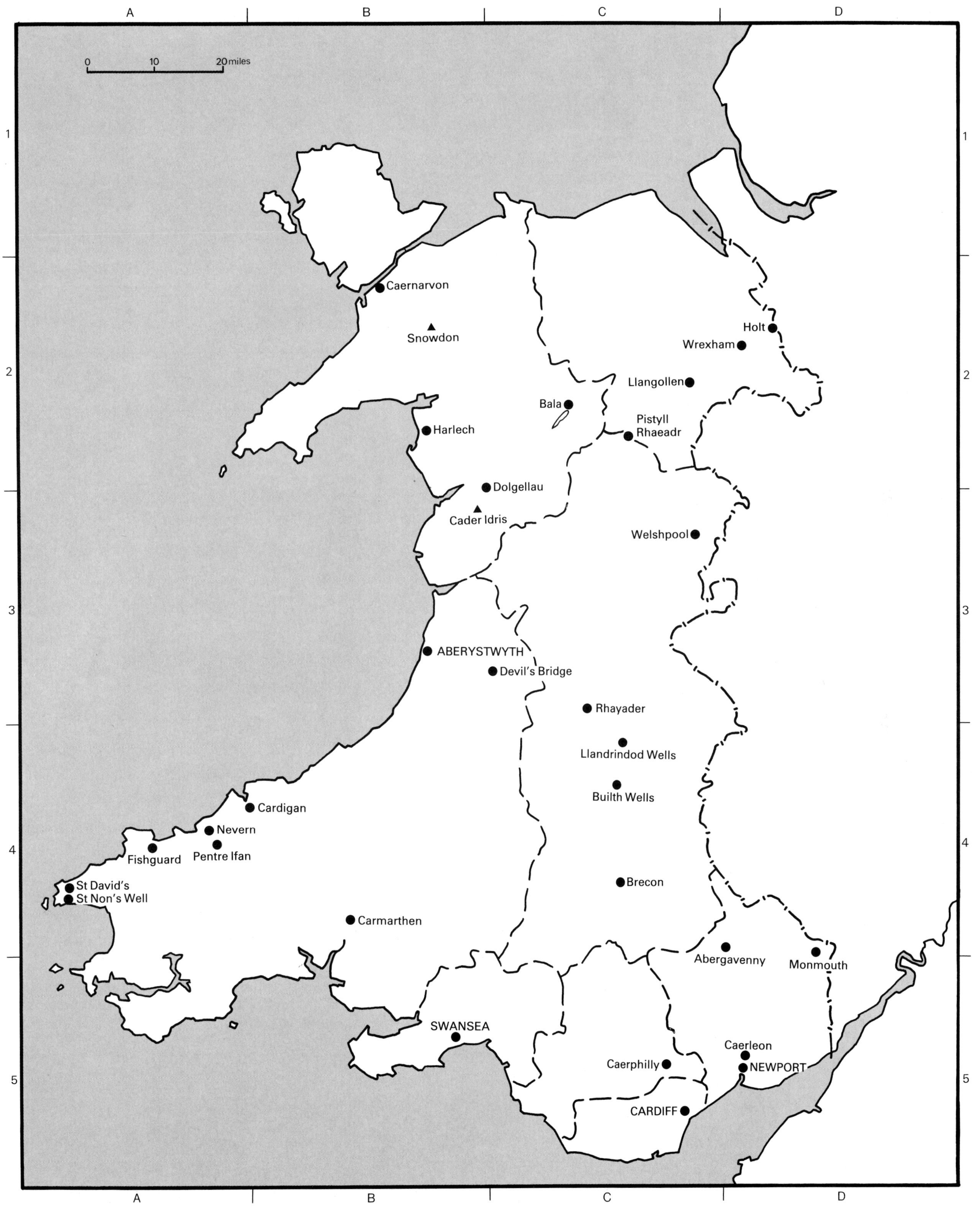

A
B
C
D
1
2
3
4
5
0
10
20 miles
Caernarvon
Snowdon
Harlech
Bala
Holt
Wrexham
Llangollen
Pistyll Rhaeadr
Dolgellau
Cader Idris
Welshpool
ABERYSTWYTH
Devil's Bridge
Rhayader
Llandrindod Wells
Builth Wells
Cardigan
Nevern
Pentre Ifan
Fishguard
St David's
St Non's Well
Carmarthen
Brecon
Abergavenny
Monmouth
SWANSEA
Caerleon
Caerphilly
NEWPORT
CARDIFF

Wales

CARDIFF, South Glamorgan C5

On the coat of arms of the city of Cardiff is the Welsh dragon, a banner (of the Lords of Glamorgan) and, of course, the Welsh leek. This leek looks something like a daffodil, and since these arms were granted in the early part of this present century the story has gained some credence that it is really a daffodil, and that this is the proper emblem of Wales. The leek has a more ancient ancestry than the daffodil, however, for the British King Cadwallader is said to have ordered his men to wear them in their caps prior to doing battle with the Saxons, that they might recognize each other in the heat of the fight. Although, in Shakespeare's *Henry V*, Fluellen appears to have confused this Cadwallader story with the fight at Poitiers, the leek is still 'to this hour...an honourable badge of service'. When in the same play Fluellen proudlyinsists that Pistol should eat the leek he has scorned, Pistol replies, 'Not for Cadwallader and all his goats'.

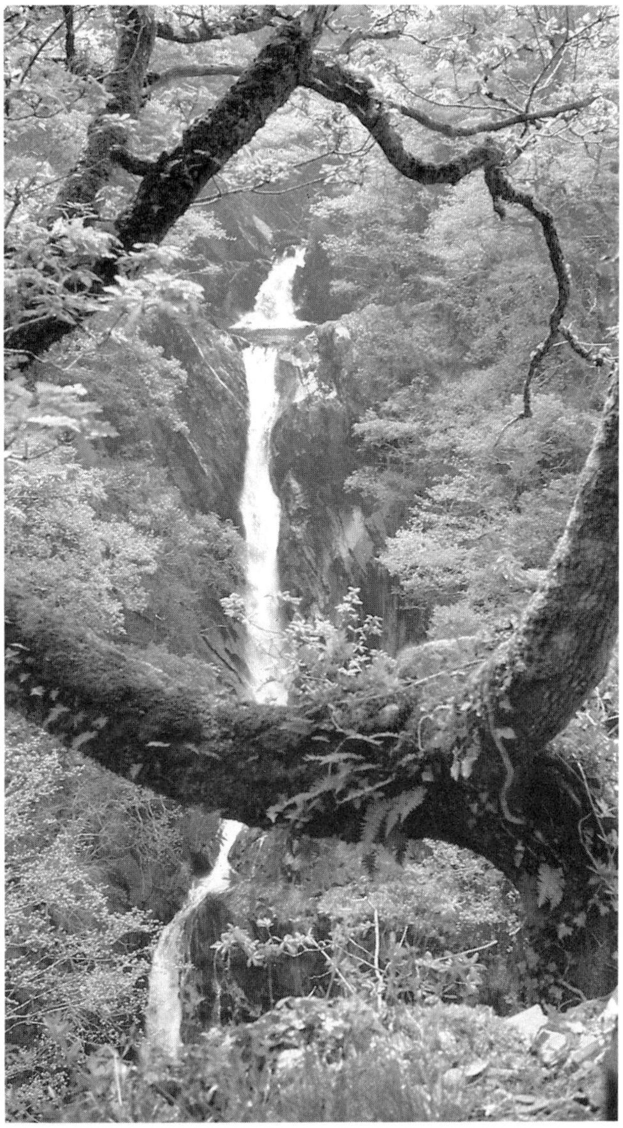

84: One of the waterfalls which run to the south of Devil's Bridge, Dyfed. The bridge is linked with legends that say it was built by the Devil, although the earliest of the triple spans was built by medieval monks.

The goats might be a reference to the arms of Wales (the coat of arms granted to Cardiff in 1906 has a goat and a sea-horse as a supporter), but some occultists insist that Wales is governed by the zodiacal sign Capricorn, the image for which is sometimes a goat. The traditional image for Capricorn is actually a goat-fish, with a curling tail (page 18), and one wonders if the goat and the sea-horse of the Cardiff arms are merely the old Capricorn severed into two pieces, but still the guardian of Wales?

CAERLEON, Gwent D5

This town, which was the Isca Silurum of the Romans, is claimed by many as the original site of King Arthur's Round Table, the legendary 'Camelot', which has been confused with Camelford, and may even have been the prehistoric earthworks known as Cadbury Castle. However, the first literary mention of Arthur's Round Table is in Wace's French rhymed verse 'Le Roman de Brut', written several centuries after the semi-mythological Arthur lived (see WINCHESTER). Brut was a mythical King of the Britons, whose ancestry traces back to the famous Aeneas. He accidentally killed his father, and took refuge first in Greece then in Britain. It was in recognition of the power of ancient Troy that he called the capital he established in Britain 'Troynovant' (New Troy). This was the mythological name for pre-Roman London. Another 'King Arthur's Round Table' is found at EAMONT BRIDGE.

CAERNARVON, Gwynedd B2

In Caernarvon Castle is the Eagle Tower, which is supposed by many to be the place where the first Prince of Wales, Edward II, was born in 1284. This is quite wrong, as documents exist which show that the tower was built many years afterwards on the instruction of this same Edward, long after he had become king. Popular legend has Edward I standing with the new-born child on a balcony, proclaiming to the Welsh that this would be their future native king. It is said (perhaps jokingly) that Edward I presented the child as one who could not speak English — implying of course that the king of Wales should speak Welsh, a notion with which the Welshmen of that time would heartily agree. However, the story is a fabrication, for the castle itself was not completed until well over thirty years later.

DEVIL'S BRIDGE, Dyfed C3

To the south of the triple bridge over the waterfall-gorge of the Mynach at Devil's Bridge (Dyfed) are a number of beautiful waterfalls (figure 84), linked with local legends, the whole area being associated with Devilish legends. The earliest medieval stone bridge, which is now arched by two of later construction, was said to have been built

85: Devil's Bridge.

by the Devil himself — though the fact is that it was constructed by Cistercian monks from nearby Strata Florida Abbey. It is possible to climb the steep pathway alongside the waterfalls and experience the powerful elemental forces of the area in a most personal way, with spray from the falls on the face, the din of the several waterfalls in the ears, and a kaleidoscope of trees all around: for all the organised tourism, it is surely one of the most lovely places in Wales.

HOLT, Clwyd D2

In the church of St Chad at Holt, in Clwyd, is a font which, as the historian E.E. Dorling says, tells 'for those with eyes to read it, the tale of the great ones who in times past ruled the country-side'. The font is octagonal, bearing 24 surfaces each carved with designs of a highly symbolic nature, many of them of heraldic origin. Each

86 (facing page): The prehistoric Pentre Ifan is by far the finest dolmen in Wales, with a capstone almost 17 feet in length.
87 (left): The highest waterfall in Wales is the impressive Pistyll Rhaeadr.

88: St Non's Well overlooks St Non's Bay, about one mile south of St David's.

of the 24 designs tells a story of its own, and an account of these is well-told by Dorling, but the one which we shall select is that area which shows three men in a boat. The fascinatingimage belongs to the symbolism of St Nicholas, who became the modern Father Christmas, one of the most enduring of modern mythologies. One might reasonably associate the three men in the boat with the Three Wise Men who visited the new born Child, but what has the boat to do with Father Christmas, one wonders? In fact, long before Nicholas of Bari was adopted as Father Christmas, he was the patron saint of children. He is said to have brought to life some children killed by a wicked inn-keeper. Another of his exploits was to save three young men from drowning. He also gave gifts to three unmarried women, so that they could use these as dowries to find husbands. The merging of the patron saint of children, the 'giving of gifts', and the saving of lives eventually gave rise to the idea of giving gifts to children on a holy day. This is probably why we find the image of Nicholas on a font, for baptism is the 'gift' of a 'new life' to a child.

NEVERN, Dyfed — A4

The churchyard of Nevern must be one of the most famous in Wales, for not only is it beautiful in the romantic sense of the word, and not only does it have a most lovely avenue of yews, one of which is said to weep blood (actually a resin), but in the burial ground, near to the south face of the church wall, is St Brynach's Cross, the most impressive in the land. The upright cross is richly decorated with complicated scrollwork which suggests a date of about the tenth century. The myth-makers insist that the first cuckoo to break the silence of winter sings from the top of the cross on St Brynach's day — 7 April.

PENTRE IFAN, Dyfed — A4

At Pentre Ifan, in the parish of Nevern, is a prehistoric tomb, distinguished by the three tall jamb-stones which support the long capstone (figure 86). It is by far the finest dolmen in Wales, with a capstone almost 17 feet in length and over 9 feet across at its widest point. The supporters, which are so tapered as to lend an impression of near-flight to the heavy capstone, are nearly eight feet high above the ground.

PISTYLL RHAEADR, Clwyd — C2

The mighty waterfall of Pistyll Rhaeadr in Clwyd (figure 87), is the highest in Wales. According to legend it was the bathing place of a winged serpent which lived on a diet of human flesh. It was eventually killed by the cunning locals, who persuaded it to attack a scarlet cloth, behind which they had hidden impaling spikes.

ST NON'S WELL, Dyfed — A4

This well, built into a stream which pours into the fields overlooking St Non's Bay, about one mile south of St Davids, (figure 88) is very ancient, and has a long-established tradition for healing — especially on St David's Day. Until late into the last century, it was the practice for locals to dip their children in the waters.

89: This recess and statue of the Virgin Mary is placed opposite St Non's Well itself.

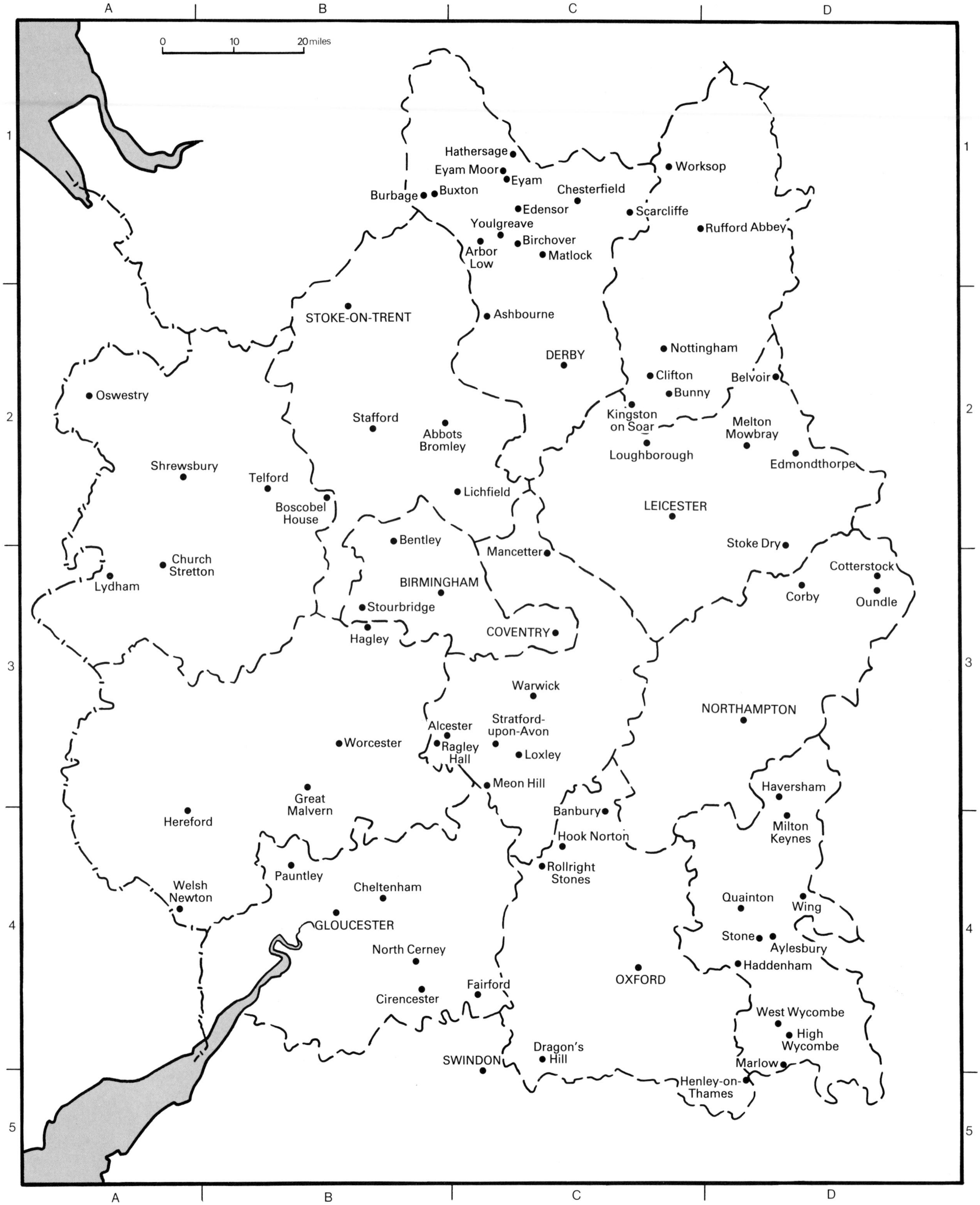
A
B
C
D
1
2
3
4
5
0
10
20 miles
Hathersage
Eyam Moor
Eyam
Burbage
Buxton
Chesterfield
Edensor
Youlgreave
Birchover
Arbor Low
Matlock
Worksop
Scarcliffe
Rufford Abbey
STOKE-ON-TRENT
Ashbourne
DERBY
Nottingham
Clifton
Bunny
Belvoir
Kingston on Soar
Loughborough
Melton Mowbray
Edmondthorpe
Oswestry
Stafford
Abbots Bromley
Shrewsbury
Telford
Boscobel House
Lichfield
LEICESTER
Bentley
Mancetter
Stoke Dry
Cotterstock
Church Stretton
Lydham
BIRMINGHAM
Corby
Oundle
Stourbridge
Hagley
COVENTRY
Warwick
NORTHAMPTON
Alcester
Stratford-upon-Avon
Worcester
Ragley Hall
Loxley
Meon Hill
Haversham
Great Malvern
Hereford
Banbury
Milton Keynes
Hook Norton
Rollright Stones
Pauntley
Welsh Newton
Cheltenham
Quainton
Wing
GLOUCESTER
Stone
Aylesbury
North Cerney
Haddenham
OXFORD
Fairford
Cirencester
West Wycombe
High Wycombe
Dragon's Hill
SWINDON
Marlow
Henley-on-Thames

Central England

ABBOTS BROMLEY, Staffordshire B2

The Horn Dance at Abbots Bromley is performed each year on the first Sunday after 4 September, in a day-long serpentine dance from farmhouse to farmhouse and through the streets of Abbots Bromley itself. Records show that the dance (it is more of a processional) used to be performed at Christmas and Twelfth Night, which has led some to suspect a connexion with the Winter Solstice, when the Sun reaches the first degree of Capricorn, the symbol for which is a horned goat or horned goat-fish. At all events, the emphasis at Abbots Bromley is on horns, for the dancers (the 'Deer Men') carry heavy antlers affixed to the effigy of a deer's head in a form which has suggested a connexion with the earliest known paintings in the world — the horned 'medicine men' painted on such cave walls as Trois-Freres in France. The six Deer Men are divided into two groups of three each, one group being of a light colour, the other dark, enacting a token warfare (as the weakening light of the Sun in Capricorn fights to regain its strength in the zodiac, perhaps). Among the other actors in this annual drama are a Fool, with traditional cap and bells, a hobby horse and a Maid Marion. As we shall see in other festivals where Marion appears, the name is a survival from an old cult; it is from 'Malkin', the diminutive form of Matilda, which was at one time used widely for a slut, a scarecrow or a grotesque puppet. For reasons which are not quite clear, the name was later given to the pagan Queen of the May, but by then it clearly had overtones of the 'old religion' which was the later witchcraft or devil-worship. As the word Malkin separated from the word Marion, the former eventually became a term used only in witchcraft (see NEWCHURCH). It was only in the later mythology of Robin Hood that this Matilda became the mistress of the folk hero (see, however, NOTTINGHAM). This Marion of the festival was probably the token fertility figure in the Horn Dance, just as the Fool was a token symbol of chaos (see HAXEY) in a dance which is no longer properly understood, but is probably linked with sympathetic magic, designed in ages past when such matters were of great importance to preserve or increase the deer under the control of a particular tribe.

ALCESTER, Warwickshire B3

In this detail of the memorial tomb to Sir Fulke Greville in St Nicholas church, Alcester, are three effigies of children born to Sir Fulke. The child in the red shroud (figure 90) died in infancy. This symbolic way of indi-

90: Detail from the tomb of Sir Fulke Greville in the church of St Nicholas, Alcester. The child wrapped in the red shroud died in infancy.

cating that a child died before its parents is only one of many. A more commonly used method is to present the child holding a skull, or to picture a skull (or some other emblem of death) above the child's head.

ARBOR LOW, Derbyshire C1

Arbor Low is sometimes described as 'Derbyshire's Stonehenge', though there does not appear to have been a series of hanging stones or 'henges' as in the Wiltshire circle. Arbor Low is of much the same period, possibly 4,000 years old, and consists of a well-formed earth bank some seven feet high and about 250 feet in diameter, visible for miles around on top of raised ground. Within this is a wide ditch, and then on the raised plateau about 50 fallen stones still marking out a circle about 150 feet in diameter. There is an air of desolation within the circle, and it is hard to believe that any of these giants were ever embedded in the earth. There are several other circles within the vicinity as well as a number of burial places, the most impressive of which is the man-made hill (a barrow burial) called Gib Hill, which may be seen from the earth banks of the main circle.

ASHBOURNE, Derbyshire C2

The church of St Oswald at Ashbourne is famous for its superb tower and spire, but inside the nave is the prone effigy of a young girl called Penelope Boothby, who died in 1791, and whose body in a posture of natural sleep was sculpted by the artist Thomas Banks. Prior to being set in the church, the effigy was exhibited in the Royal Academy; it was seen by Queen Charlotte, who is reputed to have wept at its beauty and sadness.

BELVOIR, Leicestershire D2

Belvoir Castle (pronounced 'Beever Castle') is where the famous witches of Bottesford claimed to have bewitched to death the two small children of the 6th Earl of Rutland, owner of Belvoir in the seventeenth century (figure 91). A so-called 'witchcraft memorial' in the Chancel of Bottesford Church mentions this sorcery, and the death of the two children at the hands of the local witches.

BENTLEY, West Midlands B2

The heroine Jane Lane lived in Bentley Hall, near Walsall (the seat of her brother), from which she set out to help King Charles I escape from England, by arranging for him to accompany her to Abbots Leigh disguised as a male servant. Towards this end, on 10 September, 1651, King Charles dressed in the suit of a serving-man, assumed the name of William Jackson, and brought Jane Lane's strawberry roan horse to the house front for her to ride behind him as pillion. The journey to Abbots Leigh (where Charles intended to find a ship bound for France from Bristol) took three days, and when they finally arrived, Charles was immediately

91: Belvoir Castle, where the Bottesford witches claimed to have bewitched to death the small children of the 6th Earl of Rutland.

92: The Bottesford witches were Joan Flower and her two daughters, Margaret and Philippa, who worked at Belvoir Castle. This print is from a contemporary pamphlet recording the story of their hanging at Lincoln in 1617.

recognised by the butler at the inn where they stayed. Fortunately, this butler was an old royalist soldier and willingly helped Charles, who eventually did escape to France.

For the rest of his life Charles remained a friend of Jane Lane, who married Sir Clement Fisher and received both a pension and a gift of £1,000 'to buy herself a jewel'. On the orders of the King, the Lane family were granted an augmentation to their coat of arms, including the three lions of England and a crest of the strawberry roan on which the King had escaped. This heraldic horse is holding a crown, as a symbol of its famous rider. See also BOSCOBEL.

BIRCHOVER, Derbyshire C1

Stanton Moor on the plateau above Birchover and Stanton Lees was used in prehistoric times as a vast necropolis and contains many interesting burial mounds, several stone circles, at least 70 stone cairns, a large number of free-standing stones and some natural outlandish rocks, which were clearly used for cult purposes. Several of the cairns and mounds have been excavated and have revealed human cremations, as well as fascinating bronzes, urns, flints and other prehistoric objects, some of which are lodged in the Heathcote Museum at Birchover, and others of which are in Sheffield City Museum. Without doubt, the most famous of the Stanton Moor circles is the so-called 'Nine Ladies', which consists of nine uprights (somewhat ruined by the proximity of a huge metal 'Ministry of Works' notice) with a diameter of about 33 feet. While the circle is now entirely flat in the centre, there are records of its surrounding a mound. One of the stones (which are all less than three feet high above the ground) is marked with a curious carving which somewhat resembles an anchor or possibly an early cross, suggesting some attempt to Christianize the circle or to expel the pagan 'demons'. The outlier to this circle is called the King Stone. To the west of Stanton Moor, beyond the Stanton-in-Peak road which runs northward, is the remains of the 'Doll Tor' circle, which consisted of six upright stones (only four of which are still standing), near to which excavations in 1931-33 revealed five human burials, with collared urns, along with adjacent cremations. As with the nearby ROBIN HOOD'S STRIDE to the west, there are indications that many of the interesting natural rock-formations with which the moors are littered were used for ritual worship in ancient times. Behind the 'Druid Inn' at Birchover is a large outcropping of rocks which include a couple of rocking stones. Inevitably, the outcropping is called 'Druid Rocks', though it certainly had nothing to do with the historic Druids.

BOSCOBEL HOUSE, Shropshire B2

Boscobel House, about four miles east of Tong, is a timber-framed medieval structure in which King Charles II is said to have found refuge, prior to escaping to France. Nearby is the famous Royal Oak in which he is said to have hidden after the Battle of Worcester. The 'Oak Apple Day' which is supposed to celebrate the King's escape is certainly derived from a pagan festival, reminding us that the oak was once held so sacred by the ancients that there were laws forbidding people to fell them. It is said that acorns were once held to have magical power, because they grew from the sacred oak tree; they were once threaded on strings and used as amulets. The tree under which the Babes in the Wood are supposed to have hidden was an oak (see WATTON). This was destroyed by lightning in 1879.

BUNNY, Nottinghamshire C2

In the Church of St Mary's at Bunny is the memorial monument to Sir Thomas Parkyns, who died in 1741 (figure 93). To the left of the monument is a life-size effigy of Parkyns in life, adopting the uncompromising stance of a wrestler, a reminder that he was known in his day as 'the Wrestling Baronet', and was author of a book with a Greek title (following the conceit of the times) which was, in English translation, *The Cornish Hugg Wrestler*. Not surprisingly, Sir Thomas is depicted with hands pushed menacingly outwards, as though he were ready to start one of his wrestling bouts. To the right of the same monument is a smaller image of Sir Thomas, this time lying prone on the floor, having been thrown by Old Father Time, that same Death who inevitably throws all men; even the image of Death has suffered the rapacity of time, however, as the scythe which he once held has been removed. As the inscription says:

> That TIME at length did throw him it is plain
> Who lived in hopes that he should RISE again.

The huge Saxon font in front of the memorial is said to be nearly 1,000 years old; it was discovered in use as a cattle trough in a field in Bunny Moor, and was brought to the church in 1916. It is recorded in M.H. Hill's *A Brief History of Bunny and Bradmore* that in 1963 a diviner named Dixon, who lived on Bunny Hill, presumably using a divining rod, discovered gypsum, as a result of which the digging of gypsum was established as a local industry.

BURBAGE, Derbyshire B1

The 'Cat and Fiddle' Inn, high on the A537, almost straddling the Cheshire-Derbyshire borders, to the south-west of Burbage, is perhaps one of the most famous of inns in Britain, partly because its height above sea-level is almost 2,000 feet and makes it one of the highest in England but also because of its name. The inn sign, which shows the cat fiddling against a huge full moon is replete with (unconscious) symbolism, for the cat was in ancient Egyptian times linked directly with the Moon, and was worshipped as a goddess under the name Bubastis; this association may be derived from the distinctive eyes of the cat, which appear to wax and wane like the moon itself.

The connexion between the fiddling cat and the Christian religion continues the ancient honouring of spiritual beings, though in this case the person honoured is no longer a goddess but a saint. It seems that the phrase 'cat and fiddle', which is preserved so beautifully in children's nursery rhymes might be a corruption of the French 'Catherine Fidele' (faithful Catherine), one of the names of a saint. However, the less imaginative among the scholars say that the phrase is from a popular game called 'tip-cat', and the fiddle (sometimes itself called a 'cat') used to attract customers. Another possible meaning has been derived from the fact that women of dubious repute were once called 'cats', so that a place where the cat and the fiddle were to be found meant something akin to 'wine, women and song' — not an unreasonable expectation in such a remote place as the 'Cat and Fiddle'.

CHESTERFIELD, Derbyshire C1

In the eastern-end Lady Chapel of the church of St Mary and All Saints is a late-sixteenth-century tomb without explanatory inscription, but which no doubt pertains to the local Foljambe family. The corpse is represented in a shroud, while above there is a triptych carving depicting Old Age to the left, Death (with dart and shovel) in the middle, and an extremely large child symbolizing Youth to the right.

The world-famous crooked spire of Chesterfield is eight-sided, but there is a most curious optical illusion arising out of the herring-bone tilings of lead, which give the impression from below that the spire consists of 16 faces. No-one has been able to determine precisely when the spire twisted into its present crooked distortion, though a traveller of 1679, who recommended Chesterfield and this church 'only for its ugliness', claimed to be able to see the warping of the spire at a distance of three miles. Many legends account for the warping — the most original being the one which insists that the spire twisted itself in order to see the miracle of a virgin going towards the altar for marriage. Another story tells how the Devil was resting on the spire while Mass was being said below when the incense caused him to sneeze — and his attempt to keep a grip with his claws and tail caused the structure to twist round. The weight of lead supported by the warped timber is well over 30 tons — with an overhang of over eight feet to the southwards and nearly four feet to the westwards — yet the whole structure has been pronounced perfectly safe by specialists.

CHURCH STRETTON, Shropshire A3

The Shropshire legends of Edric Wild are as extensive and variable as the more northerly legends of Robin Hood, but the gist of the story is that he was a hero who lived in the eleventh century — one of those who sided with the Welsh and rose up against William the Conqueror. He is especially remembered because of his strange meeting with his ideal woman — a fairy indeed — whom he had chanced to see in a fairy gathering and kidnapped. Within days of this act she had fallen in love with Edric and the two were married, on the under-

93: The tomb of the 'Wrestling Baronet' Sir Thomas Parkyns, local landowner, Latin translator, philanthropist and wrestler, who died at Bunny in 1741.

standing that Edric would never mention her fairy origin again. Unfortunately, Edric did eventually speak of her fairy folk and his wife vanished, though not before she had given birth to a son whom they named Aelnoth, who lived to a ripe old age and (according to legend) bequeathed the manor of Lydbury North to the bishopric of Hereford. As the quasi-historian Walter Map recorded in the Middle Ages, 'We have often heard of demons, incubi and succubi, and of the dangers of mating with them, but rarely or never do we read that the offspring of such unions ended their lives happily, as did this Aelnoth.' Legends tell how the ghost of the forester Edric Wild haunts the hills around Church Stretton in the form of a diabolical hound with burning eyes. To the north of Shrewsbury at Bomere Heath was a pool in which dwelt a magic fish that guarded his sword. The modern historian Charles Kightly records the Shropshire story that Edric did not die at all, but, along with his train of followers, awaits the call to serve England in her hour of need. Just before the Crimean War, the ghostly troupe were said to have been seen riding in the darkness at Minsterley, the whole band dressed in greens and whites, with Edric riding a white horse, his fairy-wife Lady Godda with golden locks flowing to her waist. A similar group was sighted in 1914, though none in 1939.

CIRENCESTER, Gloucestershire B4

On Querns Hill, Cirencester, are the remains of what is generally believed to be a Roman amphitheatre, though the present remains would suggest that it was in fact an ancient earth fortification, perhaps used by the Romans for their games. To the south of the amphitheatre, standing in isolation, is an eighteenth-century obelisk (figure 95) which none of the locals appear to know anything about.

94 (above): Late 14th-century alabaster effigy of Dame Alice Nevill in the church of St Mary the Virgin, Clifton.
95 (far left): Obelisk to the south of the remains of the Roman amphitheatre on Querns Hill. Cirencester was called Corinium by the Romans and was the second largest of their British cities.

96 (left): Detail of a charnel chamber with bones and skulls on the memorial to the first three wives of Sir Gervase Clifton, in the church of St Mary the Virgin, Clifton. It is dated c.1631.

CLIFTON, Nottinghamshire C2

In St Mary's church, Clifton (which is now almost a suburb of Nottingham), is a collection of impressive monuments which record an almost unbroken family tradition relating to the Cliftons. The most peaceful is the fourteenth-century effigy of Dame Alice Nevill (figure 94), whose elegant coiffure is preserved in a decorated hair-net, her head supported by a pillow held in the hands of an angel. Less tranquil is the sculpted charnel chamber at the foot of the 1631 memorial to the first three wives of Sir Gervase Clifton (who had seven wives), with its grisly *memento mori* of skulls, skeletal hands, and bones (figure 96). The tall crossing tower of St Mary's is decorated with four gargoyles, one of which has what must be the longest tongue of all such British figures; it is over 18 inches long, and appears to be made of lead.

COTTERSTOCK, Northamptonshire D3

Typical of the witchcraft literature of the early eighteenth century is a pamphlet which tells the story of two Northamptonshire witches who were executed in 1705. According to this pamphlet, young Ellinor Shaw of Cotterstock gained herself such a reputation for evil-doing that by the time she was 21 she was the talk of the whole neighbourhood — in Glapthorn, Benefield, Southwick, Oundle itself, 'and many Parts adjacent'. Seemingly, in order to revenge herself on the people who mistrusted her, she and her friend Mary Phillips of Oundle decided to enter into a contract with the Devil. On 12 February, 1704, at precisely midnight, the Devil obligingly appeared in the form of 'a black tall Man', persuading Ellinor Shaw to pawn her soul to him for a year and two months, during which time he would help her to attain anything she desired. When she agreed, he produced a little piece of parchment, by which their consents were to be registered. Having pricked their fingers, he wrote the document in their own blood, which they then signed.

COVENTRY, West Midlands C3

Popular legend says that Lady Godiva rode naked through the streets of Coventry. The story tells how, having agreed to ride through the streets in order to reduce taxes (imposed according to some legends by her husband), or to bring some other benefit to the townspeople, everyone agreed not to watch the spectacle. All people would leave the streets, and close their doors and window shutters in order to save embarrassing the lady. However, one man did secretly watch her during this naked ride, and he was ever afterwards called 'Peeping Tom'. The lady's husband was Leofric, the eleventh century Earl of the Mercians, not at all the cruel ruler depicted in the story but indeed the historic founder of Coventry Priory. However, there is no documentary evidence in support of the Lady Godiva story, which does not appear to have circulated until almost three centuries after the death of Leofric, while the account of the peeping tailor was not added for nearly seven centuries.

The earliest surviving painting of Lady Godiva riding naked through the streets is in the Flemish style, dated 1586, and almost certainly commissioned by the City of Coventry. Most modern scholars point out that there is much doubt as to what was meant by the phrase 'mounted naked' — it could possibly have referred to the idea of Godiva riding through the streets stripped of her official attire of rank, or even to her riding without a saddle. Again, there is something of a problem in regard to the deed itself, for in the days of Leofric the town of Coventry was not at all the huge and beautiful city which it became in later centuries, and it is doubtful that there would have been much for the lady to ride through. However, by the nineteenth century, when Tennyson wrote his poem on Godiva, there was no doubt that she rode naked ('clothed on with chastity') through a city crowned with 'fantastic gables' and gothic arches, and that Tom peeped through an auger-hole, to have his eyes 'shrivell'd into darkness in his head'.

In modern times there is a 'Lady Godiva Clock' designed by Trevor Tennant in the Broadgate. The clock mechanism is so designed that on the strike of the hour an effigy of the naked Lady Godiva rides along a trackway upon a white horse while Tom peers down from an opened door above, holding his hands to his hurting eyes. In the centre of Broadgate itself is a statue of Lady Godiva riding her horse — though this life-size figure has none of the beauty of the statues by William Calder Marshall (c.1854) or Thomas Woolner (1878) in the local museum. Nearby, a late-medieval effigy built into a modern passage-bridge across the shopping precinct is pointed out as being that of Peeping Tom. The local museum has several interesting full-life images of this Peeping Tom, as well as some excellent statues, paintings and engravings of the event which led to his fame. It is said that at one time there were many such Peeping Tom effigies in different parts of Coventry. Paintings and engravings of these Toms have survived into modern times, though the earliest mention of him is no older than 1659. However, as the useful guide by Clarke and Day (1882) records, when the Flemish-style picture of 1586 was cleaned in 1976 there was discovered underneath the layers of yellow varnish the shadowy image of a man peering down from a window in one of the ornate buildings behind the naked woman. Is this an indication that the Peeping Tom story is much older than is generally suspected? The Lady Godiva festivals and processionals (figure 98) appear to have been started as a result of the growth of interest in the story sparked off by Tennyson's poem, and have continued even into the present decade (the last on record at the time of writing being in 1982).

Astrology appears to have flourished in Coventry in former times, and there are survies along a trackway upon a white horse while Tom peers down from an opened door above, holding his hands to his hurting eyes. In the centre of Broadgate itself is a statue of Lady Godiva riding her horse — though this life-size figure has none of the beauty of the statues by William Calder Marshall (c.1854) or Thomas Woolner (1878) in the local museum. Nearby, a late-medieval effigy built into a modern passage-bridge across the shopping precinct is pointed out as being that of Peeping Tom. The local museum has several interesting full-life images of this Peeping Tom, as well as some excellent statues, paintings and engravings of the event which led to his fame. It is said that at one time there were many such Peeping Tom effigies in different parts of Coventry. Paintings and engravings of these Toms have survived into modern times, though the earliest mention of him is no older than 1659. However, as the useful guide by Clarke and Day (1882) records, when the Flemish-style picture of 1586 was

97 (*below*): An engraving of Peeping Tom, from around 1826.
98 (*facing page*): Lady Godiva by William Holman Hunt, from Moxton's edition of Tennyson's *Poems*, 1859.

99 (facing page): A modern statue of the naked Lady Godiva in the centre of Coventry. She is guarded by elephants with turrets on their backs, derived from the heraldic tradition.
100 (left): A lion as part of the decorative heraldic treatment on the facade of the City Hall in Coventry. The crest of the city arms is a cat. Early 19th century.
101 (bottom left): The spire and interior of the cathedral church of St Michael, bombed in 1941 and now used as a car park, alongside the new Coventry Cathedral designed by Sir Basil Spence in the 1950s.
102 (below): One of the bronze elephants which guard Lady Godiva in the city centre.

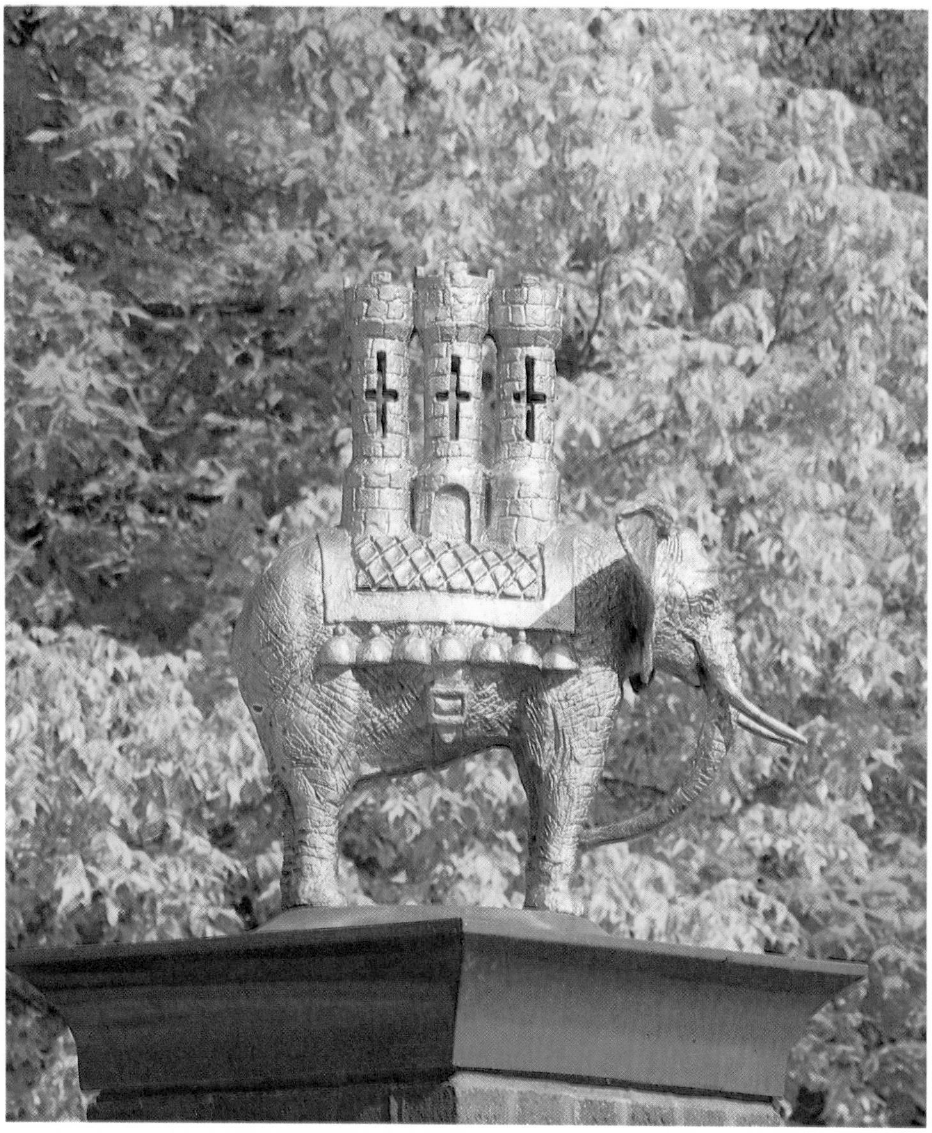

to any longitude or latitude whatsoever'.

The armorial bearings of Coventry are almost a study in secret symbolism themselves. The arms depict a golden elephant (on a background of red and green) bearing a triple-towered castle (figure 00). This is said by some to represent the Christ bearing the whole world, though others see a more esoteric meaning in the symbolism, linking it with the stories of the prowess of the elephant in the ancient bestiaries. The foe of the elephant was said to be the dragon, so that the elephant was ranged with Adam and Eve as being under constant threat from the great dragon who was Satan. The link with the dragon-slaying elephant is entwined with local mythology, however, for Coventry was said to have been the birthplace of St George, the archetypal dragon-slayer. Indeed, the reverse of the earliest seal used officially within the city showed St George slaying the dragon; on the obverse is the elephant and castle.

Another strain of secret symbolism is also linked with the bestiary treatment of the elephant. It was believed that elephants had no knees and, on the strength of this, ivory-hunters would induce elephants to lie down so that they would be rendered helpless and thus have their ivory tusks removed without much difficulty. The elephant (it was claimed) would go to sleep leaning against a tree, and so the cunning hunters would saw the tree almost through at the base in the anticipation that when the elephant leaned against it, the tree would fall, bringing with it the heavy elephant, who would then be unable to get up. It seems that the armorial bearings once had a tree among the symbols, but this was eventually dropped. The local historian, Mary Dormer Harris, points out that the name Coventry was almost certainly derived from that used for a special tree, 'Cofa's Tree'. This was perhaps associated symbolically with the tree in which the great dragon Satan lived, and from which he set out to attack Adam, Eve and the golden elephant. The delightful image of a golden elephant is found in many different parts of Coventry, but perhaps the most impressive are those gilded images flanking the statue of Godiva in Broadgate (figure 99). The cat on the crest of the armorial bearings was probably a 'cat-a-mountain' or wild cat (some of the early designs preserved in the museum would suggest a lynx, or a spotted cat), and this alone makes the armorial device unique among city arms. The cat is said to be a symbol of watchfulness. The supporters to the arms were granted in 1959, and depict the black eagle of Leofric and the Phoenix arising from the flames. This latter bird was adopted to symbolize the New Coventry arising from the ashes of the Old, after the destructive bombing of the last war.

DRAGON'S HILL, Oxfordshire C4

The curious natural formation below the white horse of Uffington (figure 82) is said to mark the site where St George killed the dragon. The top of the hill is said to have been so poisoned by the blood of the dragon that it will no longer grow vegetation — in fact the top soil has long been eroded, to leave the chalk surface open to the skies. From historically-based mythologies we learn that the founder of the West Saxon kingdom, Cerdic, slew Natanleod at this spot, along with 5,000 of his soldiers. Natanleod was called the 'Pendragon'.

EDENSOR, Derbyshire C1

Strange memorials which make use of skeletons and shrouded figures are found in many parts of Britain, but one of the most interesting is that in the Cavendish chapel at Edensor, which combines both skeleton and shrouded figure in a single tomb. The memorial is to William, first Duke of Devonshire (died 1625) and to Henry Cavendish (died 1616). The former is represented in a shroud, though with his face visible, while Henry is represented as a full-length skeleton set out on a plaited straw matting (figure 103). Of William, the Latin inscription says, 'He was not merely the best man of his own, but of every age, nor can his character be suppressed or spoken of without difficulty... he claimed no honours and yet obtained all.' To the east end of the church exterior is a most remarkable carving of a demon (or so it seems) holding down beneath its feet another demon, with bat-like wings.

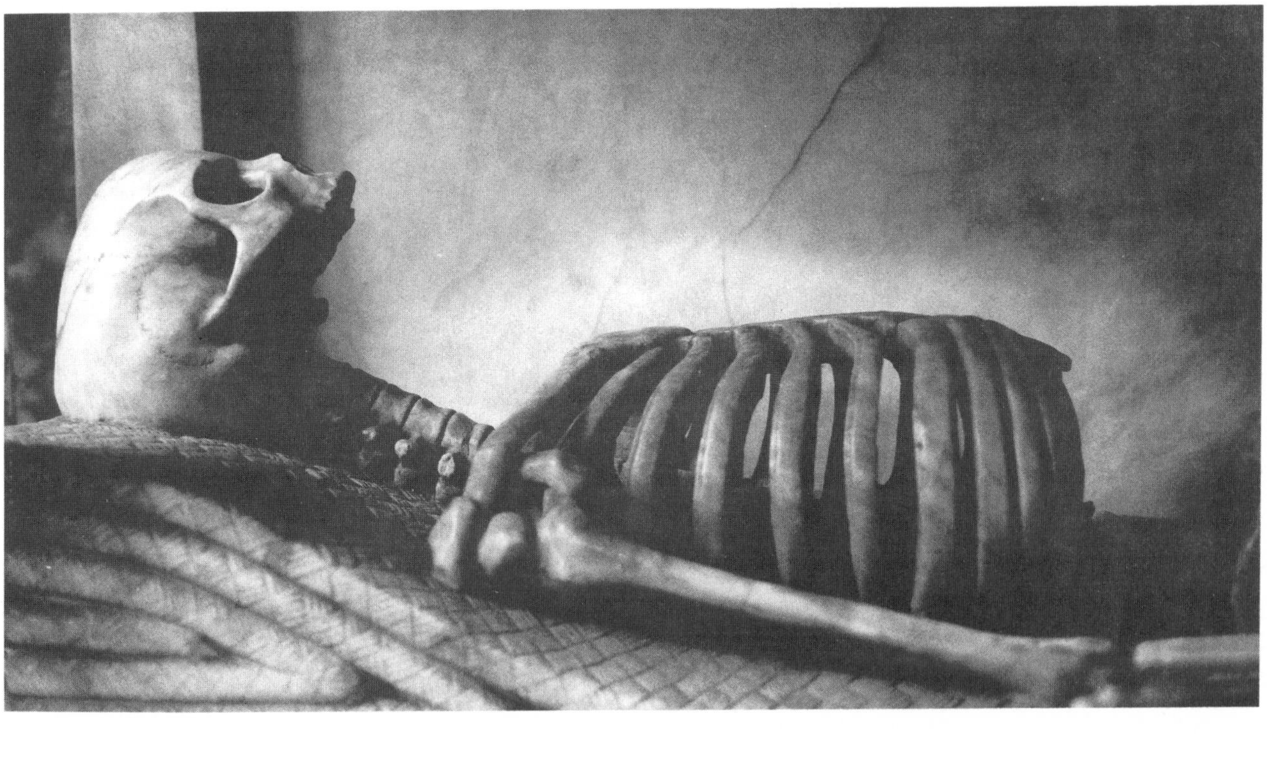

103: The tomb of William, 1st Duke of Devonshire (died 1625) and of Henry Cavendish (died 1616) in the Cavendish chapel at Edensor.

In the church of St Edmund at Fenny Bentley is the strange memorial to Thomas Beresford and his wife, dated 1473, in which both figures are completely shrouded, with the shroud knotted over their heads. Their small children are also bundled up in similar shrouds. In the church of St Mary at Weston-upon-Trent there is a memorial to Richard Sale (died 1615) which contains within an oval the skeleton holding an hour-glass, and leaning upon a shovel. Beneath the image is a Latin inscription (Ecce nosce te ipsum. Ut sum tu eris) meaning 'Behold, know yourself: as I am, you will be'.

EDMONDTHORPE, Leicestershire D2

In St Michael's Church at Edmondthorpe is the seventeenth-century memorial tomb to Sir Roger Smith. He and his two wives are shown in life-size and realistic imagery. The lower effigy represents Lady Ann, who was reputed to have been a witch with the magical power to turn herself into a cat at night (a popular guise adopted by witches, according to the general view). One night, when so transformed, her own butler, anxious to rid the kitchen of the unwanted feline, struck at it with a cleaver and wounded it in the paw. When the cat returned to its human form, the wound was seen in the same place on her hand. Is this elaborate story merely an attempt to explain the dark stain and break on the wrist of this effigy? It is unlikely that a lady of the seventeenth century (no matter what her social rank) would have escaped the law had she really been a witch — or even had she been suspected of being a witch.

EYAM, Derbyshire C1

The terrible plague of 1665 arrived at the remote village of Eyam in Derbyshire by way of a parcel of clothing. As soon as the cause of the rapid deaths was realised, the rector of the village, William Mompesson, arranged to seal off the community to prevent the plague spreading into the neighbourhood. He asked the neighbouring villages to leave food for his flock at strategic points, and forbade those in his charge to have commerce with any other living souls outside the village, drawing an imaginary line one mile from its centre to mark the point of no exit. To avoid contagion as much as possible (in days when the cause of the plague was not understood), the rector preached in the open air, in a place now called the Dell, using a natural rock as his pulpit. In this way, and with this incredible fortitude and self-sacrifice, the plague was prevented from spreading to the rest of the county. Every person remained faithful to Mompesson's wishes; of the 300 villagers of Eyam, 267 died.

On Wakes Sunday, the last Sunday of August, the anniversary of the day on which the first signs of the plague became evident, an open air service is held in the Dell, called as a result Cucklet 'Church', in memory of this extraordinary devotion. In the village church is a

104: This 19th-century gravestone in Eyam churchyard is to the memory of Ann Carr, who died in 1859.

105: The effigy of Lady Ann in St Michael's Church, Edmondthorpe, showing the left wrist stained dark red.

106: The village of Eyam, famous for the way its inhabitants behaved in the face of the plague of 1665.

107: The Mompesson memorial window in the parish church at Eyam.

chair inscribed with the first three letters of Mompesson's name, the date 1665 and the name of the village.

In 1985 a triple-lancet memorial window was given to the church by Mrs C.M. Creswick in memory of her husband. It was designed by Alfred Fisher of Kings Langley, and is now called 'the Plague Window'. The details within the window show different incidents during those terrible days (figure 107), including the story of the lovers Roland Torre and Emmot Sydall who were separated by the plague. Mompesson himself survived the plague, and is buried at Eakring near Newark. His wife Catherine succumbed, however, and her grave is to the south of the sundial door of the church, with a touching Latin motto.

Above the external south door of the church (figure 106) is an eighteenth-century sundial designed to tell the time in various parts of the world in comparison with the local time. Marked on the slab are certain sigils for the signs of the zodiac, and the names of different places with corresponding times (London, Jerusalem, Mecca, Mexico, and so on). On the corbels supporting the sundial are carved the Latin 'Ut Umbra' and 'Sic Vita' (Life passes like a shadow).

EYAM MOOR, Derbyshire C1

On the edge of Eyam Moor is Highlow Hall, said to be one of the most haunted houses in Derbyshire and once the seat of the Eyre family, whose memorial brasses are now the pride of HATHERSAGE church. One ghost of Highlow Hall is said to be that of a mason who was playing dice when he should have been working on the restoration of the hall, and who was killed (perhaps a little unjustifiably) by Robert Eyre, whose memorial brass is still in the church (figure 114). Another haunting spirit is that of a Miss Archer, who was said to have committed suicide after being jilted by Nicholas Eyre.

On Eyam Moor, on land belonging to Highlow Hall,

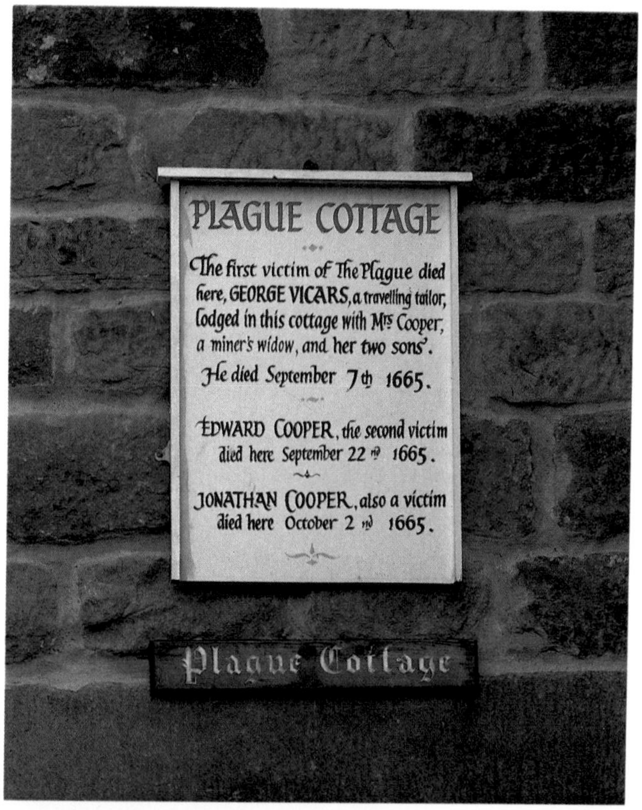

are the remains of a Roman road, leading to a ditched area called Wet Withens, near to which is a stone circle hidden in thick bracken. It has 16 small stones within a circular bank, the circle being 100 feet in diameter. The circle is on private land, and difficult to find without precise directions.

FAIRFORD, Gloucestershire C4

St Mary's at Fairford is world-famous for the collection of stained glass in its west windows, but the many impressive gargoyles on its external walls are also worthy of attention, as this demonic head (figure 109) indicates.

GLOUCESTER, Gloucestershire B4

In the Cathedral of Gloucester is a beautifully preserved life-size effigy of Edward II (figure 111), built by his son Edward III. The face of the effigy is said to have been copied from a death mask which had been made almost as soon as the King had died under the red-hot spit used by his torturers; this explains the grimace and sense of pain within the immobile features. The story of this effigy, resting in its exquisitely sculpted canopy, is one of the strangest in history, for it merges into mythology and

108 (left): Notice relating to the deaths of two Eyam inhabitants during the plague.
110 (above): Disposing of plague victims.

109: A gargoyle on the south wall of St Mary's church in Fairford, built in the later part of the 15th century.

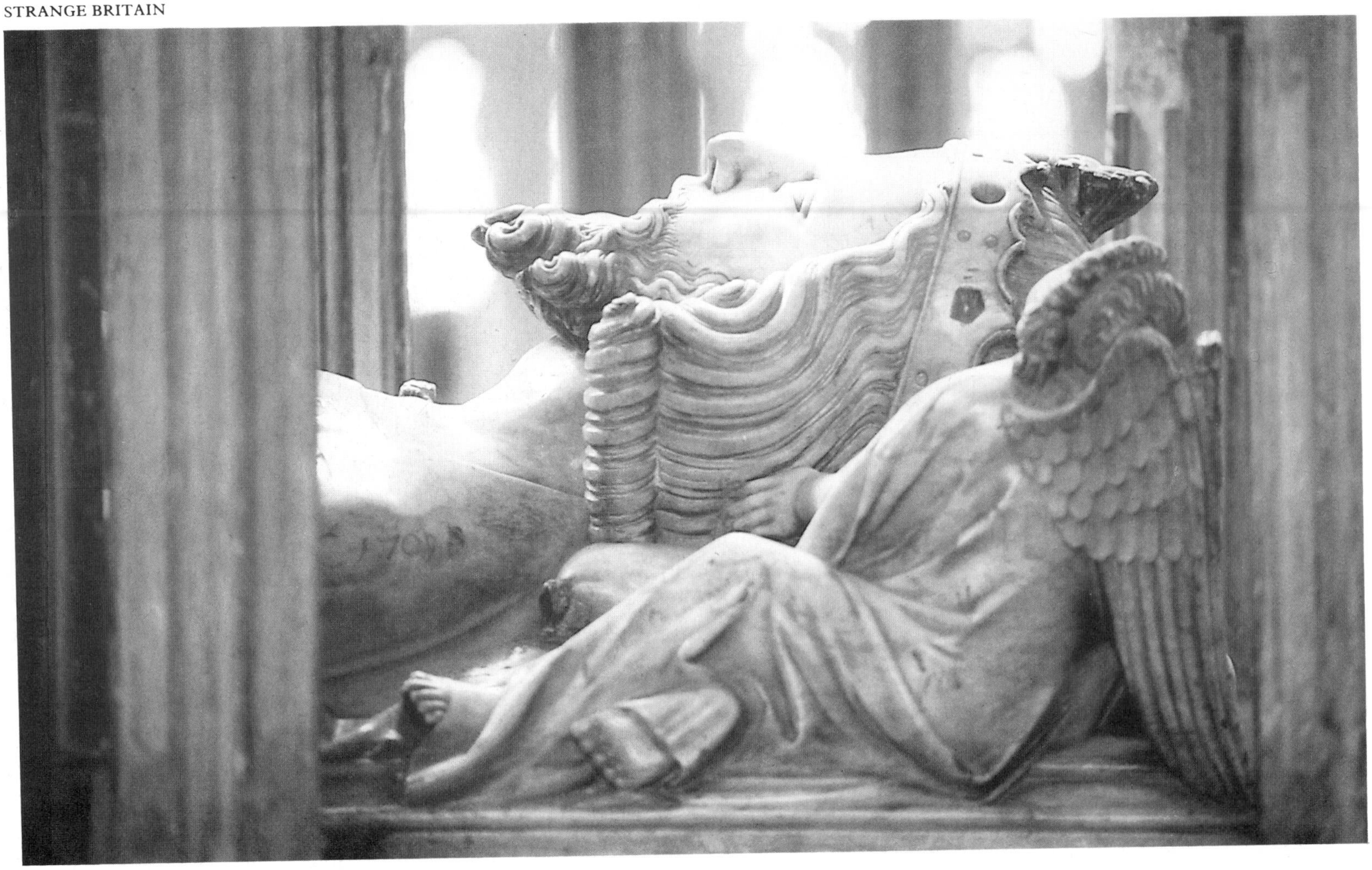

111: The effigy of Edward II in Gloucester Cathedral.

magic in a unique way. The story begins with the murder of the ineffectual Edward II at Berkeley Castle in 1327 on the orders of Queen Isabella and Roger Mortimer. The abbeys nearest to Berkeley — Bristol and Malmesbury — refused to bury the body, mainly for fear of the two powerful murderers, and by the time the Abbot of Gloucester, 'moved by pity', allowed it to be interred in the cathedral, the corpse was already far decayed.

It was soon rumoured that the tomb was a miracle-worker, and that sick people could be cured magically by being placed near to it, with the result that the dead Edward, who had been ineffectual in life, became effectual in death as a Saint. His son, Edward III, who had been born at Windsor in 1312, was more adroit in political and military matters and introduced order into the chaos which his father had left behind. It was he who commissioned and paid for the tomb of his father in Gloucester, to mark the place of pilgrimage of the sick to the 'martyr Edward', leaving behind one of the most impressive alabaster effigies in Britain. It is said that pilgrims to this tomb were so numerous that the small charges made were sufficient to enable the Abbot to reconstruct the east end, the clerestory, and parts of the nave of the Cathedral itself. The castle at Berkeley, where the foul murder of Edward II was committed, is said still to be haunted by the spirit of the troubled king. Edward had not been one of the wisest of rulers, preferring the companionship of low-born men to that of his peers (for example, he appears to have befriended Robin Hood — see KIRKLEES) — nor was he one of the most competent of fighting men. When he led an army of conquest against Scotland in 1314, he managed to have 28,000 men defeated by about a third of that number under Robert the Bruce at the English disaster of Bannockburn.

HADDENHAM, Buckinghamshire D4

The 'Legend of Silly Haddenham' in Buckinghamshire tells how, in the days when the breeding of ducks was the main source of income for Haddenham, one local built a roof over a pond to keep ducklings dry in the rain, as a result of which the hamlet was afterwards called Silly Haddenham. The duck industry began to peter out shortly before the last war, when the installation of drains lowered the water-table in the whole area, thereby drying-out the ponds. Although attempts have been made to construct special ponds since then, it has not been possible to keep ducks in any numbers for the past few years. In 1987, however, one pond was connected to the mains supply in such a way as to fill up whenever the water table dropped, and there is now the possibility that the not-so-silly Haddenham will soon be in business with its ducks once again.

HAGLEY, Hereford and Worcester B3

Sir Thomas Lyttleton was said to have been an extreme profligate, even by eighteenth-century standards, and is chiefly remembered now because of a tale concerning a warning given to him by the ghost of one of his mistresses that he was shortly to die. It is recorded that Sir Thomas, sleeping in his ancestral home at Hagley, in Worcestershire, was awakened by the sound of something like a bird fluttering around his bedroom, and then saw standing at the foot of his bed, 'the figure of a female whom he had seduced and deserted, and who, when so deserted, had put an end to her own existence'. The spectre pointed to a clock, and then announced that in three days' time (to the very minute) Lyttleton would be dead. He told many friends of this ghastly vision, and when the time drew near they attempted to bring back confidence to his troubled mind by putting the clock forward an hour. He was relieved that the time passed without incident and then went to bed calmly. When the hour had passed, he died without a sound. A painting, many times copied in print and lithographic form, was based on a verbal reconstruction of the event of the ghost's appearance, the year following his death. This print (figure 112) is certainly one of the most famous of all eighteenth-century ghost pictures.

HATHERSAGE, Derbyshire C1

The grave of Little John, the amiable giant who served Robin Hood so faithfully, is in the churchyard of Hathersage parish church, the place marked by a distinctly modern headstone (figure 113). In the centre of the lengthy grave is a second stone which records that it is in the care of the Ancient Order of Foresters Friendly Society. There should be little surprise to find the grave here, for Little John was said to have spent the last few years of his life in Hathersage, living in a small cottage

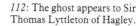

112: The ghost appears to Sir Thomas Lyttleton of Hagley.

113 (top): The memorial stone on Little John's grave at Hathersage.
114 (above): Brass rubbing of Robert Eyre's memorial.
115 (below): Memorial brass to Sir John d'Abernon.

near the east end of the church. It is said that Little John's cuirass, his green cap and yew bow (six feet long, and tipped with horn), along with a couple of arrows, used to hang inside the church. The antiquarian Ashmole reported it still hanging there in 1625, near to the famous Eyre monuments of brass, which are still one of the great treasures of Hathersage church (figure 114). The bow was eventually moved to Cannon Hall near Barnsley; a photograph taken before 1950 shows a gentleman holding the bow outside Cannon Hall, but it would appear to be more than six feet long. The useful guidebook by the Rev. Hulbert of Hathersage Vicarage records that the bow was removed to the Scottish home of Mr Simon Frazer, and was still there in 1980.

Some historians have claimed that Little John's real name was Naylor. One most curious chance is that the ancient bow is said to have been last used to shoot a deer by a Colonel Taylor, in 1715; it took 160lb to draw the bow to the full. Whether it is the grave of Little John or not (the initials I.L. were still visible on the stone as late as 1792), there may be no doubt that a giant of a man was buried there, for when the grave was opened by Captain James Shuttleworth, who had just returned from the American War of Independence, in 1784, he found at a depth of over two yards a human thigh-bone over 32 inches long. A strange story is told about this bone: it seems that Captain Shuttleworth kept this thigh-bone and hung it near his bed. On a later occasion, when he had broken one of his own limbs while out hunting, his nurse told him that he would continue to do so as long as he kept dead men's bones out of their grave. He therefore gave it to his clerk to rebury but, instead of doing this, the clerk put it in his own window, with an explanatory label as to whose bone it was. Sir George Strickland stole it from this place.

In the immediate neighbourhood of Hathersage are many places named after the famous outlaws. On the Longshaw estate is 'Little John's Well', on Abney Moor is 'Robin Hood's Cross', on Offerton Moor there is 'Robin Hood's Stoop', and the distinctive 'Robin Hood's Cave' on Stanage Edge overlooks Hathersage. The group of brasses in St Michael's and All Angels is among the finest in the country, and is related to the ancient family of Eyre. The name has entered our literary heritage through the inspiration of Charlotte Bronte, who called her heroine 'Jane Eyre' after staying in what used to be the old vicarage opposite Hathersage church. The brass rubbing in figure 114 is of Robert Eyre, part of a monument which includes his wife, four children, and an inscription with a coat of arms and a couple of banderolles, all dating 1656. This Robert Eyre is said to have lived at Highlow Hall, said to be the most haunted house in Derbyshire. There are excellent facilities in the sacristy of the church for anyone to make their own rubbings for a very reasonable fee.

HAVERSHAM, Buckinghamshire D3

Set in the chancel floor of the church of St Mary at Haversham is an interesting plate memorial of 1605 to John Maunsell which depicts the 'dead image' of Maunsell in skeletal form. This kind of gruesome effigy began to appear in the late fifteenth century (an excellent three dimensional example is found at WORSBROUGH, another at HATFIELD) but the example in Haversham is of an especially fine quality. More frequently, the deceased were represented as corpses in covering shrouds, as for example the Henry Millner memorial (1635) in the church of SS Peter and Lawrence at Wickenby. In other types, the shrouds are open and one is offered a glimpse of the corpse, as for example in the two effigies of the early sixteenth century in St Andrew's church at BIDDENDEN. In the church of St Andrew at Oddington, Oxford, the memorial brass to Ralph Hamsterley (1518) depicts a shrouded skeleton being devoured by worms. Prior to the 'cadaver' images, which were no doubt influenced by the popular 'Dance of Death' prints which circulated widely after the invention of printing in the mid-sixteenth century, it was more usual for effigies and brasses to represent stylized images of the deceased as they were seen when alive. The oldest effigy brass in Britain (dated 1277) is in St Mary's church at Stoke d'Abernon, which building the ubiquitous Pevsner described as a 'classic example of bad restoration'. This brass (figure 115), which is over six feet long, depicts Sir John d'Abernon in full chain-mail armour, his feet resting on a lion which bites at the base of his spear; the copper shield is enamelled with blue, and has been neatly set into the brasswork. Next to this oldest brass is a memorial to his son, dated 1327. Also in St Mary's at Haversham is a long vamping horn, which was used to encourage the choir to sing with more gusto.

LOUGHBOROUGH, Leicestershire C2

A throwback to the medieval practices enshrined in the story of the Boy Bishop of SALISBURY is the annual 'Mothering Service' in Holy Trinity Church, Loughborough. By special arrangement, the service is given over entirely to children, and a boy takes the place of the vicar to preach to the congregation, helped by boy curates and other young people. The child-service of Loughborough recalls the fact that Mid-Lent is a time for taking stock, and for recalling the innocence of Christ. Mothering Sunday, which was originally observed on the mid-Sunday of Lent, was not linked directly with mothers, but with the mother-church — that is, with the parish church where one was baptized. There was once a Church ordinance which required all priests and congregation to visit their mother churches on the mid-Sunday in Lent, and naturally this became a time when families would gather together. During this time the fast of Lent was broken with the Simnel Cake, a word which has come from the Latin 'siminellus' which means 'fine quality bread.' Devizes shares with Shrewsbury and Bury the distinction of making Simnel Cakes of a recognised and distinctive form. The Devizes Simnel is in the form of star, the Shrewsbury has a thick crust, and the Bury Simnel is round and flat, with a rich mixture of spices, currants and candied peel. The traditional Simnel Cake is supposed to be ornamented with scallops, which are supposed to symbolize the feeding of the 5,000, the Gospel of the Day on Mothering Sunday. The west doorway of Holy Trinity is decorated with symbolic devices from the arms of individuals and families connected with the church — a collection of the most unexpected symbols, from fish to sheep and beer barrels (figure 121).

LOXLEY, Warwickshire C3

Early manuscripts claim that Robin Hood was born at Loxley, which in some accounts became Lockesley. He is said to have died and been buried in the park at KIRKLEES. All this would suggest that Robin Hood, for all his name is sheathed in legends and derring-do, was an historical character — which is precisely the conclusion which some modern researchers (such as Valentine Harris) have reached. The earliest written mention of Robin Hood occurs in *Piers Plowman*, in the 1377 text, while the earliest complete ballad which has survived was printed by Wynkyn de Worde about 1495, shortly after the printing press had been brought to London (see, however, OXFORD). The internal evidence of this 'Lytell Geste of Robyn Hode' points to a source earlier than 1400:

> Robyn, was a proude outlaw,
> Whyles he walked on grounde,
> So curteys an outlawe as he was one
> Was nevr none yfounde.

None of the early poems mention his wife (or mistress) Maid Marion or the fat monk Friar Tuck, but the 'King' and the 'Sheriff' play an important part in the stories. It would appear that both these characters were later additions from Morris Dance characters; the lady in question appeared in other poems quite unconnected with Robin Hood as late as 1500. For a survey of Robin Hood material, see BARNSDALE, FOUNTAINS ABBEY, HATHERSAGE, KIRKLEES, NOTTINGHAM and SKELBROOK.

122: Sherwood Forest, home of Robin Hood.

LYDHAM, Shropshire A3

About five miles north-west of Lydham, the ancient stone circle of Mitchell's Fold, with superb views which extend even into Wales, is (according to local myths) named after a witch. According to eighteenth-century legends, before the witch came this 75-foot circumference circle of 14 stones had no name, but was the haunt of a beneficent white cow such as we find associated with the largest of the northern stone circles at CALLANISH. It was said that when living was difficult, because of natural or political forces in the land, a white cow would appear and stand in the middle of the circle. Everyone who cared to milk her could do so, provided that they filled only one bucket at a time; under these conditions the white cow never ran dry. However, a witch by the name of Mitchell sought to do evil to the community by milking the white cow into a sieve, so that she eventually ran dry and vanished. What the eighteenth-century legends ignore is that the circle appears to have been called Midgley's Fold in earlier times, and was associated not with a white cow but with a giant who kept his cows within the fold. The magical white cow appears in many guises, and in many different stories — it is even said, for example, that the cow of Mitchell's Fold did not vanish, but was transformed by the witch into the Dun Cow which was killed by Guy of WARWICK.

MANCETTER, Warwickshire C3

Almost immediately after the death of her husband Prasutagus, in the first century AD, Queen Boudicca of the Iceni tribe found herself being harrassed by the Romans who then occupied the greater part of Britain. The ultimate indignity, when she herself was flogged and her two daughters raped, persuaded Boudicca to rebel against the Romans. In the first sweep of this rebellion, Boudicca completely destroyed the Roman settlements of Colchester, London and St Albans, putting to death well over 70,000 Romans. Eventually she and her tribesmen were confronted by the Roman Suetonius Paulinus, at a ridge which some historians locate at the village of Mancetter, where hints of a battle have been found by archaeologists. While the Roman soldiers were outnumbered by 10 to 1, they managed to completely destroy the Iceni hordes. It is said that 80,000 Iceni died in the battle, while the Romans suffered only 400 losses. Boudicca, in despair at the disaster, took her own life. Undoubtedly Boudicca had been a courageous Queen, but the fight between her tribesmen and the Romans had been made inevitable by the rapacious cruelty of the Roman occupiers, and she had no alternative but to rebel. Her initial success against the Roman settlements of Colchester, London and St Albans was probably due to the fact that these places were only poorly garrisoned, the main Roman legions being occupied in advances to the west. However, whatever the reasons for the war, and whatever the outcome, the fact remains that Boudicca entered with vigour into British mythology as the most important symbol of feminine courage and endurance. Could this have been connected with the mystery of her name, which would suggest that she was associated with a Celtic goddess? Boudicca's name meant 'Victory', and it has been remarked that the name of the goddess openly invoked by Boudicca prior to the last battle was 'Andrasta', whose name also meant 'Victory'. This suggests that the Queen's name was not a personal one at all but perhaps a religious title, which means that from the point of view of the tribesmen who followed her, she was a goddess. Indeed, in his fascinating study of British folk heroes, Charles Kightly points out that there was actually a Celtic goddess named 'Boudiga', as proved by the fact that a Romano-British merchant of York and Lincoln erected an altar in her name as late as AD 237. 'She has close links, therefore,' writes Kightly, 'with Brigantia ('the High One'), the ruling war-goddess of the Brigantes, whom the Romans also called 'Victoria', and with the terrifying Irish Morrigan ('Great Queen'), the triple war-goddess whose three persons were Nemain ('Frenzy'), Badb Catha ('Battle Raven') and Macha ('Crow'), whose sacred birds were fed on the stake-impaled heads of the slaughtered.' Forgotten, save by specialist historians, for many centuries, Boudicca did not enter into popular British mythology until 1780, when the poet Cowper resurrected her ancient fame and created a new image of her in the form of a Druid bard's 'prophetic words' which foretold her role in the making of the coming mighty British Empire:

Then the progeny that springs
  From the forests of our land,
Arm'd with thunder, clad with wings,
  Shall a wider world command.

Regions Caesar never knew
  Thy posterity shall sway,
Where his eagles never flew,
  None invincible as they.

It was Cowper who gave life to the mythological view of the rebel queen, and the myth grew to such an extent that towards the end of the reign of Queen Victoria (who bore the same ancient name and ruled 'a wider world'), the huge statue of the horse-drawn chariot and its fierce queen was erected at Westminster Bridge, on the north bank of the River Thames, which was itself named after a Roman goddess. As with so many folk-heroes, it is claimed that Boudicca did not die, but still sleeps awaiting the call for feminine valour when Britain is next hard-pressed. In contradiction of this belief, her ghost (as sure a sign of death as anything) has been reported in places as far apart as the two extremes of the vast Iceni territory in which she fought, and several places have been claimed as marking the site of her grave. Some have suggested that Boudicca's resting place is marked by the magnificent Stonehenge — though the fact is that this monument was at least 2,000 years old when the Iceni queen died. Others claim for her burial-place a mound on Parliament Hill Fields, in London. Some say that her ghost is still seen on the Essex hill fort of AMBRESBURY BANKS. Charles Kightly records that as recently as 1950 her ghost, driving a chariot through the grey mists, was seen near the village of Cammeringham. To the east of Mancetter, on the old Roman Road of Watling Street, is the site of Manduessedum, a rectangular earthworks some 120 yards by 200 yards, with an enclosed area of about six acres. The defensive wall was supported by a 9-foot ditch twice as wide, and walls over 9 feet high and over 25 feet thick. This defence-works was constructed just before the Iceni rebellion, and would support the popular tradition that the battle took place in this area.

For mention of a few relics of the Boudicca rebellion, see SAXMUNDHAM.

123: The relic hand of St James of Compostela, preserved in the church of St Peter in Marlow.

MARLOW, Buckinghamshire D4

The miraculous relic of the hand of St James is kept in a reliquary in the lovely church of St Peter in Marlow. This relic (figure 123) was among the most important of those in England during the Middle Ages, and was originally in the possession of Reading Abbey, to which institution it had been given by Henry I. So highly was the relic held in popular esteem during the Middle Ages that people would make pilgramages to Reading in order to see the hand, or to seek its healing power; in many cases pilgrims would gather at Reading in order to begin their long pilgrimage to St James's shrine at Compostela in Spain. A most interesting medieval manuscript dated to the end of the twelfth century has survived into modern times and gives a list of 28 miracles (mainly of a healing kind) which were attributed to the hand. It seems that in cases of sickness, in which the healing power of St James was sought, the hand would be dipped into holy water, and this would be used either as a medicine to be taken internally or to be bathed upon specific wounds. In one case, a head tumour was cured by making a sign with the hand over the head of the sick man, and then binding the head with a cloth moistened with the holy water. The earliest of the dated miracles in the manuscript relates to a healing which took place in 1156, in which a sheriff of Surrey named Mauger Malcuvenant (who was on the point of death and ready to receive extreme unction) was 'fed' by monks with a few drops of the holy water and was miraculously cured. A most interesting translation of the list of cures has been published by Brian Kemp.

MEON HILL, Warwickshire C3

As with so many hills which were adopted by the ancient pagans as the sites for defensive earthwork forts, Meon Hill (which rises to some 600 feet) is said to have been built by the Devil, and the hoard of nearly 400 currency bars found in the centre of the fort in 1824 was called 'Devil's money'. As we might expect in a place associated with the Devil, Meon Hill is said to be haunted by phantoms and goblins; the running of the spectral hound (in this case a black dog) is supposed to presage a disaster in one of the local villages such as Mickleton or Upper and Lower Quinton. It is believed, with some justice, that Meon Hill was the site of one of the few modern witchcraft murders, when on 14 February, 1945, the elderly Charles Walton was found murdered with a pitchfork stuck through his neck, and deep into the earth. His body had been slashed with a rough sign of the cross — a sign generally believed to indicate a ritual witch-slaying. Part of the popular nonsensical gossip held that Walton had bred huge toads and trained them to work the land with miniature ploughs; similar stories were told of some Scottish witches, who were even

124: The medieval graffito of a manticore on the south wall of North Cerney church. The graffito is said to be 16th century in origin.

named after their familiar toads. Newspaper reports of the time tell how a black dog was found hanging near to the body of the murdered man.

NORTH CERNEY, Gloucester B4

On the south wall of North Cerney church is a medieval graffito of a manticore (figure 124). A true manticore is a fabulous beast with the body of a lion, the head of a man, porcupine quills, and the tail or sting of a scorpion. It is said to be the demonic reversal of the four beasts which make up the four fixed signs of the zodiac — the lion of Leo, the human head of Aquarius and the scorpion of Scorpio, with the wings of the eagle turned into the featherless quills of a porcupine.

NORTHAMPTON, Northamptonshire D3

The swimming of a witch was a semi-legal procedure by which a suspect was lowered three times into water with the right thumb tied to the left big toe. If the person floated, then he or she was regarded as being guilty of witchcraft and was (in theory at least) arraigned for trial, but more usually killed by the mob. If the victims sank, then they were regarded as being not guilty, though sometimes they drowned in the process. While in theory the test was supposed to be an appeal to God (like all the ancient 'trials by ordeal'), it was often aided by the mind of man, who devised various cunning strategems for ensuring that those on trial did not sink. The popular notion of 'swimming' as a sort of pre-trial of witchcraft seems to have its roots in the pagan concept of ordeal which entered into Christian law even in Anglo-Saxon times, so that by the tenth century the notion that a 'trial by water' could be used as a general test of criminality was enshrined in law. As the historian of witchcraft Rossell Hope Robbins points out, this trial by water (called 'Iudicium acquae') was abolished under Henry III in 1219, though it did continue in 'unofficial' use for long after. Its particular application to the crime of witchcraft was founded on the popular belief that water, being a thing of baptism, would refuse to take into its own essence the darkness of a witch who had, by definition, renounced baptism. While swimming as a pre-trial for witchcraft existed in rural areas, it was not actually admitted as legal evidence until the trial of Arthur Bill and his parents, all accused of witchcraft, at Northampton in 1612. Curiously enough, one of the most famous contemporaneous illustrations of such a swimming — that of Mary Sutton of BEDFORD (figure 125) — was from the same year of 1612. This legal application of the ancient ordeal was finally done away with a hundred years later at Leicester, at which trial it was recorded that the two suspects 'Swam like a cork... or an empty barrell, tho: they Strove all they could to Sinke'. This trial (actually, a pre-trial to determine on commitment) is sometimes described as the last witch-trial in England, and it is significant that the matter was not proceeded with. Much of the prejudice of the older trials was still found in the evidence adduced against the couple, however; it was maintained that a white witch who had been approached for remedy against the black magic practised by the pair had boiled the urine of those afflicted, which had caused the 'witches' to helter-skelter into the room. It is significant, however, that these appeared 'sometimes in the Shape of a cat & and sometimes a dog who would run in panting...' By 1717, the attitude of the law had changed sufficiently to warn that anyone who caused the death of a suspected criminal by swimming would themselves be indicted with murder. A famous case of unofficial swimming at Longmarston, in 1751, resulted in a naked suspect being drowned, and the ring-leader, named Colley, was later hanged in chains.

NOTTINGHAM, Nottinghamshire C2

Although the historical Robin Hood appears to have had little to do with Nottingham (see KIRKLEES), the grip of legends and myths has been too strong for most people, who suppose a most intimate connexion between the folk hero and Nottingham Forest. A fine example of this is found in *The Gentleman's Magazine* of April, 1796. 'A few days ago, as some labourers were digging in a garden at Fox-lane, near Nottingham, they discovered six human skeletons entire, deposited in regular order side by side, supposed to be part of the fifteen foresters that were killed by Robin Hood.' Again, in a list compiled for Nottingham Public Libraries by Violet Walker is a note to the effect that, 'There is in the Public Library a cross-bow bolt which was found in the skull of a skeleton unearthed in St Michael's churchyard during excavations about a century ago. Thirteen skeletons were unearthed lying side by side head to foot; it would seem likely that they were those of thirteen persons whom

125: Swimming a witch, from *Witches apprehended, examined and executed*, 1613.

126: Witches riding on a huge sow to visit a sick friend. From the pamphlet 'The Witches of Northamptonshire', 1612.

127: Robin Hood, from the frontispiece of the earliest printed ballad, 'A Lytell Geste of Robyn Hode', published around 1530.

Robin Hood and his men were recorded to have shot and buried in St Michael's Churchyard.' Both these stories are recorded with some humour by Valentine Harris in *The Truth About Robin Hood*. As Harris points out, the riddle of how six corpses became thirteen, or why the longbowmen (as the outlaws were famed) should use the much slower crossbow to kill their victims, remains unsolved. In the original story (or poetic myth) Robin killed fifteen foresters, but in the hands of historians he finishes up having thirteen killed by his band prior to burying them in the churchyard. A more serious miscounting is that provided by Dr Margaret Murray, who is anxious to demote Robin Hood to being less a local hero and more of a cult figure with dark associations, for she claims that he was always accompanied by a band of twelve companions, 'suggestive of a Grandmaster and his coven.' In fact, most of the ballads claim Robin's companions were more numerically substantial — 'seven score ... yeomen' being mentioned in one. This is not the only error made by Dr Margaret Murray in *God of the Witches*. The truth is that the legends of Robin Hood, no doubt rooted in a historical reality, have given rise to very many personal interpretations of history and mythology. For further information on Robin Hood, see BARNSDALE, FOUNTAINS ABBEY, HATHERSAGE, KIRKLEES, LOXLEY and SKELBROOK.

The seventeenth-century astrologer William Lilly cast a horoscope in connexion with King Charles I's approach to Nottingham in August, 1642, when it was believed that he would take the city. From a consideration of the horoscope, Lilly came to the conclusion that Charles' plans would come to ruin, and indeed predicted that the King would be imprisoned, and 'all the remainder of his life, after this August 22d, 1642, was a mere labyrinth of sorrow; a continued and daily misfortune'. Lilly could see from the fact that the Moon was at that time near to the violent fixed star Antares that the King faced a violent death, while the approach of the war-like Mars to the evil star Algol, 'which is said to denote beheading', might indicate the nature of that death. The horoscope, besides revealing the fate of Nottingham, also set out the main destiny of the King. According to records, a metal branks, used to punish people for scolding, or to stop people screaming out, was still kept at the County Hall as late as 1821, in which year the local Judge ordered that it be destroyed. The branks was a metal face-cage which could be locked over the head in such a way as to force a

128 (right) & 129 (facing, top): The ever-popular Robin Hood has been portrayed in many guises and situations.

metal strip into the mouth, and thus prevent the wearer from making any sound whatsoever. This diabolical instrument was often used as a short-term punishment, someone guilty of abuse being compelled to wear it for a few hours. The last recorded use of the Nottingham branks was when a blind beggar named James Brodie, who had been convicted of murdering his guide-boy in Nottingham Forest, was compelled to wear it in prison. Prior to his execution he had made so much noise that the authorities were compelled to fix the branks in order to literally make him hold his tongue. An old wood engraving shows a particularly savage example of a branks used in Chesterfield. It is 9 inches high, almost seven inches across the hoop, and incised on the metal is the date 1688. The historian William Andrews remarked in 1881 that this year was 'memorable in the annals of Chesterfield and the little village of Whittington' nearby, for in that place and time the 'Glorious Revolution' was planned. 'Strange,' he continues, 'that an instrument of brutal and tyrannical torture should be made and used at Chesterfield, at the same moment that the people should be plotting for freedom at the same place.' For a more cruel branks, see FORFAR.

OSWESTRY, Shropshire A2

The name Oswestry is derived from 'Oswald', the name of the Saint-King who raised the Christian cross before doing battle with the British King Cadwallader. Oswald was killed at Maserfield in Shropshire, in the great battle against Penda of Mercia. At his death, his shield (bearing a cross and four golden lions on red) was carried from the battlefield to a place where the monastery which bears his name was built. Oswald's seal shows the King himself holding a sword in his right hand and a tree in his left — it is said that the word for 'tree' in English is the same as the old word 'try' for 'place' (as for example in Bantry, the 'place of Ban', or in COVENTRY, 'the place of the Convent'), so that the symbol reads Oswald-tree (the place of Oswald), to mark the name Oswestry.

OXFORD, Oxfordshire C4

Brasenose College actually takes its name from a corruption of 'brasenhuis', a Dutch word for 'brewhouse', one of which used to occupy the site of the College. However, a sort of mythological conceit was for the students to take as an emblem a brass nose, which is now incorporated into the arms of the college as an heraldic pun. It seems, however, that the original brass nose was at Stamford for well over 500 years, for in the thirteenth century many discontented students went to this town in an attempt to establish a rival university. Those from Brasenose took with them their curious mascot. Although the students soon returned *en masse* to Oxford, the emblem remained on the Stamford gateway until 1890, when the building was sold to the College. This curious interlude resulted in each candidate for a degree at Oxford having to take an oath not to lecture or attend lectures at Stamford, this oath not being rescinded until 1827.

It is generally believed that William Caxton introduced printing into England in 1477 at Westminster, and that the first book printed in this country was his *Dictes and Sayenges of the Phylosophers*. However, there is much evidence to show that there was a printing press being used in Oxford for some years before Caxton returned to England with his knowledge of the printer's art. It is said that this press was established by a man called Corsellis.

130: The stained glass of Quainton church contains this lovely image of an angel holding the Arma Christi, symbolic of Christ's Passion.

131: Ragley Hall is a large 17th/18th-century mansion set in its own park.

PAUNTLEY, Gloucestershire B4

The considerable splendour of the 'Whittington' home at Pauntley, where Dick Whittington of London-mayoral fame was born, is a sure sign that his was not a 'rags to riches' story. When the carved figure of a boy holding an indistinguishable animal was found in the foundations of a house in Westgate Street, Gloucester, it was said (on no evidence whatsoever) to be the image of Dick with his cat. The image is now in the Gloucester Folk Museum.

QUAINTON, Buckinghamshire D4

In the parish church at Quainton is a beautiful stained glass image of an angel holding the Arma Christi, symbols of Christ's Passion. Across the road from the church is the Old Rectory (now a private dwelling) in which a cutting of the famous Sacred Thorn of Glastonbury grew. The tract of cultivated land behind the Rectory is said to be haunted by a ghostly rider.

RAGLEY HALL, Warwickshire B3

In the seventeenth century, Ragley Hall (figure 131) was one of the most important meeting points for the English Rosicrucians who influenced the direction of British history, such as Christopher Wren, Henry More, Ezechiel Foxcroft and Ralph Cudworth. These meetings were organized by the wife of the owner, Lady Ann Conway, herself an author on occult subjects, who was taught the secret art by the Dutch Rosicrucian Franciscus von Helmont.

ROBIN HOOD'S STRIDE, Derbyshire C1

The huge rocks dominating the west of the B5056 look like the ruins of an old castle, with unsafe towers and crumbling walls, hanging defiantly on the edge of the hills. On closer inspection, however, the enigmatic structure turns out to be a vast pile of rocks, built neither by men nor giants — natural outcroppings shaped by millennia of weathering (figure 132). The exotic forms of the rocks, and the distinctive energies which radiate from them, explain why, in prehistoric times, they were used as a centre for cult worship.

The nearby grave barrows (one of which may be seen from the top of the Stride, with its once-covered stone uprights now uncovered) indicate that Robin Hood's Stride was once a religious centre, but in addition to this we find that the surface of some of the upper rocks has been carved with the distinctive cup marks which were used in forgotten prehistoric rituals. It is quite possible that the religious rites practised here were linked with the 4,000-year-old cairns, circles and standing stones of Stanton Moor, above BIRCHOVER to the east of the valley, visible from the top of the Stride. The origin of the name is obscure, but the rocks appear to be linked with Robin Hood only through the popular imagination.

132: Robin Hood's Stride appears to have no connection with the outlaw and has been naturally formed by thousands of years of weathering.

S.
PA

ROLLRIGHT STONES, Oxfordshire C4

The eight-foot-high 'King Stone', the important outlier of the Rollright stone circle complex, is chained like some mighty beast behind the metal fencing of the 'Ministry of Works' (figure 135). This outlier, and the related circle of 53 stones (which have the usual reputation of being uncountable), along with the denuded uprights and capstone of a chambered long barrow called the 'Whispering Knights' (figure 134), is about half a mile north-east of Little Rollright.

133 (facing page): Robin Hood's Stride.
134 (below): The so-called 'Whispering Knights' are the capstone and uprights of a long barrow.

135 (facing page): The King Stone of the Rollright stone circle is 8 feet high.
136 (above): The 12th-century effigy of Lady Constantia and her child in St Leonard's church, Scarcliffe.

RUFFORD ABBEY, Nottinghamshire D1

The ruins are said to be haunted by the ghost of a monk who has a skull rather than a face beneath his cowl. There is one recorded case of a man having died from fright as a result of 'seeing the Rufford ghost'. For a less dramatic case — of a man receiving a broken leg as a result of witnessing a spirit — see LEWTRENCHARD.

SCARCLIFFE, Derbyshire C1

In the church of St Leonard in Scarcliffe is a very touching memorial to Constantia de Frecheville, who died in 1175. The lady's head is represented as lying on the back of a couchant lion, while her child reaches in adoration to her face (figure 136). There must have been some intention on behalf of the twelfth-century sculptor to evoke the images of the Virgin and Child. Below the effigies is a long scroll of Latin Leonine verse, which is now badly damaged, but which mentions her name ('Constant and kind, rightly called Constance') and the fact that her child is buried with her. The local legends tell how she was 'a queen or lady' who was lost in the nearby wood with her child. In danger of dying from fatigue, she heard the sound of the curfew bell being rung in Scarcliffe church, and was thus guided to safety. In gratitude, she left a bequest of land to pay for the curfew bell to toll in perpetuity. The bell is rung during Christmas week.

STOKE DRY, Leicestershire D2

Tourists in British villages are so often invited to believe that witches took an active part in local politics and community life that they may well be relieved to find the note pinned in St Andrew's Church at Stoke Dry. The short notice requests them not to believe the popular legend that a previous vicar sealed a witch in the tiny room above the porch and starved her to death. The historical truth is (perhaps) that some details of the famous Gunpowder Plot were worked out in the church (if not in that room) for one of the plotters, Sir Everard Digby, was a local parishioner, and some of the Digby family memorials are still found in the church.

STONE, Buckinghamshire D4

The Norman font in the church of St John the Baptist in Stone is one of the great iconographic mysteries of the medieval world. Contained in a panel surrounded by interfaced decorations is a most curious scene: two naked men fight a monster, seemingly aided in their task by a huge bird, which may well be a dove. One of these men appears to be standing upon a snake, his own leg being bitten by what is probably a lizard or a salamander. Watching this fight is a fire-breathing dragon sitting up on his haunches, as though enjoying the contest; at his back is a vertical fish, one of the most frequently used symbols of Christ. The meaning of the carving is now lost, and is not explicable.

137: The mausoleum at West Wycombe, with the finial of St Lawrence's church towering above it.

WARWICK, Warwickshire

Warwick Castle is said to be haunted by the ghost of the Dun Cow. The Dun Cow was supposed to be similar to that of LONGRIDGE which provided 'milke for all and sundry', but it was eventually enraged by the greed of one man and turned wild, killing several locals until it was finally slain by the heroic Guy of Warwick. On display in the Castle itself is a huge fossilized rib, said to have been taken from the cow after it had died. However, experts say that it is the fossilized rib-bone of an elephant, herds of which roamed the area many thousands of years ago.

WELSH NEWTON, Hereford and Worcester A4

In the graveyard of the Norman church of Welsh Newton, between Monmouth and Skenfrith Castles, is the grave of a priest, Father Kemble, who was martyred at HEREFORD in 1679. The grave, located by the preaching cross, is itself marked with a large cross. Beside this slab is another tomb containing the body of Catharine Scudamore, who is said to have recovered her hearing when she prayed at the grave during one of her pilgrimages. A relative of the same family of Scudamores had been cured of a malignant sore throat by putting around her neck the preserved cord which had been used to hang the martyr. The interesting thing is that the Scudamores were all related to Captain Scudamore, who had originally apprehended the unfortunate priest.

Father Kemble had been fond of his pipe, and when the time came for his execution his last request was to smoke a pipe of tobacco, which he did along with the Under-Sheriff. This act gave rise to a local Herefordshire custom, by which the last smoke in company was called a 'Kemble Pipe'.

WEST WYCOMBE, Buckinghamshire D4

The strange oriental-design gold-encased bulbous finial on the church of St Lawrence (figure 139) is said to have been designed by Sir Francis Dashwood, whose eccentric behaviour, and interest in black magic, has made him one of the more infamous of local characters. The engraving of him worshipping Venus (in the place of the cross) is intended to be a double symbolism, for Venus is the patron deity of women. The finial is supposed to be large enough to accommodate nine men in a modicum of comfort, and local legends insist that Sir Francis would hold black magic masses, and even orgies, inside it.

138 (facing page): Sir Francis Dashwood worshipping Venus. An engraving after Hogarth.

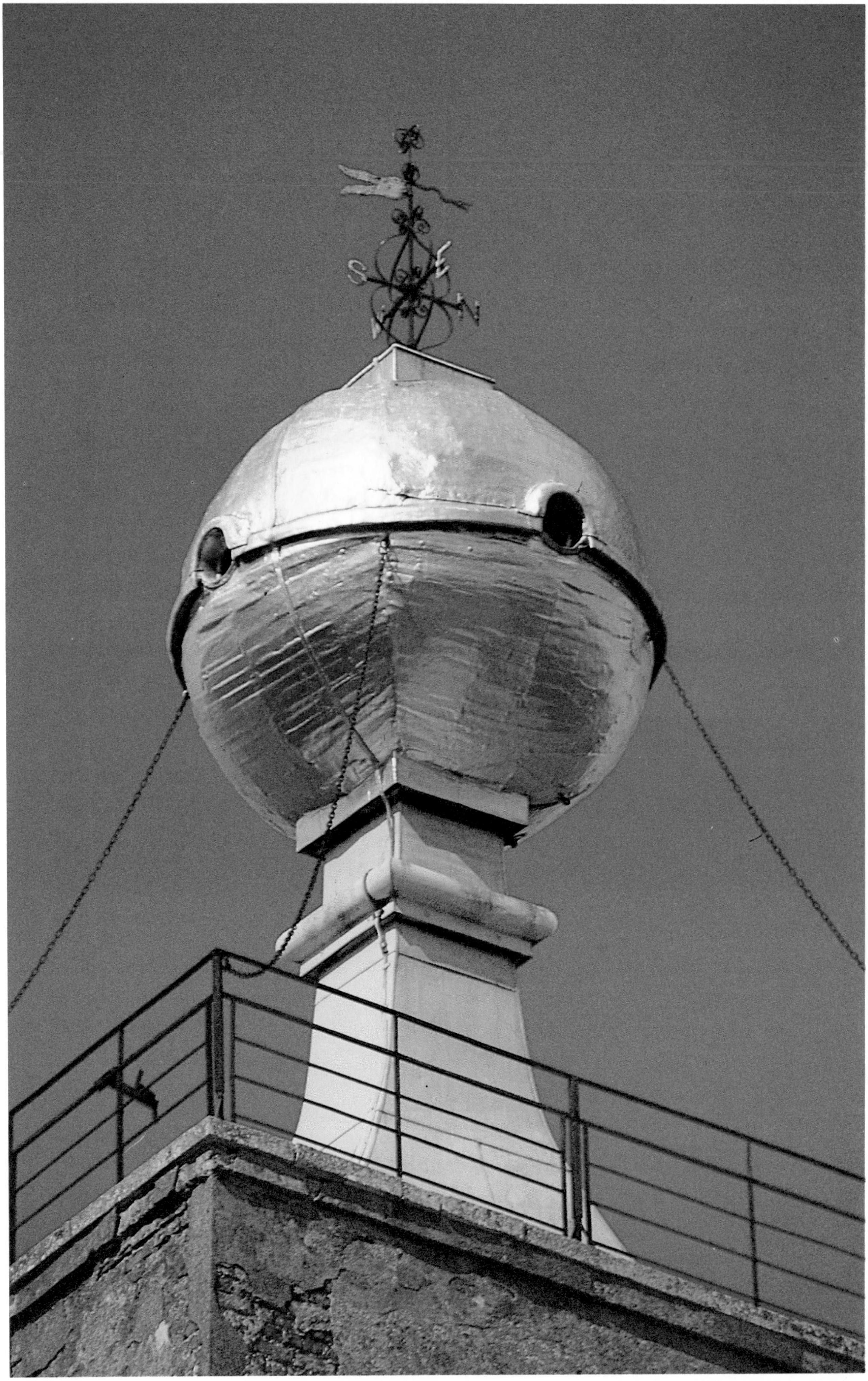

139: The gold-encased finial of St Lawrence's church, West Wycombe, is said to have been designed by Sir Francis Dashwood and can supposedly accommodate nine men.

WING, Buckinghamshire D4

In the churchyard of All Saints, in Wing, is a high medieval cross topped by a beautiful image of St George riding a horse and killing a dragon (figure 140). The symbolism is an excellent one to have on a Christian cross, for in the occult tradition St George is a sun-symbol (linked with the other dragon-killer St Michael, who is the archangel of the sun), while the dragon is a symbol of the moon, which in ancient times was believed to wrap itself around the earth. This solar-lunar symbolism above the cross is reflected in medieval paintings and woodcuts which show the sun and moon above the cross on which hangs the crucified Christ.

YOULGREAVE, Derbyshire C1

Twelfth-century All Saints parish church in Youlgreave possesses a unique font — the only one in England with an integrated stoup for holy oil or water. This stoup is supported by a two-legged salamander, the elemental fire-being of the medieval alchemists (figure 141). Although the font is Norman and probably thirteenth-century, it was not designed for Youlgreave but was originally at nearby Elton, from which church it was ejected during the rebuilding of 1812, eventually to find its way to Youlgreave. All Saints has some magnificent stained glass from designs by the Pre-Raphaelites, and many interesting symbols — note especially the dog poppy-heads in the choir and the demonic creatures in the chancel and nave roof. Over the entrance arch to the seventeenth-century 'Bull's Head Hotel' in Youlgreave is a magnificently-carved bull's head, said to be the work of William Shimwell.

140: The churchyard of All Saints church in Wing, Buckinghamshire.

141: The two-legged salamander which supports the unique font in All Saints parish church, Youlgreave.

A
B
C
1
2
3
4
0
10
20 miles
LINCOLNSHIRE
Blakeney
King's Lynn
NORFOLK
NORWICH
Watton
PETERBOROUGH
Norman Cross
Bungay
CAMBRIDGESHIRE
ELY
Diss
St Ives
Bury St Edmunds
SUFFOLK
Saxmundham
Woolpit
Winston
CAMBRIDGE
Bedford
IPSWICH
BEDFORDSHIRE
Saffron Walden
Dovercourt
Walkern
COLCHESTER
HERTFORDSHIRE
ESSEX
St Osyth
Hatfield
Ambresbury Banks
GREATER LONDON

Eastern Counties

AMBRESBURY BANKS, Essex B4

According to local traditions, the Iron Age fort to the north end of Epping Forest, about three miles south of Epping Upland, was the place where Queen Boudicca (or Boadicea) and her two daughters poisoned themselves after the terrible battle of MANCETTER. Some say that the ghost of the Queen is sometimes seen standing on the high ramparts of the settlement fort, where the earthworks are still seven feet high in places, fronted by a ditch which is over 10 feet deep. Boudicca's spectral chariot has also been reported at Cammeringham.

BLAKENEY, Norfolk C1

The church at Blakeney is one of the few in Britain to have two towers. The slender spire at the north-eastern angle of the chancel was said to have been built to act as a guide to mariners, as a sort of lighthouse or point of reference.

Another two-towered church is the former Benedictine Abbey church at Wymondham (pronounced Winnd'm), which was the object of a quarrel between the lay congregation and the monks who worshipped within it. Eventually the church was divided between the two communities, and in 1445 the lay congregation obtained permission to build their own tower at the west end.

BEDFORD, Bedfordshire A3

The 'swimming' of Mary Sutton at Bedford as a suspect witch in 1612 has resulted in one of the most well-known of all witch-pictures (figure 125). This old woodcut shows Mary being lowered into the waters of a mill-stream by two officials, her right-hand thumb tied to her left big toe (for an account of this ordeal, see NORTHAMPTON). The fact that the picture is in what historians call 'continuous representation' explains the curious happenings around the ordeal of swimming, for the artist has felt free to include in his illustration the various imagined crimes (committed at different times and in different places) for which Mary was being swum as a witch. The figure in the tiny boat in front of her is supposed to be Mary herself, who was accused of sailing on water in a sieve (the two animals swimming with her are almost certainly her familiars). The pig to the right is 'mad' — supposedly driven into this state by Mary's art of black magic. Equally, the cart with the broken wheel, which has discharged its cargo of sacks on the ground to the fury of the carter, was damaged by Mary's evil-doing. As we see from the illustration, Mary Sutton floated, and she was tried, found guilty and hanged for witchcraft. The illustration itself is from a rare pamphlet entitled *Witches Apprehended, Examined, and Executed*, published in 1613.

BUNGAY, Suffolk C2

In a terrible storm of 1577 it is said that a demon-dog broke into the parish church at Bungay and killed three of the worshippers. The incident is 'memorialized' in the curious weather vane which takes the form of a black and savage hound. In this part of the world the spectral hound which haunts lonely country districts (see, for example, DARTMOOR) is called Old Shuck, or Black Shuck, the name said to be derived from the Anglo-Saxon 'scucca', which meant 'demon' or 'Satan' (scuccagyld is actually 'devil worship'). Shuck is said to prowl at night-time, to be the size of a pony and to have fire-red eyes as large as saucers. His appearance is usually said to forbode evil or even death — usually 'death in the family'; this is especially so of the Black Shuck seen on the Wicken Fen. As a relief from the canine demonology at Bungay, note the interesting spandrels on the door of St Mary, which show a knight seated on a lion he has slain, and a lion playing with its cubs.

BURY ST EDMUNDS, Suffolk B3

King Edmund, who was to become the most famous of British martyrs, was captured by Ingvar the Boneless of the Danish army in AD 869 at Hellesdon or Hoxne. His captors insisted that he share his lands with the Vikings, and when he refused they tortured him in the most painful of ways, first flogging him, then using him for archery practice, and then sacrificing him to Odin by cutting his ribs away from his spine. Finally they beheaded him, and flung his head into a thorn tree. Legend tells how when his friends sought out the King's remains they heard the head shouting out, 'Here, here', and discovered it being guarded by a white wolf. His mourners eventually found the mutilated body, and took it to the place now called Bury St Edmunds, where the great Abbey was constructed. For many years St Edmund was regarded as the patron saint of England, and the special protector of sailors. One of the most ancient stories of his saintly prowess tells how, when the Danish King Sweyn Forkbeard insisted on Bury paying tribute in 1014, he died suddenly at Gainsborough, screaming that St Edmund was piercing him with a spear. (See also WINSTON)

CAMBRIDGE, Cambridgeshire B3

In the Old Court of Queen's College, Cambridge, is one of the most complicated and extremely attractive sundials in the country. Records indicate that it was *in situ* in the middle of the seventeenth century, but whether it was precisely of this design or not is difficult to say. The board on which the shadows of the gnomen are cast is decorated with the 12 zodiacal images, and from the

142: The ruined medieval walls of the Abbey at Bury St Edmunds look like monstrous forms within the parklands of the former Abbey grounds.

143: A wooden demon with cloven hooves on a mock-Tudor building in the centre of Bury St Edmunds. It overlooks the square where (according to some) the Bury witches were hanged. However, the demon itself is probably 19th-century.

positions of the shadows it is possible to determine the sun's altitude, the date, the time of sunrise and sunset, and in which arc of the zodiac the sun is placed. The sundial is seemingly unique in also being a moon-dial, for, whenever the light of the moon is strong enough, it is possible to calculate the exact time of night.

COLCHESTER, Essex C4

One of the most curious and persistent of medieval myths was that the city of Colchester was founded by one Coel, the 'Duke of the Britons', and that his daughter Helen (born in AD 242) was the mother of Constantine, who became the first Roman Emperor to openly support Christianity. The historical Helen, who was indeed the mother of Constantine, is reputed to have discovered the original cross upon which Christ had died, which accounts for the fact that the coat of arms of Colchester bears the image of the rude cross, while the corporation Seal carries a picture of Helen herself. The Emperor Constantius, who married Helen, and who was the father of Constantine, died in YORK. The legends which link Coel, the 'Old King Cole' of the nursery rhymes, with Colchester are purely fictitious, just as is the derivation of the name 'Colchester' from 'Cole's caester' (Cole's Castle). The original Colchester was a Roman settlement and then a 'Colonia', and it is from this latter word that the name of the city was derived, long before 'King Cole' came upon the scene; the supposed 'Cole-Caester' had nothing to do with the 'castle of Cole', being rather a 'Colony-Castle'. Constantine was actually born at Naissus, as his surviving horoscope records, and after service with the Roman Emperor in various parts of the Empire he joined his father Constantius in Britain. When the latter died in York (25 July, 306) he was proclaimed Emperor by the Roman legions in the same city. The historical truth — that the most influential man to espouse early Christianity was made Roman Emperor in Britain — is somehow more remarkable than the curious stories connecting Helen and her son with Colchester. Charles Kightly, who has dealt in some depth with the mythology of the city, points out that while the legends of Helen and King Cole are obviously fictitious, even so there are records showing that well into the nineteenth century the inhabitants of the High Street drew water from 'King Coyle's pump', and sincerely believed that the Roman gateway had been 'King Coyle's Castle'. The development of mythology has its own laws and logic; at about the same time that the rebel Queen Boudicca was being embraced as a Brittanic hero in Cowper's poem 'Boudicca' (published 1780), the famous Gibbon in his *Decline and Fall of the Roman Empire* (1782) dismissed completely the long-enduring mythology of King Cole and his daughter Helen. The origin of the 'Colchester King Cole' is hard to trace now, but there is fairly secure evidence to show that, during the early fifth century, parts of Scotland and northern England did fall under the rule of a British king named Coel. Perhaps most curiously of all, men who were regarded as the 'sons of Coel' who were historical rulers in the areas around Carlisle and the Solway Firth (stretching as far south as Rochdale), probably under the names of Urien and Owain, became the Welsh folk-heroes who were absorbed into the early strains of Arthurian legends, where Sir Yvain is said to be the son of King Urien, the owner of magic ravens. Kightly suggests indeed that this Yvain was probably the original 'Ewen Caesarius' of PENRITH. (See also COYLTON)

DOVERCOURT, Essex C3

According to Christian legend, Dovercourt church once had on display a miraculous speaking cross, which attracted so many people that it was quite impossible for the crowds to get into the church. In the anonymous play *Grim, the Collier of Croydon* we have the lines:

> And now the rood of Dovercourt did speak,
> Confirming his opinion to be true.

The phrase 'a Dovercourt' is often used to denote a confused babble of noise, and some explain this as referring to the crowds of people visiting the rood. Other authorities, however, suggest that the village was famous for its chattering women.

ELY, Cambridgeshire B3

In the annals of British mythology, Ely is remembered as the centre of the rebellion of the folk-hero 'Hereward the Wake', in whose day Ely was an island set in the midst of boggy and dangerous fenland marshes. Hereward is mentioned in the Domesday book as a Lincolnshire landholder, but in fact little is known about him. What history lacks, mythology has supplied and embellished into a vast saga of derring-do. It seems that Hereward did in fact take part in a Danish raid upon Peterborough in 1070, resulting in the destruction of what had been the most wealthy of all British abbeys. Shortly afterwards he appears to have formed the centre of a rebellion against the Norman overlords by taking refuge in the swamp-surrounded Ely. So redoubtable was the courage of Hereward and his supporters, and so well-protected were they by marshes and fenlands, that the Normans were unable to dislodge them, even when the wicked Ivo Taillebois called into their service the powers of an old witch (later called 'Pythonissa') who was hired to cast spells on the island defenders even as the Normans attacked. Hereward and his followers were eventually driven from Ely as a result of treason, and nothing more is heard of him from a historical standpoint. However, legend tells of his later exploits in which the supernatural plays an important part. On one occasion, while hiding in the vast forests which then stretched through Lincolnshire, he and his party found themselves completely lost. However, a huge white wolf appeared, and ran ahead of them to lead them through the labyrinth of dark trees; even as they followed, their lances began to glow like candles to light their way. The story is in some ways symbolic, for in his day the white wolf was the symbol of St Edmund (see BURY ST EDMUNDS), who was then the patron saint of the English and sought to guide those who fought on his behalf. Hereward is often credited as being owner of the Manor of Bourne, but this is not recorded to his name, while other manors (such as Witham-on-the-Hill) are. The mystery of the title 'the Wake' seems to be derived from an attempt, made centuries after his death, to link Hereward with a Norman family (tradition insists that he was finally reconciled to William the Conquerer), for the Norman family of Wake was established in England immediately after the Conquest. We see, then, that the title has nothing to do with the idea of Hereward being 'especially watchful or awake'; indeed, he was not called Hereward the Wake until about three hundred years after his death. As the historian Charles Kightly records, the Anglo-Saxon word 'wak' means 'timid', and this is almost certainly the origin of the modern 'weak' — a quite inappropriate title for such a hero as Hereward. In the legendary account of his life, Hereward died fighting manfully against impossible odds, the last Englishman to continue organized rebellion against the Norman invaders. He was reputed to have been buried in Crowland Abbey church.

HATFIELD, Hertfordshire A4

In the church of St Etheldreda, Hatfield, is one of the most complex of all those British monuments which include the image of a skeleton effigy. This is the monument to Robert Cecil, first Earl of Salisbury, who (like the two-tier monument at WORSBROUGH) lies fully-dressed on the top tier of the tomb, and then in skeletal effigy on the lower tier. The top tier is supported by beautifully-carved representations of the four Virtues. The monument was designed and carved by Maximilian Colt about six years before Robert Cecil died (1612), and (according to the practice of the day) the Earl posed for preliminary drawings in order to ensure a good likeness in the upper effigy.

Near to the Cecil monument is the effigy of a thirteenth-century knight in armour and, on the floor, covered by a shroud, the effigy of William Curll, dated 1617. The symbolism of the reversed torch and the Mercurial caduceus in the Heaviside monument by Thomas Banks is intended to be an allegory of death and of medicine, respectively. The Burne-Jones windows in the south transept are among the most beautiful of all Pre-Raphaelite designs.

Lady Caroline Lamb is buried in Hatfield churchyard. She is now remembered mainly because of her unhappy infatuation with Lord Byron, and for her novel *Glenarvon* (1816, but republished with the title *The Fatal Passion* long after her death) which contains a caricature portrait of the poet. It was her chance meeting with Byron's funeral cortege, in 1824, which is said to have finally unhinged her already delicate mind, and she never fully recovered before her death in 1828.

NORMAN CROSS, Cambridgeshire A2

To the west of the A1, at Norman Cross, is a high column bearing a bronze model of an eagle (figure 144). It was raised in memory of the 1,800 French soldiers and sailors who died here, in the barracks built on this site in 1796 as a prison to house those captured during the Napoleonic Wars.

PETERBOROUGH, Cambridgeshire A2

In the early nineteenth century there was a custom linked with St Catherine (whose day is 25 November) for the girls who lived in the workhouse to make a procession through the city, wearing white dresses tied with scarlet ribbons, the leading one dressed as a queen with crown and sceptre. They would stop at the main houses, sing songs and beg for money. It has been suggested that since most of these girls worked as spinners, the ritual was linked with St Catherine as the patron saint of this trade. However, some historians say that the ritual is popularly supposed to be derived from Katherine Parr, one of the wives of Henry VIII, who came from Northamptonshire.

The locals of Peterborough called the day of the ritual 'Candle-day', and some say this is because 25 November was when they had to start using candlelight to work at their lace-making and spinning. It is likely that the link between spinners and St Catherine arises from the fact that St Catherine of Alexandria is reputed to have suffered martyrdom on the wheel, and the work of spinning is done at a 'wheel'. St Catherine's day used to be the holiday of wheelwrights.

ST IVES, Cambridgeshire A3

There is a legend that when Robert Langley was stranded in the snow, and had given himself up for lost, he was saved by hearing the ringing of the bells of All Saints, and as a mark of gratitude left money after his death in 1656 to provide bread for the town's poor. The 'Langley Bread', which is still distributed, is no longer bread, but groceries, handed out in the first week of January to the elderly. Another last will and testament resulted in a very different custom in St Ives, known as the 'distributing of the Bibles' by means of a lottery, in a ritual which takes place during the middle of June. The local Dr Robert Wilde left £50.00 to provide copies of the good book for the poor children of the parish, with the proviso that they were to dice for the same. Twelve children throw dice near the school by the church for six available copies of the Bible; the will stipulated that the dicing should be done at the altar, but ecclesiastical propriety deemed otherwise.

ST OSYTH, Essex C4

In the late sixteenth century, a local woman Ursula Kempe earned her living as a sort of day-nurse, and had some fame for curing sick children by means of 'natural magic'. After a quarrel with one of the villagers, Ursula was arrested and charged with witchcraft. Her initial denials were ignored, and gradually the unfortunate woman was led to confess to diabolic rites which involved several of her acquaintances and a whole bevy of suspect witches were arrested in the neighbourhood. Ursula was committed for trial at Chelmsford and was eventually found guilty of murdering three people by witchcraft between 1580 and 1582. She was hanged, but in the light of modern reason it would appear that the old woman had nothing to do either with the deaths or with witchcraft. Her popular fame in modern times seems to rest on the fact that her bones were exhumed from the burial ground at St Osyth parish church in 1956 and transferred for exhibition in the witchcraft museum at Polperro.

SAFFRON WALDEN, Essex B3

The fame of the Saffron Walden maze, and of the fighting giants Tom Hickathrift and the Wisbech Ogre on the parget-work of the Old Sun Inn, have tended to obscure the fame of the Saffron Walden Monster. This monster was a cockatrice, hatched from a cock's egg by a toad, and vested with the power to kill all on whom it looked with its glance. The hero who liberated Saffron Walden was a famous knight who despatched many such creatures by walking among them in a special armour made from reflecting mirrors, 'whereby,' writes the seventeenth-century natural historian Topsell, 'their owne shapes were reflected upon their owne faces, and so they dyed.' The maze, on Saffron Walden common, has a convoluted pathway over 1,500 metres in length. The maze is so large that it is difficult to see the formal pattern clearly from the ground, but in the church of St Mary, whose tower may be seen from the maze, is a most lovely tapestry kneeler in crewel wool, which reveals the pattern clearly (figure 145).

144: The bronze eagle on a stone memorial shaft at Norman Cross.

145: Plan of the Saffron Walden maze (located on the Common) on a woollen kneeler inside the church of St Mary the Virgin.

SAXMUNDHAM, Suffolk C3

A life-size bronze head of the Roman Emperor Claudius was found in the River Alde near this village in 1907, and may well have been part of the loot taken from Colchester after the sack of the Roman city by Boudicca, Queen of the Iceni — see MANCETTER. Some scholars suggest that the head was hacked from a figure which stood in the destroyed temple in the city. It would have been a natural enough thing for the marauding Iceni to hack off this head, for the Celts were renowned as head-hunters among their enemies, and very many skulls have been found in places where ancient battles were fought. In the London Museum there is a large number of such skulls which were collected from the Walbrook stream, and which archaeologists assume were thrown there after the ritual decapitations following Boudicca's destruction of the Roman settlement of London in the first century AD. The Saxmundham bronze head is now preserved in the British Museum, London.

WINSTON, Suffolk C3

In 1983, a hoard of witchcraft paraphernalia was discovered in two chimney cavities in Barley House Farm in Winston, all dating from the last part of the seventeenth century. Among the finds were about 20 pairs of shoes, some of them stuffed with straw, which means that they were probably fertility symbols. More gruesome were the two mummified bodies of kittens and a rat, a bird's wing (perhaps a goose), and a pig's trotter, almost certainly placed there to avert witchcraft. Some of these finds are now on display in the Moyses House Museum in BURY ST EDMUNDS, where there are also a couple of 'bellarmines' which were used as witch-bottles. These bottles were filled with curious objects (often sharp nails, and the like), urine and human hair or nail-parings. After being filled with such things, the bottle was usually buried beneath the house threshold, or under the stone flags in front of the fire-hearth, as a protection against witchcraft or the evil eye.

146 (left): Stained glass depiction of 'Our Lady of Woolpit' in St Mary's Church.

WOOLPIT, Suffolk C3

The stained glass of 'Our Lady of Woolpit' in St Mary's Church, (figure 146) was probably placed in the church as a memento of the famous sacred well of Woolpit. This has now fallen into disuse, though there is still a ready supply of water in the region where it healed people in the past.

WALKERN, Hertfordshire A4

In 1712, the trial for witchcraft of Jane Wenham, known locally as the 'Wise Woman of Walkern', was famous. Jane Wenham appears to have been a very ordinary woman who gained a reputation she did not deserve. When a local farmer named Chapman accused her openly of being a witch, she obtained a warrant against him and won a case of defamation. Shortly afterwards, however, a servant at Walkern parsonage claimed that she had been bewitched by Jane Wenham, who was promptly arrested and later tried at Hertford. As Montague Summers, the historian of witchcraft, observes, in spite of the preliminary investigation into the case, 'the one charge brought was that Jane Wenham entertained a familiar in the shape of a cat'. Less easy to substantiate than the ownership of a cat was the 'Devil's unguent made of dead men's fat' which was supposed to have been found under her pillow. It is a sign of how much the fear of witchcraft had declined by the second decade of the eighteenth century that this 'evidence' was not immediately siezed upon by the judge as a sign of depraved witchcraft. Although he found her guilty, she was immediately reprieved and soon pardoned. There appears to have been no reason why Montague Summers should read into the flimsy evidence against Jane that it was 'very probable that Jane Wenham was a medium possessed of hypnotic powers, one who had attempted to meddle with dark secrets'.

WATTON, Norfolk B2

The 'Babes in the Wood' story is claimed for the locality of Watton, and the device of the two children sleeping beneath an oak tree (see BOSCOBEL) has been adopted as a sort of unofficial village coat of arms or logo (figure 147). The device below the two children is actually a rebus, which shows a hare (in former times a 'wat') jumping over a barrel (in former times a 'tun'), giving the combination 'wat-tun'.

147: The 'Babes in the Wood' have been incorporated into the village sign at Watton, Norfolk.

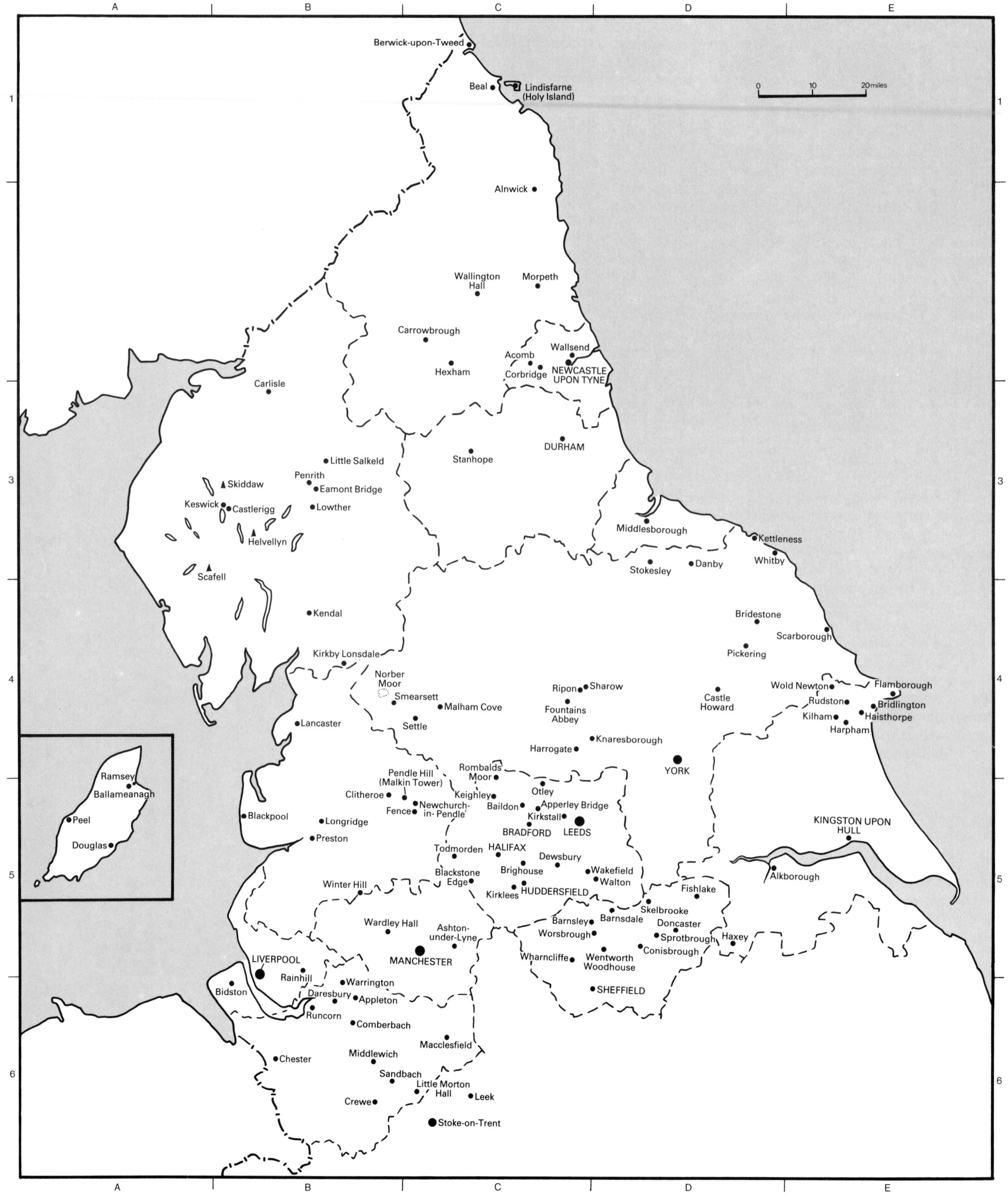
A
B
C
D
E
1
3
4
5
6
0
10
20miles
Berwick-upon-Tweed
Beal
Lindisfarne
(Holy Island)
Alnwick
Wallington
Hall
Morpeth
Carrowbrough
Hexham
Acomb
Corbridge
Wallsend
NEWCASTLE
UPON TYNE
Carlisle
DURHAM
Stanhope
Little Salkeld
Penrith
Eamont Bridge
Lowther
Skiddaw
Keswick
Castlerigg
Helvellyn
Scafell
Middlesborough
Kettleness
Whitby
Stokesley
Danby
Kendal
Bridestone
Scarborough
Pickering
Kirkby Lonsdale
Norber
Moor
Smearsett
Malham Cove
Settle
Lancaster
Ripon
Sharow
Fountains
Abbey
Knaresborough
Harrogate
Castle
Howard
Wold Newton
Flamborough
Rudston
Bridlington
Kilham
Haisthorpe
Harpham
YORK
Ramsey
Ballameanagh
Peel
Douglas
Pendle Hill
(Malkin Tower)
Clitheroe
Fence
Newchurch-
in- Pendle
Rombalds
Moor
Keighley
Otley
Baildon
Apperley Bridge
Kirkstall
BRADFORD
LEEDS
Blackpool
Longridge
Preston
KINGSTON UPON
HULL
Todmorden
HALIFAX
Dewsbury
Brighouse
Wakefield
Walton
Blackstone
Edge
Kirklees
HUDDERSFIELD
Alkborough
Winter Hill
Fishlake
Skelbrooke
Barnsdale
Barnsley
Worsbrough
Doncaster
Sprotbrough
Haxey
Conisbrough
Wardley Hall
Ashton-
under-Lyne
MANCHESTER
LIVERPOOL
Rainhill
Wharncliffe
Wentworth
Woodhouse
SHEFFIELD
Bidston
Warrington
Daresbury
Appleton
Runcorn
Comberbach
Macclesfield
Chester
Middlewich
Sandbach
Little Morton
Hall
Leek
Crewe
Stoke-on-Trent

The North

ACOMB, Northumberland C2

In the village of Acomb lived Moses Cotsworth, whose work in the nineteenth century was instrumental in forming many of the notions connected with the modern view of stone circles and related lore. Cotsworth's mn interest was calendrical form, attempting to persuade people to move from the complex modern calendrical system of 12 months per year to one of 13 months. In the course of researching the background to these reforms in such places as Egypt and the Middle East, he began to conceive of the hidden purpose of the stone circles and standing stones as calendrical markers and regulators of a particular kind, and almost incidentally offered some useful insights into the design of the mysterious 'Clog Calendar' (figure 148), which was widely used in ancient times for measuring the passage of the days and relating these to the festivals. Many of Cotsworth's notions are widely accepted today, but when he first published his findings, in his remarkable book *The Rational Almanac*, he was laughed to scorn. Among his more interesting proposals was the recognition that the degree of 360 divisions of a circle was derived from the lunar-width measurement of a sunrise/sunset arc at the latitude of the pyramids. He took the moon's vertical diameter of 31', and divided this into the tropical arc (the variation between solstice points) of 46 minutes and 54 seconds to obtain 90 links or lunar (31') repetitions, which he proposed was the earliest method of measuring sky curves and angles and from which eventually developed the notion of there being 4 x 90 'divisions' in the entire circle of the sky. He showed that the central tower of the Minster at YORK was orientated in such a way as to reflect the sunrise-sunset on the longest and shortest days — thus, for example, the shortest day sunrise (Dec 22nd) is on the SE corner of the tower, while the sunset is on the SW corner. He developed notions of SILBURY HILL as a sighting point for calendrical measurements, and saw the construction of this extraordinary mound as being done for much the same purposes as the pyramids. For more on Cotsworth, see STONEHENGE.

The Clog Calendar shown here has nothing to do with the wooden-soled footwear called 'clogs', yet both terms come from the Middle English word 'clog' which meant a thick piece of wood. The calendar was marked on a long piece of thick wood in the earliest times, but was by the late medieval period also drawn on strips of paper in a form closely resembling that reproduced by Moses Cotsworth of ACOMB. The hieroglyphics, signs and symbols cut along the edge and face of the clog determine the dates of the major ecclesiastical and state festivals throughout Europe. The earliest references to the Clog Calendar indicate it is not related to the standard solar system (now in general use) but to the lunar system, for which reason the Clog Calendar was called an 'Al-monaght' or 'Al-mon-heed' (the word 'mon' meaning moon), from which we derived our word Almanac. The year begins on 1 January; the outer runic-like symbols indicate lunar phases, the corner relates to the perpetual calendar, and the four notched corners relate to the four quarters of the year (although illustrated as four sticks, the notches are actually cut on to the four edges of a single clog.) The symbols on the right-hand face relate to religious festivals, saints' days and even important agricultural dates. For example, the heart at the bottom of the first clog marks 25 March, the religious festival of the Annunciation (see MARCH, page 19). The 'falling man' at the top of the fourth clog represents St Edward the King Confessor, who was crucified head downwards and has his Saint's Day on 13 October. The simple hayrake near the bottom of the second clog corresponds to 11 June as a farming activity.

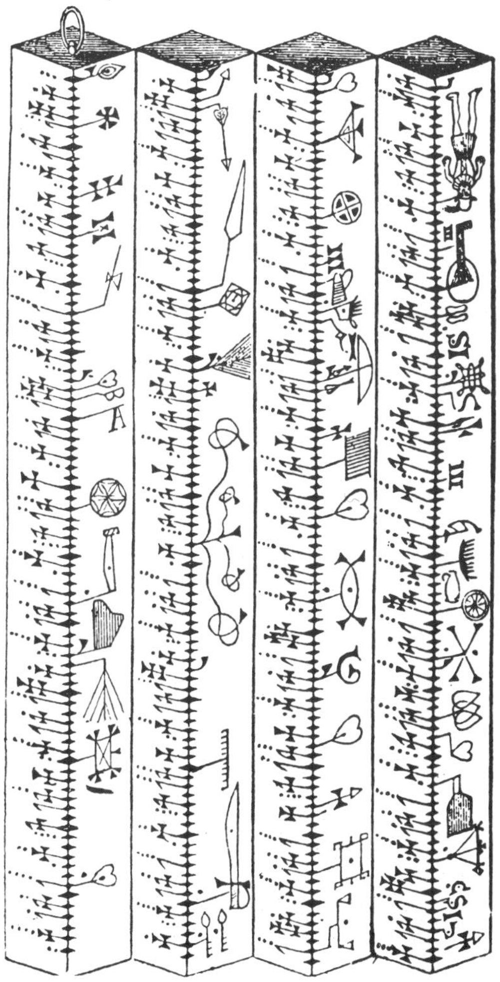

ALKBOROUGH, Humberside D5

The turf maze at Alkborough, set on the brow of a hill overlooking the valley of the Humber, with the Humber Bridge itself almost in view, was probably designed and cut in the thirteenth century by monks from Spalding Abbey. Mazes were often used in ecclesiastical art during that time (especially in the huge marble pavements of the cathedrals), perhaps as sacred 'dancing grounds' (figure 149). The name 'Julian's Bower', which is used of this maze and of others, is said to be derived from Julius the son of Aeneas, who supposedly introduced mazes to the west. The Alkborough turf maze is echoed in several parts of the village; a copy (over six feet in diameter) is set in stone in the floor of the porch in the nearby church of St John the Baptist, as well as in a stained glass roundel above the Christ in the central part the east window. In the burial grounds to the south-west of the village, to the left of the grounds, near the wall, another maze-copy in metal has been affixed to a gravestone set up in 1922 (figure 150).

APPERLEY BRIDGE, West Yorkshire C5

It was in the River Aire below Apperley Bridge that the infamous Prophet Wroe was publicly baptized by John Brunton of Bradford in the presence of 30,000 spectators, some of them most unfriendiy to the convert. In later times it was claimed that he had promised to walk over the waters without wetting his feet, and that the waters would part to make way for him, as they were said

to have done for Moses — but most prophets gain a reputation they do not deserve. Whatever his intentions, he was baptized, and although for days the weather had been overcast and snowy, as one might expect in January, the sun did shine out at the moment of his baptism, as he had said it would. When he stepped into the cold water, some of the younger male spectators, who were sitting on the branch of a tree, cried out, 'Drown him!', perhaps in jest — but Prophet Wroe took the matter seriously, especially when a former apprentice of his cursed him. Wroe commanded the young men to come down in the name of the Lord — which they immediately did when the bank which supported their tree collapsed, and they were also unwillingly 'baptized'.

Wroe had been born at Bowling (near Bradford) in September, 1782, and eventually, after a severe illness, began to have intense visions, hearing voices telling him what to do in the name of the Lord. He eventually became a contender for the leadership of the strange sect of Southcottians, who awaited the second coming of the Messiah (the 'Shiloh') from the womb of Joanna Southcott. It was his canny realization that the Shiloh would not come forth from that particular womb which led him to announce to the Southcott Society in Bradford, in August 1822, that the Messiah would not come. On the following Sunday he had one of his contrived epileptic fits, and lay as if dead; later he said he had been visited by an angel, who had ordered him to become a prophet. His bizarre travels to convert the Jews took him through many parts of Europe, but there appears to have been only one convert (that a Methodist minister) in the whole of that time.

Wroe was a con-man of the highest degree, though sometimes his tricks were seen through. For example, in Pudsey he undertook a 14-day fast, but the suspicious among his followers found him hiding in a cornfield, eating new potatoes with a mutton chop, and drinking wine. He was set on a donkey, carried in triumph through Pudsey, and ducked repeatedly in a horse-pond until people feared for his life. The incident lost him many of his adherents, but he carried on with his 'religious work'.

His biggest confidence trick is still memorialized in Wrenthorpe, near Wakefield, for he fleeced many of his followers of sums of money large enough to build himself a pleasure-house 'fit for Solomon', which was later called 'Melbourne House' and is now a home for the elderly. Fit for Solomon or not, some of the expense was for the time prodigious — Australian cedar and Spanish mahogany were especially imported, while the ordinary glass in the windows was removed, to be replaced by plate glass. Wroe died in Australia at the age of 82, conning to the last: the Melbourne Society, who had fostered his ideas and financed him royally, complained that he had not kept faith with them, as he had promised not to die.

APPLETON, Cheshire B6

The 'Bawming of the Thorn' in Cheshire's Appleton during July is a sort of late continuation of the May Day rites of maypole dancing, but in this case the villagers dance around a live tree which has been decked with flowers. The original tree (replaced at the end of the last century) was itself an ancient one, and was said to have been grown from one of the cuttings of the GLASTONBURY thorn, much like the more famous one at QUAINTON. The word 'bawming' is local dialect for 'adorning'.

149 (facing page, top): The maze pattern of 'Julian's Bower' appears in metal on a gravestone in Alkborough cemetery.
150 (facing page, bottom): The Alkborough maze ('Julian's Bower'), whose pattern appears in the floor and a window of the local parish church.
151 (left): The Prophet Wroe, infamous confidence trickster of the 19th century.

ASHTON-UNDER-LYNE, Greater Manchester C5

It is said that Sir Ralph Assheton was the most detested man in England during the reign of Henry VI, regarded by many as being the cruellest in punishing and fining tenants who had failed in their difficult tasks. After his death, his own son left sufficient money to establish a procession which would commemorate the unfortunate reputation of his father and remind all of his wicked ways. It was ordered that a pageant be held in which a Black Knight, in full armour similar to that worn by Sir Ralph, should parade the town. At the end of the pageant the figure is hanged near the Old Cross in Stamford Park.

152: The heap of rocks at Baildon, claimed by some to be a fallen cromlech, was once called locally 'Robin Hood's House'. Mythology insists he used to live here, near the edge of the haunted Baildon Moor.

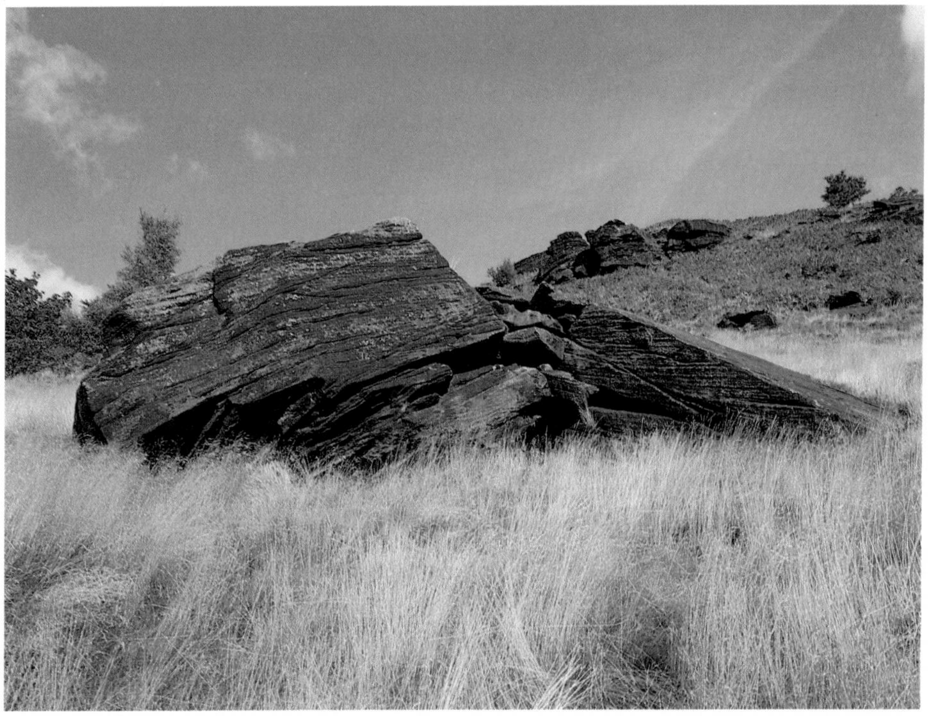

BAILDON, West Yorkshire C5

Above and below Baildon are groups of stones which were once associated with the outlaw Robin Hood. Just above Baildon Green, some way up the hill above what used to be a mill (it is now largely ruinous, though used as a garage) is a group of rocks formerly called 'Robin Hood's House'. One historian of Baildon, who wrote about this place in 1910, suggested that it was 'unquestionably a cromlech, of the type of "Kit's Coty House" in Kent', but this is very unlikely as it has no signs at all of being a fallen monument. On one side is a huge mass of stones which have obviously fallen from the cliff above and embedded themselves into the hillside. The other stones (to the eastern side) may have been placed there by man, but there is no clue as to what purpose they served. It is not possible to enter the 'house', and the name is obviously a fiction: the locals of Baildon no longer call it by the ancient name.

Above Baildon itself, at the top of Trench Wood, is a large stone with a bowl-shaped cavity which was once called 'Robin Hood's Seat'. The cavity was formed by water-erosion, and once again there is no historical reason why it should be associated with the outlaw. On the plateau above Trench Wood, on Brackenhall Green, is a rough stone circle called Soldier's Trench (figure 153). This was once much larger, but part of it was destroyed to make room for the modern road. The circle consisted of two double series of stones, measuring 50 yards from north to south and almost 40 yards from east to west. Until quite recently there was a stone circle some 27 yards in diameter on the site of Weecher, but this was destroyed when the reservoir was built. The moors beyond Baildon are covered in earthworks, cairns and those curiously marked stones which bear cup-and-ring marks (figure 152).

From the many remains on Baildon Moor, it is clear that it was once a sacred site for the practice of ancient cults, and in the nineteenth century some historians (who linked such cults with the dark practices they imagined were followed by the Druids) attempted to show that the name Baildon was actually derived from the same word which gave us Beltane, for the May Day festivities. This communal word was Baal, or Bail, the name given to an ancient god who was later regarded as being one of the most terrible of demons. The demonic word survives still in the name Belphegor, a demon who in medieval lore flew over the world in a hopeless search for a married couple who had found true happiness. It is found also in the name Beelzebub, the 'Lord of the Flies' of popular demonology.

BALLAMEANAGH, Isle of Man A5

In a field by the old cemetery in Glen Auldyn is the 'Cabbal' or 'old Chapel', which actually overlays a prehistoric pagan burial site. The archaeologist Kermode tells us that in former times people practised here a curious form of divination. Those who wanted to know who would die in the coming year would gather in the place at St John's Eve, and watch. He records that one night people saw 21 small lights come dancing up the glens: that year saw a great epidemic, and there were 21 deaths. A similar practice is observed (for similar reasons) in the porches of certain churches in the North of England, though it is more usual for the observance to take place on St Mark's Eve, or at Halloween.

BARNSDALE, South Yorkshire D5

It is known from Court Rolls of the Manor of Wakefield that a man named Hood lived in the locality during the reign of Edward II, and that the scene of his exploits (initially at least) is set in what used to be called the West Riding of Yorkshire, in the area circled by Huddersfield, Wakefield, Barnsdale, Doncaster and Rotherham (see, however, KIRKLEES). Barnsdale, which has come down to us as Robin's favourite haunt, was infamous in that period for being infested with brigands and outlaws, probably because many of the soldiers who had served

under the unsuccessful Earl of Lancaster in the battle of Boroughbridge in 1322 took refuge in this area. Indeed, the mention of a little-known place ('the Sayles') in early ballads points to this area in a most striking manner for the Sales was a small tenancy in the Manor of Pontefract, just north of Barnsdale. It is also known that King Edward II made a progress through Lancashire and Yorkshire in 1323, living for some while in York, Pickering, Liverpool and Kirkby, among other places; his journey appears to have formally terminated at Nottingham. Documents preserved in the Exchequer for Edward's reign mention one 'Robyn Hode' (sometimes Robyn Hod) several times as being one of the servants of the King, shortly after that long progress through the north of England. All these historical facts, along with others, have led Valentine Harris to conclude that 'Robin Hood was a minor robber inhabiting Barnsdale, who attained a reputation for piety, generosity and skill in archery during his lifetime. He may very possibly have been the Wakefield Robert Hood, in view of the locality of his grave and his relationship with the prioress of Kirklees, but we have no absolute proof.' For further information on Robin Hood, see entries in the following: FOUNTAINS ABBEY, HATHERSAGE, KIRKLEES, LOXLEY, NOTTINGHAM and SKELBROOK.

153: Soldier's Trench, the remains of an ancient stone circle above Baildon village.

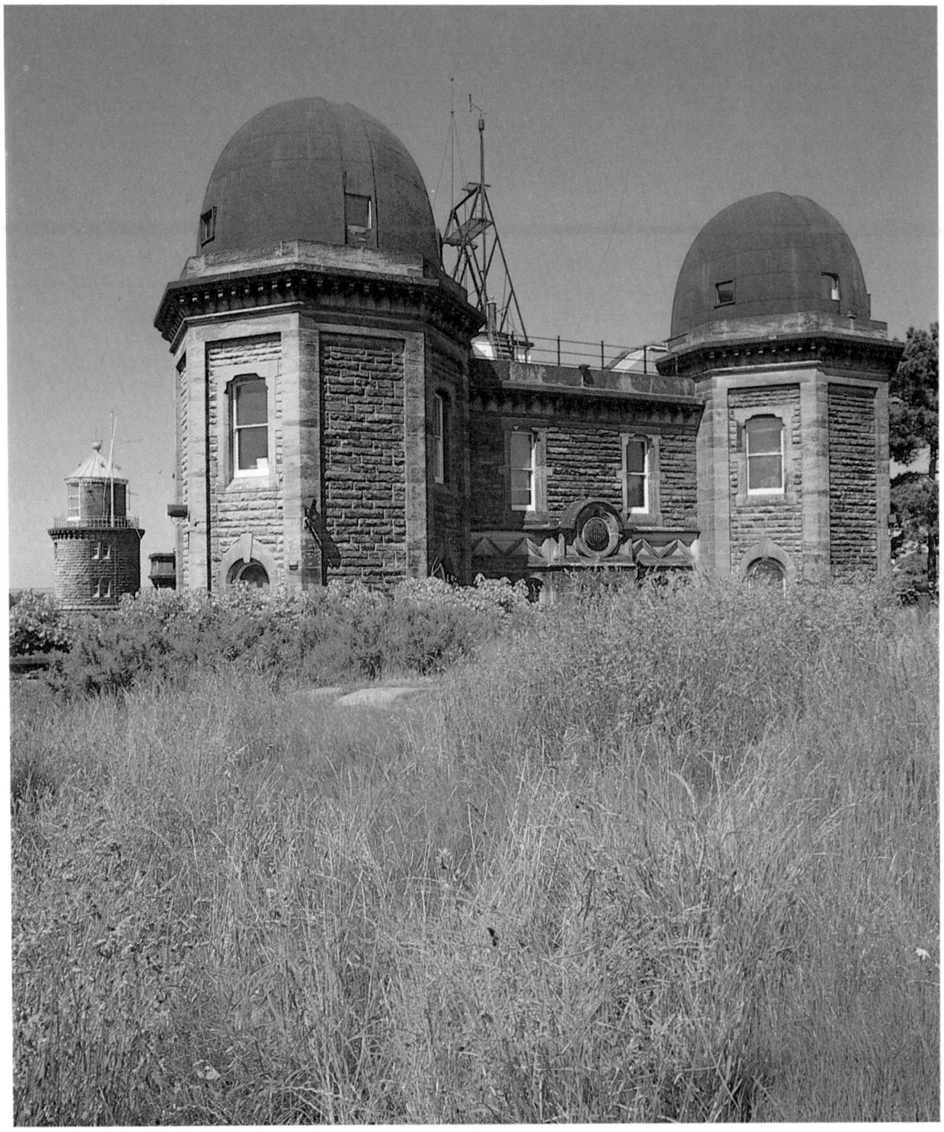

BIDSTON HILL, Merseyside B6

Bidston Hill was once a most important religious or ritual centre, and there are still traces of prehistoric carvings and cup-and-ring marks on the exposed surfaces of the rocks. The carving of a horse which is often pointed out as being 'prehistoric' is, however, probably no earlier than the seventeenth century, though a deeply incised 'sun-goddess' is probably 4,000 years old. At the southern end of the hill is the observatory and tidal institute (figure 154), now owned by Liverpool University and used to provide tidal predictions for over 160 ports world-wide. At the northern end is the Bidston windmill (figure 157) which was originally built in the seventeenth century.

BLACKSTONE EDGE, West Yorkshire C5

Along Blackstone Edge, near Todmorden, is an ancient paved roadway which leads over the crest of the hill in a direction approximately parallel to the present road to Ripponden (figure 156). The stone 'pavement' of this road is about 18 feet broad, and is of a distinctive construction, with a central continuous troughing of large stones, almost four feet wide. It is said that this road was built by the Romans and formerly connected Mancunium (Manchester) with Olicana (Ilkley), the road being a relatively secure pass across inhospitable moorlands which were held by the tribes of Brigantes from whom the Romans had wrested the land. Confirmation of the Roman origin are the many finds of Roman coins in the locality, particularly at Stoodley Pike, most of them relating to the reigns of the Emperors Hadrian, Antoninus Pius and Gallienus.

On the Yorkshire side of the hill-road, a curious formation of flat natural rock is incorporated into the high-

154 (above): The observatory and tidal institute at Bidston Hill.
155 (below): Stoodley Pike, built to commemorate victories against Napoleon.
156 (below, right): The so-called 'Roman Road', probably a pack-horse track, over the top of the moors at Blackstone Edge.
157 (facing page): Bidston windmill marks the furthest extreme of the outcroppings on the Hill.

way. This is known locally as 'Dhoul's Pavement' (Devil's Pavement). The roadway marked one of the most important crossings of the southern Pennines until the first turnpike road of 1735 bypassed the Roman section, to follow an easier gradient around the spur of the hill. The second turnpike, established round about 1780, was designed to be even less steep, and formed the basis for the later main road between Rochdale and Lancashire. Blackstone Edge was one of the important beacon hills, on which fires were burned to pass news of important happenings across the Pennines — two related beacon points were Pendle Hill and Thievely Pike.

158 (below): 'Pity poor Bradford', an engraving illustrating the vision of the Earl of Newcastle. From *The Old History of Bradford*, 1776.
159 (facing page): The Bridestones near Levisham, North Yorkshire.

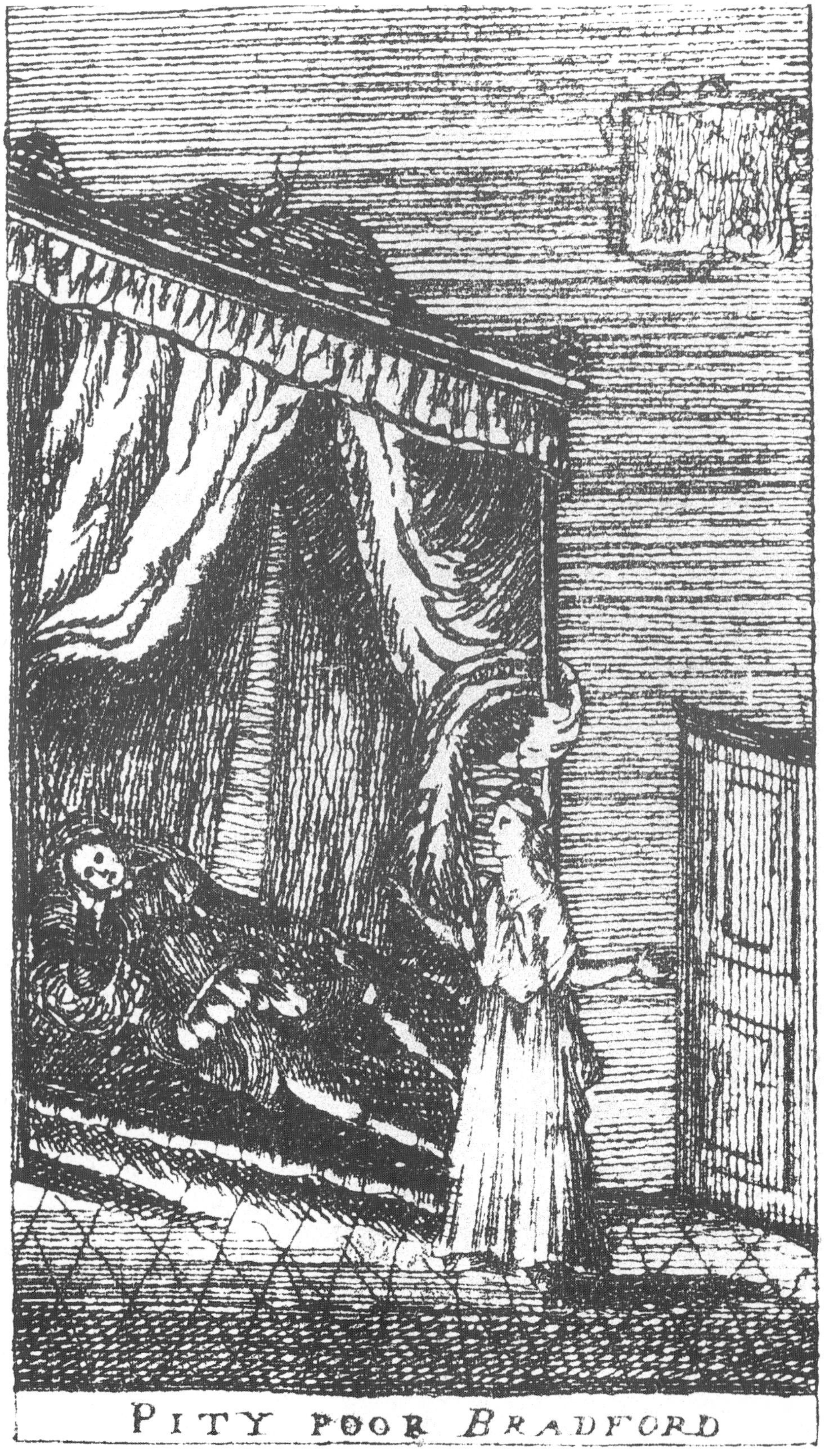

BRADFORD, West Yorkshire C5

The name of Bradford points to its original siting before it became one of the industrial hell-towns of the north, with hundreds of factories pouring smoke into the air. The older part of the town was near the head of an open valley in the uplands, down which a beck descended towards a marshy flat below. This beck still runs underground beneath the jungle of buildings above, and may still be traversed. The traveller was obliged to cross this broad stream, which was not drained until the eighteenth century when a canal was made to connect the city with Liverpool. This crossing or ford became the 'brad ford', or broad ford. What the area now lacks in romance or history is to some extent made up for by the legend of the boar. The story tells how the area was under constant threat from the ravages of a fierce boar, which none could kill. To obtain a reward offered for this deed, a local did slay it and, being unable to carry the enormous beast, cut out its tongue as proof of his valour and went off to claim the reward. Meanwhile another fellow happened upon the dead creature, and hoping that he might claim the money, cut off its head and carried it on a pole. The two men arrived at the chamber of the city at the same time, both demanding the reward. The pretender pointed to the head as the most certain proof of valour, but the other man said, 'But look for the tongue'. When the head was seen to be missing its tongue, the genuine hunter produced it in triumph. This, it is said, is why a tongueless boar's head is on the city arms.

There were many 'sore calamities at the siege of Bradford' in 1642, during the Civil War, and one local eye-witness, Joseph Lister, left an account of how the Earl of Newcastle ordered that when the city was taken his soldiers should 'put to the sword every man, woman and child, without regard to age, sex, or distinction whatsoever'. However, it is recorded that while sleeping in nearby Bowling Hall on the night before this projected outrage, an apparition appeared and importuned him with the words, 'Pity poor Bradford! Pity poor Bradford!' The Earl immediately countermanded his former order and, still in the words of Lister, 'forbade the death of any person whatsoever, except only such as made resistance; so that no lives were lost, save about ten persons, who fell into the hands of some desperadoes, who, contrary to the Earl's orders, satiated their revenge upon them.' A popular engraving, (figure 158), was circulated in books afterwards.

The local historian John James, writing in 1842, recorded that astrologers and fortune-tellers were plentiful in the city. He tells the story of a poor weaver named Sutcliffe who, imagining that his house was haunted by an evil spirit, asked a notorious Bradford fortune-teller, John Hepworth, to exorcise it. Hepworth mixed human blood with hair, poured it in a large bottle, sealed this hermetically, and put it into the fire. It soon exploded, and killed the old weaver on the spot.

BRIDESTONE, North Yorkshire D4

The natural outcroppings of strange rocks with waisted socles (figure 159) are ranged in a large arc over a wide expanse of National Trust ground near Levisham. The word 'Bride' has nothing to do with the modern notion of marriage, but is a corruption of Bridget — one of the Christian names given to a local pagan deity with a similar-sounding name.

BRIGHOUSE, West Yorkshire C5

Near to Kirklees Park, outside Brighouse, is 'The Three Nuns' public house, the only tangible reminder of the ancient Priory of Robin Hood fame (see KIRKLEES). Nearby, on the roadside at the junction of the Brighouse/Huddersfield-Leeds roads, is the so-called 'dumb steeple', looking much like a lost finial to a steeple (figure 160). It is probably one of the original 'doom steeples' which offered sanctuary to those fearful of judgment (the original 'doom'). The local historian Horsfall Turner records that the dumb steeple was used as a midnight rendezvous for the Luddites at the beginning of the nineteenth century.

CARRAWBROUGH, Northumberland C2

To the south of Hadrian's Wall near Carrawbrough (itself the site of a Mithraic temple of the Roman period) is a stone tank, once part of a sacred well enclosed within a Roman temple. It was probably a devotional well, for many objects were thrown into the tank and well — mainly offerings of coins, of which more than 14,000 were collected when the well was discovered in 1949. The well is now called 'Coventina's Well', because among the finds was a bas-relief showing this goddess reclining on a floating leaf.

CASTLE HOWARD, North Yorkshire D4

To the south of this most lovely of northern stately homes is a fountain, in the centre of which is a larger-than-life statue of Atlas carrying a celestial globe, with gilded figures of the zodiac (figure 161). The globe was one of the exhibits in the Paris Great Exhibition of 1889, and was purchased by the Howard family, shipped back to England, and mounted on the specially carved Atlas to become the only external zodiac in any British stately home.

CASTLERIGG, Cumbria B3

On a plateau among the hills to the east of Keswick is one of the most impressive ancient stone circles in the north of England, the Castlerigg, sometimes called the 'Carles' or 'Druids' Circle',

> ...a dismal cirque
> Of Druid Stones, upon a forlorn moor.

as Keats wrote in the nineteenth century. The 'cirque' consists of 38 standing stones arranged in an oval approximately 107 feet maximum diameter, with an inner rectangular setting of 10 stones. About 300 feet to the south-west is an outlier.

Castlerigg, like most of the stone circles of Britain, is a calendrical marker, though in this respect it is probably unique in that instead of using a large number of specially sited standing stones outside its circle as mark-points, it makes use of the distinctive shapes of the surrounding mountains. As may be seen from the diagram of the solar orientations of Midwinter sunset for STONEHENGE (page 48), the line of orientation in such circles is usually fixed by three single points (indicated by stones, one of which is usually an outlier, or

160 (facing page): The 'dumb steeple' near Brighouse.
161 (above): In the great gardens of Castle Howard, designed by Vanbrugh around 1699, is a figure of Atlas carrying a planisphere.

162: The Castlerigg stone circle near Keswick was probably built c.2,500 B.C.

stone free of the outer circumference of the circle) along a single sighting line. In Castlerigg, however, there are several orientation points with only two siting points within some of the orientations, the third (necessary to mark accurately a continuation line) being fixed by distinctive points on the surrounding hills and mountains: thus, in this remarkable circle, the stones are integrated perfectly into the surrounding horizon, to mark out the rhythms of the seasons. The simple diagram in figure 52 indicates how certain of the imaginary lines which connect two stones project to distinctive calendrical points. The single outlier, which is 296 feet from the outer stones of the circle (marked O in the diagram) is of interest for a variety of reasons. If it is viewed from the stone marked S, the imaginary line of view runs exactly across the main centre of the circle.

The most important work done on stone circles in the present century is that of Professor Thom, who has personally surveyed hundreds of such sites and has come to some far-reaching conclusions about their calendrical properties. It is therefore interesting to observe that Thom himself remarks that the curious evidence of the outlier at Castlerigg yielded one of the lines which, in Thom's words 'convinced the author of the necessity to examine the calendar hypothesis in detail'.

CHESTER, Cheshire B6

In the church of St John the Baptist in Chester is a remarkable monument to Lady Warburton, who died in 1693. The lady is portrayed as a fearsomely grinning skeleton, coyly holding up a burial sheet on which has been incised her memorial. It is said to be the work of Edward Pierce, though he also died while working on it and much of the detail was completed by John Nost.

CLITHEROE, Lancashire B5

On the interior of the south wall of the parish church at Clitheroe is a brass memorial to John Webster, once the headmaster of the local grammar school and vicar of Mytton, who was an alchemist and author of *Displaying of Supposed Witchcraft* (1677), critical of the contemporary view of witchcraft. His own view of the craft had been moulded by his acquaintance with Edmund Robinson of Kildwick, but what is of interest to us at Clitheroe is the alchemical symbolism of the brass memorial which was written by Webster himself, for this bears a most interesting astro-alchemical device.

The Latin on the memorial reads:

Qui hanc figurum intelligunt
Me etiam intellexisse intelligent
Hic jacet ignotus mundo merusque tumultu
Invidiae semper mens tamen aequa fuit
Multa tulit veterum ut sciret secreta Sophorum
Ac tandem vires noverit ignisıaquae
Johannes Hyphantes sive Webster
In villa Spinosa supermontane in
Parochia silvaae cuculatae in agro
Eboracensi natus 1610 Feb 3
Ergastulum animae deposuit 1682 Junii 18
Annoque aetatis suae 72 currente.
Sicque peroravit moriens mundo huic valedicens
Aurea pax vivis requies aeterna sepultis

(The man who understands this figure will understand that I understood it too. Here lies one unknown to the world and drowned in a tumult of (jealousy) yet always his mind was serene. He sought among the old things that he might learn many secrets of the (alchemists), and at length learn again the power of Fire and Water. John Hyphantes, or Webster, in his house of Spinosa on the hills in the Yorkshire parish where the cuckoo sings, born 3 Feb. 1610, and in that year, at the age of 72, he left behind the prison of his soul on 18 June 1682. And thus, dying he bids farewell to this world. A golden peace to the living, eternal rest to those buried in the tomb.)

The inscription is of great interest because of certain hidden meanings in the text; for example, in the last line he associates life with gold — and gold was the external object sought by the alchemists. Gold is the metal of the Sun, and the Sun is the symbol of life, so we should not be surprised to find the image of the Sun at the centre of this Seal of Solomon which bears the six sigils for the planets, and a seven-lettered inscription (figure 163).

The quintessence which the alchemist sought was sometimes called 'the secret life', and was associated with the Sun. More important, however, it was also visualized as being at the centre of the 'empty space' in the Seal of Solomon. The seven words on the outside of the magical symbol read 'Aqua cum Igna Tandem in gratium Redit', which mean 'With Water and Fire he will at length be restored to grace'. In the inscription there is an equals sign between the Latin words for fire and water, indicating the secret tradition which maintains that water and fire are (in their alchemical sense) the same powers in different states of being. Are the lines on the face of the sun 'tears', and is this intended to show the union of fire (sun) and water (tears)? There is an interesting relationship between the six planets and the corresponding words in the magical device, but this relationship is too complex to be discussed here.

COMBERBACH, Cheshire B6

This is one of the last villages in the north to attempt to keep alive the ancient tradition of Soulcaking (see NOVEMBER, page 27). 'Soulcaking' was once a thinly disguised moral play, which devolved into the enacting of a sort of Mummers' play centred on the spirited display of a horse's skull on the normal Hobby Horse body, to give the appearance of a grotesque dragon. The skull-horse of Comberbach, the actual skull of which was painted and said to have been taken from one of the horses bred from the famous 'Marbury Dun' buried in Marbury Park, was supported by *dramatis personae* resembling a hellish pantomime, from the Black Prince and Beelzebub to the Wise Woman and Quack Doctors. In some parts of England (especially Cheshire) 'soulcaking' has been demoted to the custom of begging from house to house for soul-cakes, and even for coins, as the insinuating lines of the Souling Ditties imply:

The roads are very dirty,
My shoes are very thin,
I've got a little pocket
To put a penny in.

Could this 'penny' be the oblos (the ancient Roman equivalent of a penny) which in ancient times was put into the mouth (the 'little pocket') of the newly dead to pay the ferrying charge across the river to Hades? Such an explanation would account for the curious 'horse

163: Hermetic device from the memorial to John Webster in Clitheroe parish church.

head', for the Mercury of Hades in Roman times was dog-headed, and the canine part has more than once been confused with the head of a horse. The extraordinary figure of dog-headed Mercury in the November section of the calendrical mosaic at Thrysdus would possibly indicate how easily the horse-head might be confused with the dog-head. Mercury was the messenger who went between the worlds of man, heaven and dead.

CONISBROUGH, South Yorkshire D5

The Castle at Conisbrough stands magnificently preserved in an off-white ashlar facing which changes hue with the colour of the sun (figure 164), still dominating this quiet and lovely village above the river Don. The castle, which is generally recognized as the best of its kind in Britain, was built in the late twelfth century by the de Warennes, shortly after William the Conqueror had given land and estates in the neighbourhood in recognition of the service rendered by the family during the conquest of England. In 1163, however the Conisbrogh estate passed into the royal line to Hameline Plantagenet, who married the last of the de Warennes, though he preserved their name. The keep, which is the most impressive of the surviving ruins, is still about 90 feet high, and is supported by six vast buttresses.

The church of St Peter is in parts as old as the castle, but has fragments which show it to have been a place of worship in Saxon times. Inside the church is an extraordinary Norman coped tomb-chest, highly decorated with images which include men fighting a dragon, a man apparently killed by a dragon, and the zodiacal signs Pisces and Sagittarius. It is marvellous to look upon this chest and realise that Robin Hood might have examined it, and wondered at its great age.

164: The magnificent keep of Conisbrough Castle is 90 feet high, with massive buttresses over nine feet thick. It is said to be the oldest and best in the country and dates from 1185.

Facing page:
The Lewis Carroll memorial window in Daresbury parish church contains images of the White Rabbit, Lizard and Dodo (*165, top left*), the Mad Hatter and Dormouse (*166, lower left*), Lewis Carroll and Alice (*167, top right*), and the King and Queen with the Cheshire Cat (*168*).

CORBRIDGE, Northumberland C2

Among the sad annals of northern witchcraft is the story of Ann Armstrong of Corbridge, a suspected member of a Northumbrian coven of witches, who confessed in 1673 that many of her neighbours would change shape before going to sabbats or to places where they might have conversations with the Devil. 'On Monday last at night, she, being in her father's house, see one Jane Baites, of Corbridge, come in the forme of a gray cat with a bridle hanging on her foote, and breath'd upon her & struck her dead (i.e. unconscious), & bridled her, & rids upon her in the name of the devill southwad, but the name of the place she does not know remember.' Ann herself appears to have changed her shape into that of a horse, and Jane rode upon her in the form of a cat to the sabbat.

DANBY, North Yorkshire D3

Some people in the north of England still regard many different forms of fossils and natural stones as possessing the magical properties of man-made amulets. Perhaps the most famous to be found the 'snake stones of Hilda', which are spiral ammonites believed to be the curled remains of vipers, yet there are also the tubular 'belemnites', which are fossilized cuttle-fish, used for curing cattle illnesses and for driving back black magic directed against the herds. Not exactly fossils, but certainly very ancient, are the 'awfshots' or 'elfbolts', which are found on the moors, and especially around Goathland and Danby. These are actually flint arrow-heads, used by ancient British archers. It was widely believed that fairies would use these to shoot at cattle, and so sick or disordered animals were 'touched' by these in order to bring about a cure by the homoeopathic practice in which 'like cures like'. It is these stones which Emily Bronte had in mind when she describes Catherine Linton of *Wuthering Heights* in her delirium of fever, visualizing Nelly as an old witch:

'I see you, Nelly, an aged woman: you have grey hair and bent shoulders.
This bed is the Fairy Cave under Penistone Crag, and you gather elf bolts
to hurt our heifers; pretending while I am near that they are only locks
of wool.'

A number of natural stones of alum shale, pierced with holes by the shell-fish 'borer', are called 'Haggomsteeans' or 'Adderstones', and are believed to have been made by the poisoned sting of the adder. They are hung up in barns and stables to 'prevent the witches riding off with the horses', in which practice they are called 'witchstones'. However, when they are used as magical amulets for door keys, they are called 'luckystones'. The practice of using curious stones for amuletic purposes is very ancient, and the historian Jeffrey records that there is good reason to believe that a holed 'holy stone' used to stand near the West Pier in WHITBY about two hundred years ago. Children were drawn through the 'eye' of this stone to strengthen their limbs, and lovers pledged their troth by joining hands through the stone.

DARESBURY, Cheshire B6

Charles Lutwidge Dodgson, better known as Lewis Carroll, the author of the 'Alice' series, was born at the Old Parsonage at Daresbury on 27 January, 1832, and lived in the village for the first 11 years of his life. One of the most outstanding mementoes to this remarkable man is the Lewis Carroll memorial window in the Daniell Chapel of All Saints Church, in his native village. The window was designed by Geoffrey Webb, and dedicated in 1934. The left-hand lancet window portrays Dodgson himself, with the Alice who figured in his most famous books. Below the pair is an entrancing image of the White Rabbit, the Lizard and the Dodo, as they were conceived by Tenniel when he illustrated the Alice series. Each of the five lower sections of the lancets portray animals and other beings from these fantasy books — perhaps the most striking being those of the Mad Hatter, the Dormouse in the teapot and the March Hare (figure 166), and the Duchess, Gryphon and Mock Turtle.

Dodgson died in GUILDFORD in 1898.

169: The River Calder at Dewsbury was the site of the earliest Christenings in the north of England by St Paulinus. He has left a preaching cross in Dewsbury parish church.

DEWSBURY, West Yorkshire C5

One of the strangest of customs in Britain is the one practised in Dewsbury on Christmas Eve — the tolling of the Devil's Knell on the bells of the parish church. Legends tell how Thomas de Soothill accidentally killed one of his servants, and in propitiation gave to the church a bell, later known as 'Black Tom of Soothill', which was to be rung every Christmas Eve to remind the world of his crime. The custom seems to have been observed since the thirteenth century, and a more general explanation of

the tolling has little to do with Soothill (a former village now swallowed up by Dewsbury) but with the more general intention of driving the Devil away so that he might bring no harm in the coming year. Some say that the tolling is in recognition of the belief that when Christ is born the Devil's power disappears. The number of tolls is said to be equal to the number of years in the Christian Calendar, and the bell ringing is so organized as to allow the last chime to fall exactly at the moment of midnight, thereby announcing the Birth of Christ.

In the parish church at Dewsbury is the fragment of a cross associated with St Paulinus, who is said to have passed through Dewsbury on his way to convert the Northumberland heathens, and to have preached by the side of the Calder, where he baptized some of the first British converts.

DONCASTER, South Yorkshire D5

The name is almost certainly from the Latin meaning 'Castle or City on the river Don', but an eleventh-century monk derives the name from 'Thong-ceaster', which means 'Castle of the thong', claiming a mythological origin for the city. He tells us that Hengist and Horsa agreed to purchase from the Brigantes' tribal King, who owned the area, as much land as they could encompass with a leather thong cut from a bull's hide. The king agreed, and the two wily leaders cut the hide up into such thin strips that they were able to encompass the vast tract of land on which the city has been built. The trick is an old one, and would have been well known to any monk in the eleventh century, for the *Aeneid* was popular reading — Queen Dido, the lover of Aeneas, built her vast Carthage from the Africans with the similar strips of hide.

EAMONT BRIDGE, Cumbria B3

The 'amphitheatre' to the south side of Eamont Bridge is popularly called 'King Arthur's Round Table', and is associated with the legends of the heroic and mythical king of the Britons. In the nineteenth century it was believed that the Romans used the raised circle of earth as a gladiatorial amphitheatre, while a century earlier it was a 'centre for druidic administration'. Thus, each age creates its own mythologies from the puzzles of the past, and ignores the truth that such sacred sites were in use thousands of years before the coming of the Druids,the Romans or the King of romantic idylls. The circle, 300 feet in diameter, is defined by an embankment which is still about five feet high; the entire circle and earth bank was very much disturbed in the nineteenth century, and it is only recent surveys which have revealed traces of cremation trenches near the centre of the circle. To the north of the circle is a most interesting memorial cross, with celtic designs, which bears the carved heads of three locals who volunteered to do service in the South African campaign at the beginning of this century (figure 171).

About a quarter of a mile to the west is the Mayburgh earth circle, which with its larger diameter of 360 feet across the entrenching banks — which are in places over 14 feet high — far more closely resembles a Roman amphitheatre than that near the Bridge. In the centre of the Mayburgh circle stands a single upright of a curious form (figure 170), from some angles looking much like a giant arrow head which has been embedded in the earth. The stone is 9 feet high, though when Sir Walter Scott visited the site he recorded it as an 'unhewn stone of 12 feet in height'. Only a century earlier there had been eight stones within the perimeter, but seven of these had been dragged away for building material — perhaps in earlier times there had been even more stones.

Following page
170 (top): The central upright stone in the prehistoric earthworks and banks at Mayburgh, just west of Eamont Bridge.
171: Detail of the memorial to the South African War volunteers, just north of the Eamont Bridge amphitheatre.

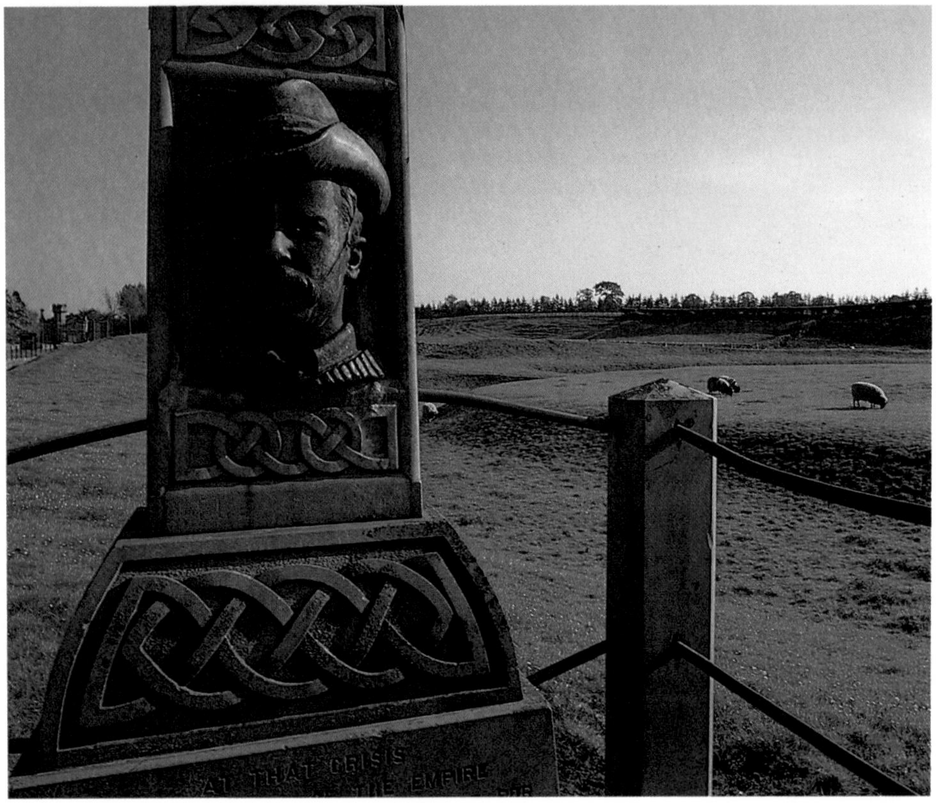

FENCE, Lancashire C5

On the night of Hallowe'en, 1632, a young boy named Edmund is supposed to have had an encounter with witchcraft. It seems that he came across two greyhounds on Pendle, both of which had chains trailing from their collar. For some reason Edmund decided to use them to hunt for hares (locally called 'malkins', somewhat reminiscent of the local MALKIN TOWER). A hare started nearby, but the dogs refused to chase it. The boy tied up the animals and started to thrash them with his stick. As the stick fell, the dogs were transformed into humans, one of whom was his neighbour Frances Dickenson, the other a boy he did not know. The woman seized hold of Edmund and promised him money if he would keep the secret of their transformation; however, the boy refused, recognizing her for a witch. The transformation scene was not complete, however, for she then changed the unidentified boy into a white horse by placing a bridle over his head, and then forced Edmund to ride alongside her. The unlikely pair rode to the house called Hoarstones at Fence, where Edmund saw witches and warlocks feasting. He escaped, and when eventually his story came out, he was taken to local magistrates.

Such was the witchcraft hysteria of the time that the boy's imaginative tale was taken seriously, and a large number of local men and women were arrested and sent for trial at Lancaster (see LANCASTER — THE CASTLE). They were all found guilty of witchcraft and sentenced to death by hanging, but fortunately the judge ordered a stay of execution. The case became very famous, and eventually a sensational play, *The Late Lancashire Witches*, was a London success. For some months Edmund was in big demand as a witch-hunter, for he claimed to be able to identify witches merely by sight. However, he was soon proved to be a liar — his tale being an adventure yarn invented by his father, who recognized the business of witch-hunting as being financially sound. One of the people aware of the extent to which Edmund was lying, and causing acute distress to the neighbourhood, was John Webster, the vicar of Mytton, whose book *Displaying of Supposed Witchcraft* (1677) was based upon his experiences with Edmund (for a note on Webster, see CLITHEROE). This batch of Lancashire witches was later reprieved by Charles I.

FISHLAKE, South Yorkshire D5

An account of a rustic attitude to witchcraft was recorded at the beginning of this century by the Reverend Ornsby about a man who used to work in his vicarage at Fishlake. A few years previously, a local tailor had asked the gardener for two small branches from the mountain ash in his gardens. When asked why he wanted the twigs, he explained that his wife had been churning milk for some hours, but the butter would not come. As a result, they knew that the cream had been bewitched and that if the cream were stirred with one twig of mountain ash, and the cow beaten with the other, then the charm would be broken. This hindering of the cream is recorded as one of the most common forms of 'witchcraft' in rural districts. In Lancashire it was (and still is) the practice to put a hot iron into the churn, to drive away the witch or the witchcraft. In Cleveland, before even attempting to make butter, the dairymaid throws a pinch of salt into the churn, then another pinch into the fire, repeating this nine times — this is a specific against witchcraft.

KIRKLEES, West Yorkshire C5

In Kirklees Park, near what used to be a Roman camp, is the grave of the outlaw Robin Hood, who is supposed to have died in 1247 in the Priory of Kirklees. It was from the upper window of the gatehouse there that he shot his last arrow to indicate the place where he was to be buried. The gatehouse, however is probably later than the fifteenth century, and in any case the site of the burial is actually 650 yards from this building. As the modern historian Valentine Harris says, the story of Robin's death-bed archery was a 'poetic invention of a later ballad writer who did not know Kirklees Park.' Local historians who wrote about the grave in 1893 provided an engraving of its state, helpfully pointing out that the uprights and crosses rivetted across were intended to keep away those who sought to prise away parts of the stonework of the tomb, as there was a popular belief that these fragments worked as charms against toothache. The historian Dr Gale, a dean of York Minster, recorded a copy of the epitaph now found on the stone wall, over 240 years ago:

> Hear underneath dis laitl stean
> laiz robert earl of Huntingtun
> nea arcir ver az hie sa geud
> an pipl kauld im robin heud
> sick utlaws as hi an iz men
> vil england nivr si agen.
> obiit 24 kal dekenbris 1247.

The date is entirely fictitious. So also is the 'old form' of spelling, and it is known that the inscription was copied on to the stone in the eighteenth century. The fact is, however, that while the grave inscription is a fiction, there was a much older tradition that Robin Hood was buried nearby. He was, the old records claim, buried 'under a great stone by the high way side'. His name, along with other names of his companions, was engraved on the stone; at either end of the 'sayde tombe was erected a cross of stone, which is to be seene at this present' (1596). A drawing made almost a hundred years later by Dr Nathanial Johnston shows the inscription, and it was explained that the reason why only a small portion of the stone now remains is that a chip from it was said to be a cure for toothache and that when the Lancashire and Yorkshire railway was being constructed in the early nineteenth century, the navvies placed pieces of it under their pillows to allay their pain. For further information on Robin Hood, see BARNSDALE, FOUNTAINS ABBEY, HATHERSAGE, LOXLEY, NOTTINGHAM and SKELBROOK.

KIRKSTALL, West Yorkshire C5

The same family of De Lacy who gave the manor of Newsam to the Templars, to give rise to the later TEMPLE NEWSAM, was also the founder of Kirkstall Abbey, which now stands in majestic ruin alongside the river Aire (figure 177). Kirkstall is now on the edge of Leeds, fringed by plots of commercial gardens on one side, by urban spread on the other, but it was the innovations of the Cistercians, who built and ran the Abbey, and who established many trades in the area, from the wool-weaving industry to coal-mining, from wood-working forestry to iron-smelting, which really founded the economic conditions that led to the growth of Leeds as an industrial city. One may see, therefore,

175: The medieval bridge at Kirkby Lonsdale is said to be haunted by the ghost of a dog, and to have been built by the Devil. The bridge dates from the 13th century.

that there is no mystery in the proximity of this most lovely of all monastic ruins within the urban spread of Leeds. Another ancient repository of history and symbolism in Leeds is to be found in the district of Adel.

KNARESBOROUGH, North Yorkshire D4

The birth-place or, more exactly, the birth-cave, of the prophetess Mother Shipton is said to be located near the Dropping Well at Knaresborough. This Mother Shipton is now associated with a few prophecies relating to the last century, which predict the coming of the aeroplane, the motor car and steam-driven ships — even with the prediction of the end of the world, which is variously dated as 1881, 1981 and 1991. These more famous prophecies were in fact nineteenth-century forgeries, yet long before the last century she was famous as a prophetess and witch. In his diary for 20 October, 1666, Pepys notes that the Fire of London still raged, and that a friend of his had reminded him that 'Shipton's prophecy was out'. According to him, the old prophetess had predicted the outbreak of this great fire which destroyed most of medieval London. It could be that Pepys and his friend were confusing the Shipton prophetess with the predictions made only a few years prior to the conflagration by the contemporary astrologer William Lilly, who had included some of Shipton's prophecies in one of his collections. This Mother Shipton was generally held to have been a witch or astrologer, and most of the illustrations from popular handbooks and pamphlets so depict her (figure 176), yet she was held in great esteem by those who knew her. It is recorded that a stone to her honour was erected near to CLIFTON (about a mile from the centre of York), among which were the lines:

Here lyes she who never ly'd,
Whose skill often has been try'd,
Her Prophecies shall still survive,
And ever keep her name alive.

The effigy near this Clifton stone was pointed out as the 'grave effigy' of Mother Shipton, but in fact it was a mutilated effigy of an armoured knight, apparently set up as a boundary stone. Another 'standing stone', called indeed 'Old Mother Shipton's Tomb' (though it is only a memorial stone) has been described by local historians — this incorporates the image of a woman's head touched by a star which stands above a Roman date. The stone, which was about seven feet high, was at Williton, and said to have come from Cumberland. The symbolism is distinctly Roman, however, even to the standard letters D M which stand for the Latin 'Deis Manibus' ('Into the hands of the Gods'), as a beginning of the commendation of the soul. Shipton has been called the 'Yorkshire Sybil', and while there is little doubt that she did not live in the tiny cave which goes under her name near the famous Dropping Well, it is fairly certain that she did originate in Yorkshire. Some historians, on very little evidence, have accepted the dubious notion that she was born in Knaresborough in 1488, but this seems to rest on a manuscript of obscure predictions in the British Library, relating to prophecies for the year 1620. More certain is that the large number of prophecies which have gone under her name did not originate during her lifetime, and that many people published poems about the future (or indeed about the immediate past, as suited their political aspirations) and hid behind the cloak of her fame. One historian, William Grainge, recorded in 1881 that a well-known 'Shipton prophecy' was:

'When carriages without horses run,
Old England will be quite undone.'

Forgery or not, Grainage continues, 'When the railway was being made between Harrogate and York, a lofty viaduct was needed to cross the river Nidd at Knaresborough, which was nearly completed, when through some deficiency in the construction the whole fabric fell into the water. The popular voice at once declared that Mother Shipton had said that "the big brig across the Nidd should tummle doon twice and stand for ivver when built the third time."' There was no second fall of the bridge. As Grainge remarks, 'This prophecy was never heard by anyone until after the catastrophe occurred.' More accurate as a prediction was the saying that Castle Hill at Northallerton would be 'filled with blood'. In latter years this has become a cemetery, and there is some extent to which the prophecy may be seen as being fulfilled. Again, records indicate she had predicted that a public road would run through the huge tithe-barn at Ulleskelf-on-the-Wharfe, and that the Keld there would be dried up — yet, as though by a miracle, the barn would continue to exist and the water spring for ever. When the York and North Midland Railway was built, it so transpired that the rails ran through the place where the barn had stood; barn and Keld were moved to another place.

176 (below): The prophetess Mother Shipton, said to be born at Knaresborough.
177 (facing page): Kirkstall Abbey, near Leeds, was founded by Cistercian monks in 1200. They established an important iron foundry, which partly explains the growth of industry in this part of the North.

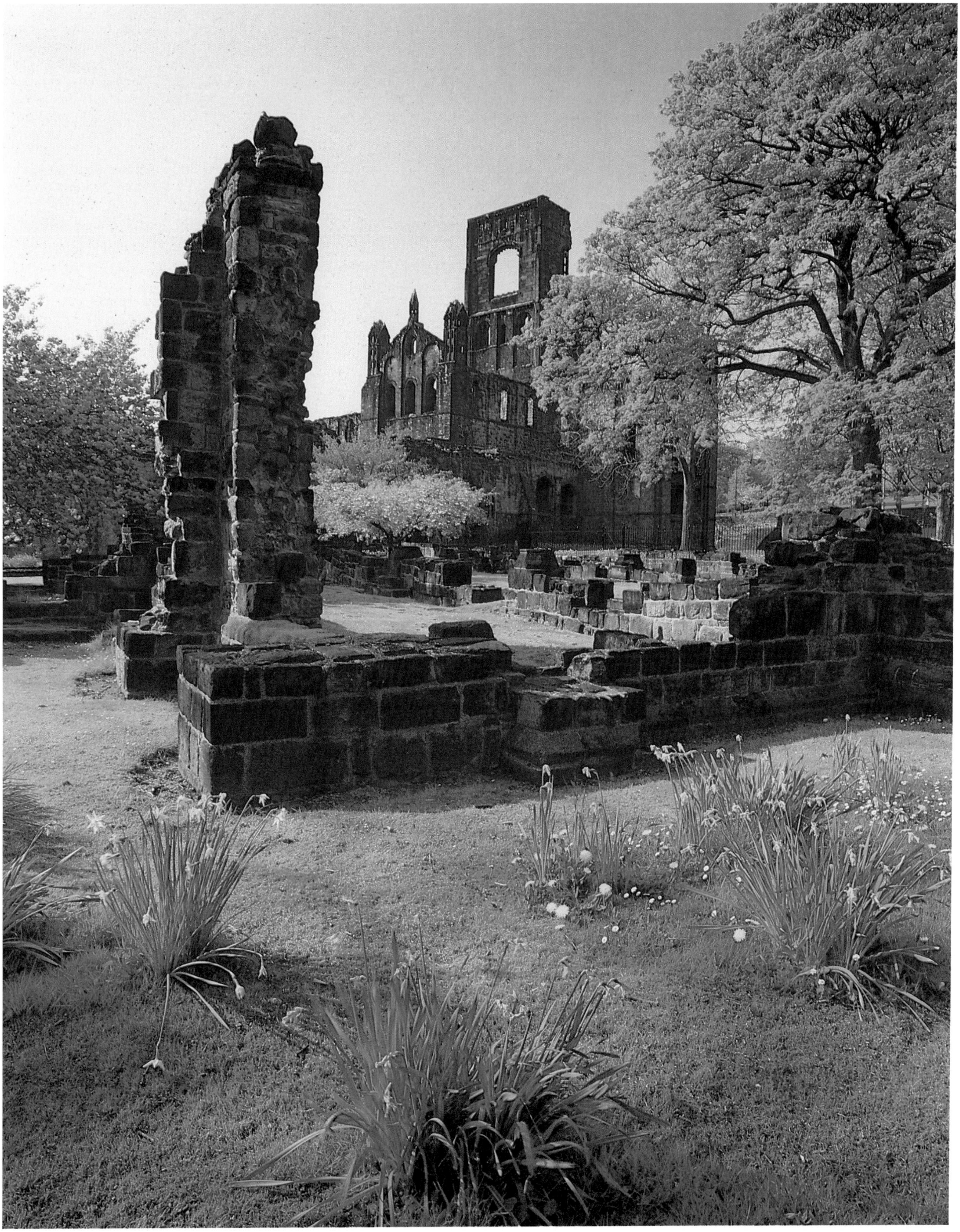

LANCASTER — THE CASTLE,
Lancashire B4

Lancaster Castle, partly a tourist attraction and partly a modern prison, is famous in legend-making because of the trials of the Lancashire witches in the seventeenth century. Among those witches who were questioned and tried in this castle, none were so famous as the old women Demdike and Chattox. The latter, arraigned for witchcraft and murder, blamed the evil influence of Demdike. They had met at MALKIN TOWER where they had been served a meal by demon familiars, during which Demdike had confessed to the murder of one Richard Assheton of Downham, and in helping in the killing by witchcraft of Robert Nutter of Greenhead. The trial began on 17 August, 1612, before Sir Edward Bromley and Sir James Altham, who eventually found Alice Nutter guilty of murder, Katherine Hewitt guilty of the murder of a Colne girl and the attempted murder of another child, and Jane and Alizon Device of Newchurch of turning Jennet Deane of Barnoldswick insane. This pair, along with a sorry collection of other men and women who had fallen foul of the strict witchcraft laws, were taken from the castle dungeons to their public hanging on 20 August.

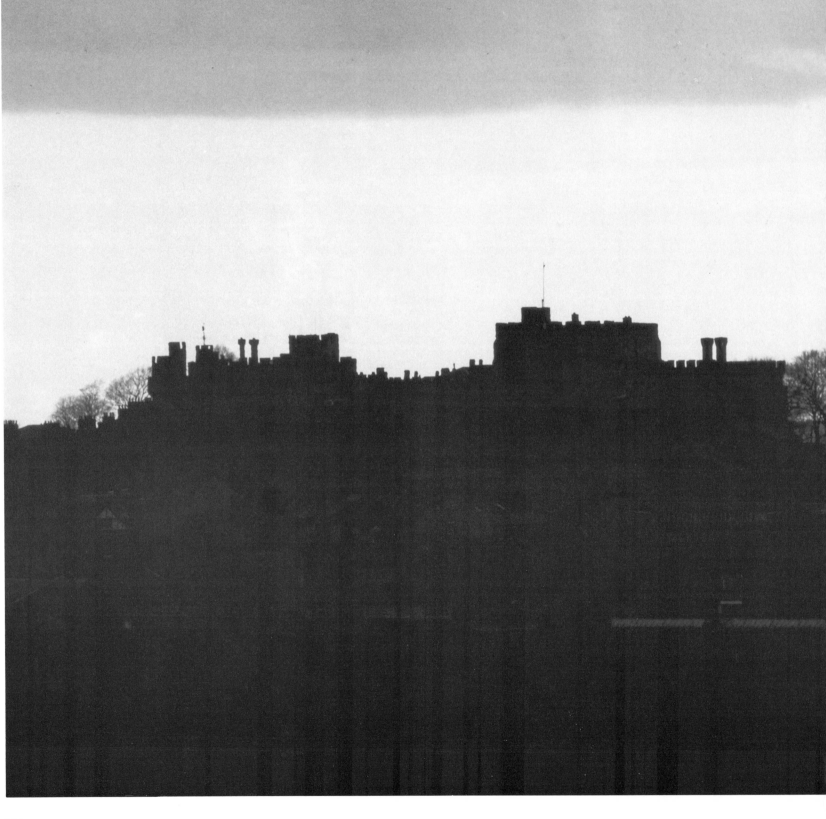

178: Lancaster Castle, now partly used as a prison. The great Norman keep was built about 1170 and a beacon on the John of Gaunt Tower signalled the approach of the Spanish Armada. George Fox, founder of the Society of Friends ('Quakers') was imprisoned here.

LEEDS, West Yorkshire C5

Within the centre of Leeds is found a plethora of quasi-hermetic symbols which we have learned to expect in any city enlarged by the Victorians, including an extremely impressive statue of the Black Prince (figure 179), and the coat of arms of the Prince of Wales. Of special interest is the extraordinary chimney which stands to the west of the railway station. This was constructed as a chimney for the Tower Works, and was built in imitation of the medieval bell-tower designed and constructed by Giotto to serve the Duomo of Florence. The tongue-in-cheek transfer of a campanile for a chimney by the architect William Bakewell in 1899 is not sacrilegious, for Bakewell did not attempt to copy any of the magical, astrological and religious symbols which Giotto placed upon his own tower; he was much more interested in the general attempt to make a chimney 'beautiful' within the neo-medieval Victorian sense of aesthetics. This curious approach to chimney design had been preceded by a full-dress copy of the Lamberti tower of Verona (for the same Tower Works) which had been designed by Thomas Shaw in 1864.

Italianate designs and concepts were not unusual at the time (the town hall in BRADFORD is entirely Florentine-Gothic in form), and so the Temple Mill to some extent broke with tradition by having the architect Ignatius Bonomi design the Mill (1838) in the form of an Egyptian temple. To this day, the Egyptian pillars and columns front the facade which impressively looks over Marshall Street, and there is a huge falcon-winged Egyptian image of Horus the Sun-god above the doors. It is said that the inspiration for this design came to

179: The old 'centre' of Leeds, with the statue of various naked ladies around the central statue of the Black Prince.

Ignatius from his brother Joseph, who was a well-known Egyptologist, but the fact is that there was a great interest in Egyptian archaeology at the time. As if the merging of Verona, Florence and Egypt were not enough to weave mythology around a single building, it is recorded that during the last century the flat roof of the Tower Works was covered in earth and sown with grass to accommodate large flocks of grazing sheep! In Headingley, the battlemented towers flanking an arched entrance are the old Bear Pits, sometimes passed off as ancient bear-baiting centres, but in fact relics from the old zoo, in which bears were kept purely for viewing.

180: Holy Island, or Lindisfarne, is overlooked by the 15th-century castle on the pyramid of rock.

LINDISFARNE, Northumberland C1

On the pyramid of volcanic rock of Lindisfarne, or Holy Island, stands a castle (figure 180) built about 1490 and eventually restored by the Victorian architect Sir Edwin Lutyens as a private house. Lutyens used some of the stones from the ancient monastery in this rebuilding.

LITTLE MORETON HALL, Cheshire C6

This hall (figure 182) is without doubt the most lovely of all Tudor buildings. Inside there is a secret room, hidden behind a chimney breast. This is sometimes said to be a 'blind', for it is not too hard to locate, while there is another, far more securely hidden secret cell below the surface of the moat, at the end of a difficult and tortuous passageway.

LITTLE SALKELD, Cumbria B3

Near this village is the ancient stone circle dominated by a vast outlier called Long Meg (figure 181). The circle of 65 stones was probably constructed about 2,500 years ago, and is now associated with many witchcraft legends, such as how Long Meg and her daughters, once living witches, were petrified and stuck on this headland for all time.

181 (right): Long Meg and her daughters, a stone circle and massive outlier (Long Meg) near Little Salkeld, was probably constructed c.2,500 B.C.
182 (facing page): The beautiful Little Moreton Hall in Cheshire.

Below: An heraldic bull on the gates of a house at Great Salkeld.

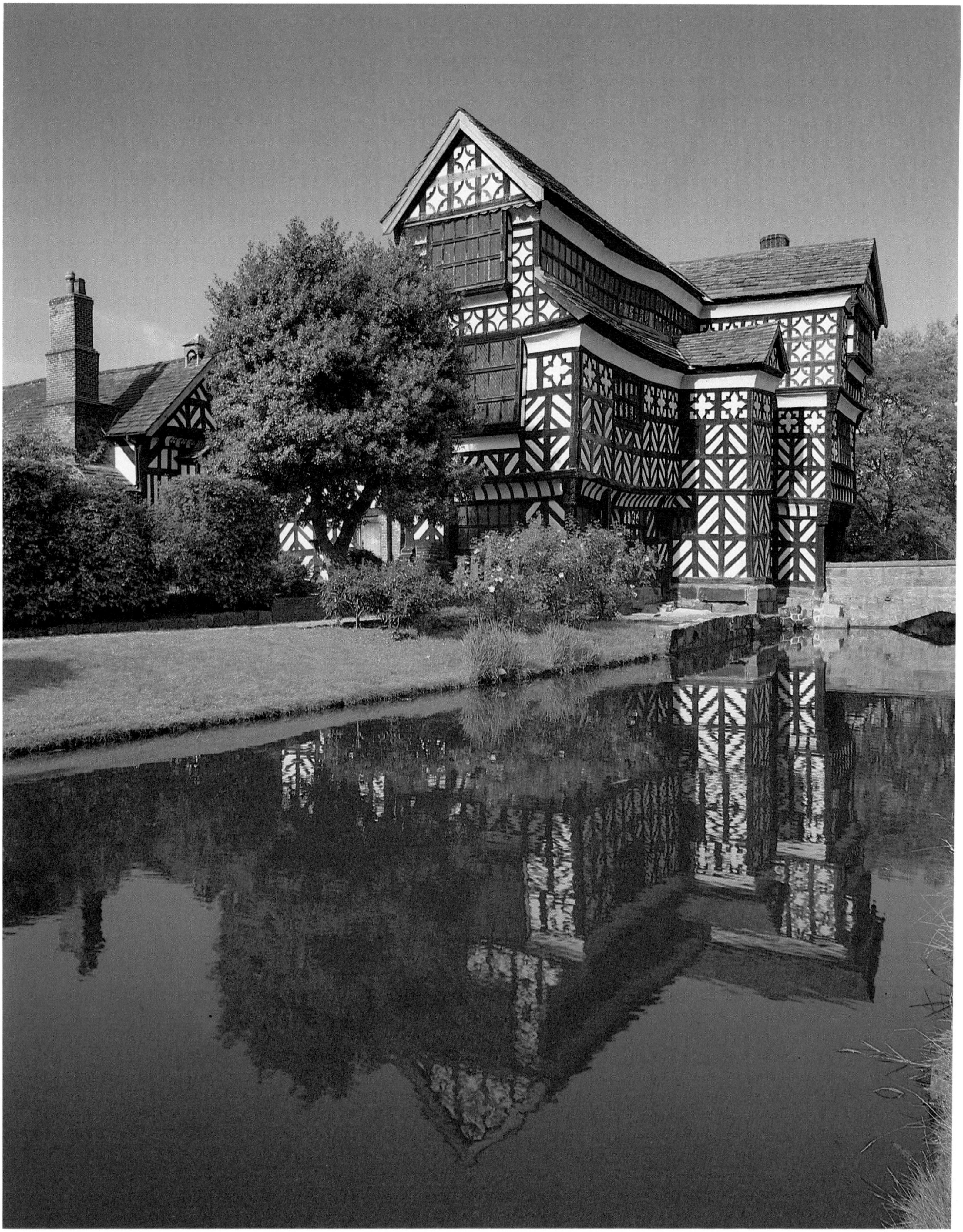

LONGRIDGE, Lancashire B5

In Halfpenny Lane, Longridge, is a house with the lintel inscription dated 1616, above which is the rib bone of what is said to be a 'giant cow'. The story goes that there was a drought in the village, and the Old Dun Cow provided milk for everyone, long after the wells had gone dry. Then, one day, the villagers found a local witch milking the cow into a sieve, allowing the milk to run dry and exhausting the cow to such an extent that it died. The locals preserved the rib as a memento of the cow which saved them all from starvation and dehydration. For another 'Dun Cow' story, see WARWICK.

LOWTHER CASTLE, Cumbria B3

Lowther is now one of the most impressive castle ruins in the north of England (figure 183), but at one time it was an important baronial hall which saw the entertainment of such guests as Mary Queen of Scots. It is linked with the early life of the poet William Wordsworth, whose father and grandfather worked for the former owners, the Earls of Lonsdale.

183: Lowther Castle, one of the great baronial halls of England. Home of the Earls of Lonsdale until 1936, it is now a splendid ruin.

MACCLESFIELD, Cheshire C6

A surprising gem of a museum is the West Park Museum in Prestbury Road, one of the few small purpose-built museums in Britain. The red-brick building was constructed on the orders of the Brocklehurst family (who were local silk-manufacturers) and opened in October, 1898. The exhibits include many Greek and Egyptian objects collected by Miss Marianne Brocklehurst during her travels abroad, and presented to the museum by her niece, but perhaps the most extraordinary thing in the museum is the high frieze which dominates the interior. This is a cast of the external frieze of the Parthenon of Athens, and includes the so-called Elgin Marbles, now lodged in the British Museum. The original frieze, from which the Macclesfield casts were taken, was carved round about 432 BC to decorate the temple built to serve the cult of Athena Parthenos (from which goddess the Athenian building took its name). The frieze is 160 metres long and one metre high, and depicts the processional of horsemen, charioteers and people who approach the heroes and gods of the ancient Greek world. The order of the Macclesfield frieze does not correspond to that of the original Parthenon frieze, but a useful pamphlet available in the museum sets out the main differences.

Those interested in strange memorials are advised to visit the parish church of St Michael and All Angels to see the Legh Pardon Brass. This is a memorial brass dated 1506 which shows Roger Legh with his children, kneeling below a vision of Pope Gregory. The extensive inscription indicates that Legh and his family gained in

184 (*left*): Malham Cove, North Yorkshire, in the snow.

recognition for their good works a pardon to last 26,000 years and 26 months — probably the most extraordinary indulgence offered.

MALHAM COVE, North Yorkshire C4

This vast amphitheatre of limestone is 240 feet high at its steepest part (figure 184), and is linked with many legends, including that of the seventeenth-century witch who is reputed to have leapt down it, to be carried to safety by her broomstick.

MALKIN TOWER, Lancashire C5

The witches of Pendle, who were condemned and hanged in 1612 (see LANCASTER — THE CASTLE), were said to have met in 'Malkin Tower', where the ringleader, the old blind and lame crone Demdike, is supposed to have lived. However, in modern times no-one is quite certain where Malkin Tower was situated, with the result that there are several claims to this dubious fame. Some say that it was to the east of Blacko Tower, near to the modern Malkin Tower Farm. Perhaps more reasonable, however, is the site on Pendle itself, near to the place where Saddler's Farm is now found. Whatever the site, it has attained a notoriety as the centre of the Pendle witchcraft, and figured in the Lancaster trials as the place where the witches met with the devil and planned their gruesome murders. Chattox herself probably lived in Higham, on land owned by the Nutters of Greenhead (a member of whom also perished in the witchcraft scourge of 1612), near to a river-bank from which she took the clay for making witch-poppets in order to bring about the death of her enemies by means of black magic. In his booklet on the Pendle Witches, Richard Catlow says that near the footbridge at the bottom of Ightenhill Lane is a ruined building, locally regarded as one of the 'witches cottages'.

MIDDLEWICH, Cheshire B6

On the carved screen of the Venables chapel in Middlewich church is a carving of a dragon with a baby in its jaws. This is the crest of the Venables family, and the curious diet is explained by a medieval legend that in ancient times a huge dragon used to dwell in the rural area around Moston (now swallowed up in the urban spread of Manchester), having made its watery nest in a local pool and laying waste the area around. The 'St George' of Moston turned out to be Thomas Venables, who undertook to kill the monster and thus deliver the villagers from their terror. When he saw the dragon, it was just about to eat a child, so he shot an arrow into its eye, which made it drop its meal, and then killed it with his broadsword.

185: On the porch of the parish church of Middlewich is this stone angel holding the Arma Christi, the instruments of Christ's Passion.

186: The 'Lamb Inn' at Newchurch, with silhouettes of witches on the facade.

NEWCASTLE UPON TYNE, Tyne and Wear C2

In former times it was believed that witches and warlocks had on a part of their body an area which was insensitive to pain and would not bleed. A whole profession of 'witch-prickers' grew up around this belief, and men (as well as women) toured the country offering themselves as able to identify witches in this way. A famous seventeenth-century case of witch-pricking was recorded in the Town Hall of Newcastle upon Tyne. In 1649, the inhabitants of this city were so worried by the witchcraft scare that they hired a Scottish 'expert' in witch-pricking to work for them, the arrangement being that he would be paid 20 shillings for each witch he discovered. After some initial advertising of the witch purge, 30 women were brought to the Town Hall and stripped by the witch-pricker, who then stuck pins into their bodies. Most of them were found to be guilty. One attractive woman was made to stand with her clothes over her head, with her naked body in full sight of everyone, while the man ran a pin into her thigh. Suddenly he let her coats fall, and then demanded whether she had any pain. She must have replied in the negative, for he put his hand up her dress and pulled out the pin, pronouncing her guilty as a 'child of the Devil', and turning his attention to those other women whom he might make guilty in such a way. A Lieutenant Colonel Hobson, who was presiding over this bizarre business, had observed that the very shame of this act had made the woman's blood contract into one part of her body, and conjectured that this was why she did not feel the pain. He therefore instructed that the woman be called again and have her clothes pulled up only to her thigh, requiring the Scotsman to push the pin into the same place. When he did this, the blood gushed out, and she was then pronounced free of witchcraft and 'not a child of the Devil'. The confidence trickster who did this pricking, and who caused the death of at least 220 women in such a way, was eventually hanged himself.

NEWCHURCH-IN-PENDLE, Lancs C5

On the front wall of the 'Lamb Inn' at Newchurch are two witch-silhouettes (figure 186), reminders of the sixteenth century, when the village and the surrounding area was infamous for its many witches. On the wall of the church near to the pub is a specially designed eye, constructed in stone and slate, intended to act as a deterrent against the evil eye of witches.

187 (right): The top of Norber Moor, looking over to the peak of Pen-y-ghent. The top of Norber is covered in flint and limestone formations.
188 (facing, top): An erratic buolder standing on its socles of limestone on Norber Moor.

NORBER MOOR, West Yorkshire B4

The large number of boulders (figure 187) which appear to have been lifted by giant hands and placed delicately on 'legs' or plinths of white limestone are called 'erratics'. They were carried to these limestone beds by glacial action thousands of years ago, and the limestone beneath has eroded to leave the harder millstone isolated, as though by some magical means.

OTLEY, West Yorkshire C5

In the churchyard at Otley is a remarkable memorial in the form of a crenellated bridge which in fact, is a miniature replica of the northern entrance to the Bramhope railway tunnel. The memorial was erected to commemorate the names of the 20 or so men who died while working on the construction of the tunnel, which (in its day) was the third longest in Britain, being over two miles in length, and dug out by hand. The castellated tower was not merely decorative, as it was used originally to house railway employees and later became a store room.

PENDLE, Lancashire C5

Pendle Hill (figure 189) is infamous as the haunt of the so-called Pendle Witches, who were tried and hanged in the early seventeenth century. Although the hill has gained much notoriety from witchcraft history, the witches themselves appear to have lived in surrounding villages, and were said to have met to practise their supposed evil-working in the Forest of Pendle, to the south of the hill.

189: Pendle Hill, meeting place of the supposed Pendle Witches in the early 17th century.

PENRITH, Cumbria B3

The so-called 'Giant's Grave' in the parish churchyard at Penrith consists of an arrangement of four hog-back gravestones flanked at each end by two much-weathered cross-shafts (figure 190), the individual stones of which are around 1,000 years old. There are many legends about the 'giant' who is buried beneath this curious grave, but the most important claim is that it covers the body of the giant 'Owen the Caesar' whom some trace to the mythological Ewen Caesarius, linked with Arthurian legends which had a shadowy beginning in historical personages. (See COLCHESTER)

RAINHILL, Merseyside B5

In the public trials of locomotives which took place here in 1829 — trials intended to decide which engines should be used to pull the first regular passenger railway trains between Liverpool and Manchester — Stephenson's *Rocket* won. However, during the trials *Rocket* knocked down the Member of Parliament for Liverpool, William Huskisson, and killed him. He was the first victim of the new-fangled railway system. A plaque marks the place where he fell.

190: The churchyard of St Andrew's, Penrith, contains the so-called 'Giant's Cave'.

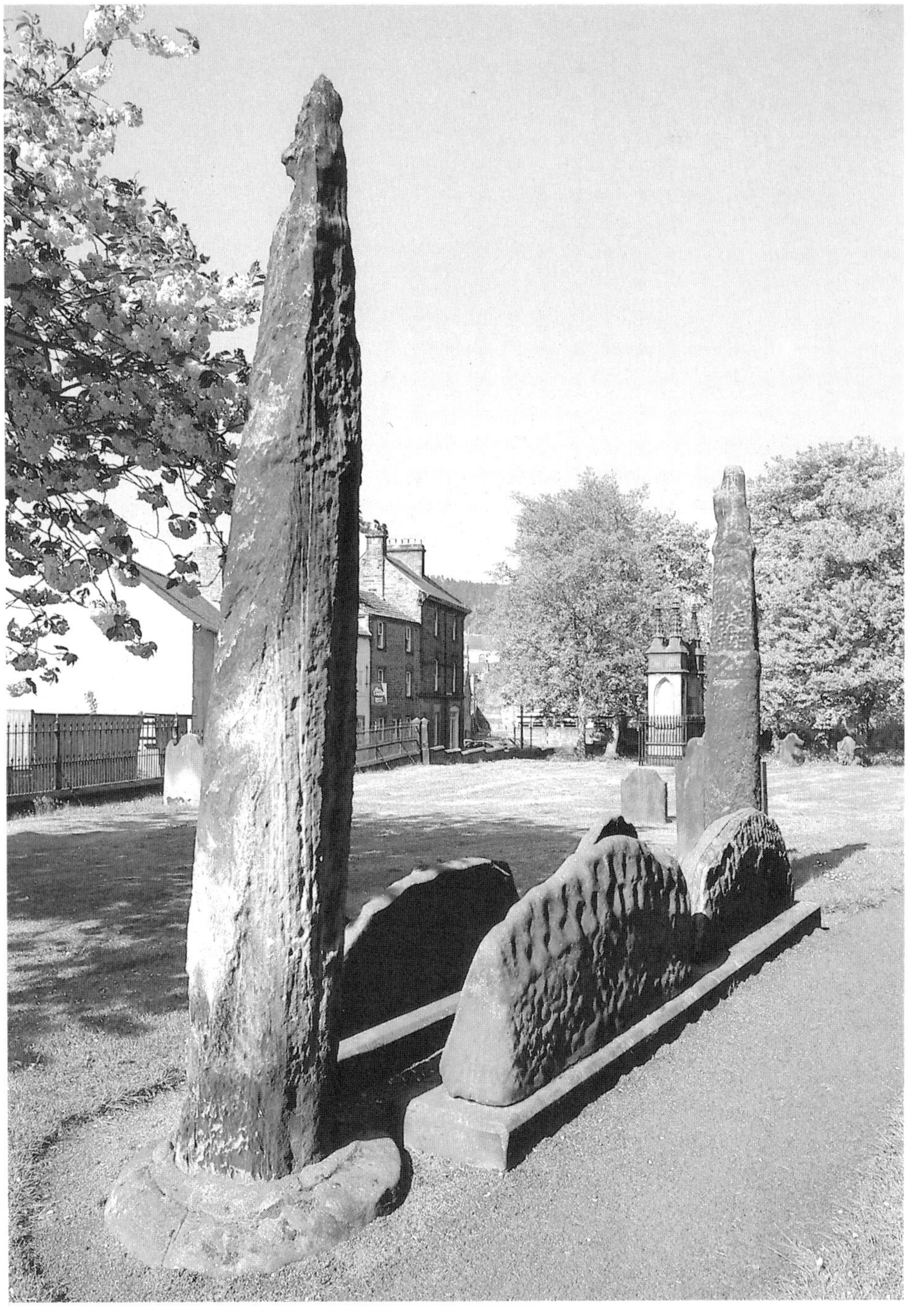

RIPON, North Yorkshire C4

Ripon Fair in August is held in honour of its patron saint, St Wilfrid (once the Bishop of York), who is simulated by a rider dressed in the garb of the holy man and mounted upon a white horse, leading a procession (including the city band) around the town. The distinctive obelisk in the central market square of Ripon is the scene of a nightly horn-blowing called 'Setting the Watch'. The City Hornblower gives one substantial blast at each corner of the Obelisk while the Curfew Bell is rung from the Minster. The original ancient Charter Horn, said to date from AD 886, is still preserved, but a modern one (scarcely more than a hundred years old!) is nowadays used for the ritual.

ROMBALDS MOOR, West Yorkshire C5

On the edge of Rombalds Moor, above Addingham, are two curiously-shaped stones, naturally eroded to a point where their tops look like pancakes (figure 191). The tops of these stones were carved in prehistoric times with incisions, cup-and-ring marks, and small wells, designed to collect pure rain water or even dew. The area of exposed rocks around these strange formations is charged with a powerful energy, and we must take it that at one time it was a centre for rituals, the purposes of which are now forgotten.

RUDSTON, Humberside E4

In the graveyard of All Saints Church in Rudston is 'the Monolith', the largest free-standing prehistoric monument still existing in this country. It is a roughly-hewn block of gritstone, said to have been carried from a source some 10 miles distant. As with all prehistoric monuments, the reason why it was erected remains a mystery, yet a tremendous effort went into its siting. While the present height is just under 26 feet above the ground, it was almost certainly another two feet higher in ancient times (part of the top has been lost due to weathering), and it was shown by Sir William Strickland in the eighteenth century that there is almost as much buried underground as is visible. It is approximately six feet at the widest point, and almost three feet thick. The name of the village is a corruption of the Old English words 'rood' and 'stane', which mean 'cross stone', and we must assume that in the early days of Christianity (even before a church had been built alongside the stone), the priests erected a wooden cross on top of the prehistoric monolith to 'Christianize' it. Archaeological surveys have shown that the area was of great ritualistic and magical importance in ancient times — even the line of the modern main street follows one of the ancient trackways (later adapted by the Romans for their road-building), while a large number of Neolithic and Bronze-Age burial mounds were once located in the area, as was the prehistoric Argam Dikes, which ran from near Reighton into Rudston village. We must assume that the monolith was the centre of this magical or ritualistic site.

191: One of the two doubler stones on Rombald's Moor, above Addingham. The stones were incised in prehistoric times with unexplained drawings.

192: The monolith in Rudston churchyard stands over 25 feet high and is the tallest standing stone in Britain. It is said to be buried to the same depth as its height.

The Romans who built their villas in Rudston left behind a number of mosaics which are now housed in the Hull Museum, one of the most lovely being that of a semi-naked Venus. Buried in the churchyard is the body of the authoress Winifred Holtby, who was born in the village and spent her childhood in the area. She attained fame with her books *The Land of Green Ginger* and the prize-winning *South Riding*. She died at the early age of 37, in 1935; on the open book which adorns her grave is the lapidary inscription, 'God give me work till my life shall end, And life till my work is done.'

SANDBACH, Cheshire B6

The remains of two Saxon crosses in the market-place in Sandbach (figure 193) are among the most interesting of such remains in Britain. The taller is about 17 feet high. They were both broken up by the Puritans in the early seventeenth century, and the parts used in various buildings. They were reassembled and erected just over 200 years later. Some images are said to show the conversion to Christianity (in AD 653) of Peada of Mercia.

CROWN
obinson's
THE CROWN
HOT and COLD
BAR SNACKS
11 30 a.m. – 2 30 p.m.
MORNING COFFEE
CHILDREN WELCOME

193 (facing page): The remains of two Saxon crosses in Sandbach market place.

194: The pyramid tomb of Piazzi Smyth in St John's churchyard, Sharow.

SHAROW, North Yorkshire C4

The pyramid tomb of Piazzi Smyth in St John's churchyard, Sharow, reminds one of Smyth's intense interest in pyramidology and Egypt in general. The tomb is a miniature of the Great Pyramid at Gizeh, and the long inscription was written by his wife.

SKELBROOKE, South Yorkshire D5

The general drift of research has suggested that Robin Hood was a real personage who came originally from the Wakefield district of Yorkshire, lived in the reign of Edward II, and even spent some time in the King's service at court. These simple historical propositions have, of course, been overlaid by a large number of legends which, although probably older than the reign of Edward II, and probably gathered from different regions, have none the less been grafted on to the story of a yeoman who turned outlaw, but was more than generous with his dubious earnings. In some of the poetical accounts he describes himself as 'Robin Hood of Barnsdale', which is indeed just north of Robin Hood's Well near Skelbrooke. For further information on Robin Hood, see BARNSDALE, FOUNTAINS ABBEY, HATHERSAGE, KIRKLEES, LOXLEY and NOTTINGHAM.

SMEARSETT, West Yorkshire B4

The 'Celtic' wall above Smearsett (title page) may be the substantial remains of a prehistoric fortification. There are the usual local legends about the wall being built by giants, reinforced by stories about how the giants placed the erratic boulders on nearby NORBER MOOR.

SPROTBROUGH, South Yorkshire D5

In the ancient church of St Mary in Sprotbrough is a strangely-carved stone seat, believed by many to have been a frithstool, which offered criminals a period of safety from legal persecution. The carvings include a sort of bust of a bearded man in the strange posture of a caryatid (figure 198), and what may be a demon with a spear to his left. The style would indicate that it was made in the fourteenth century, but it has been suggested that the carving is a re-working of a much older piece.

The church contains very many interesting puzzles and images. The clock above the organ is permanently fixed at five minutes past one, and some say that this marks the time when the donor, Sir Godfrey Copley of Sprotbrough Hall, died in 1709. On the pulpit door are three strange carvings, two of drinking vessels and one of what appears to be a pack of cards with the six of diamonds face up. This last raised carving may in fact be a book, perhaps even the bible, and the two drinking vessels may be a reference to the Eucharist, but the closeness of the 'book' to playing cards and the resemblance of the drinking vessels to a beer-mug and a dice-jar have led to one or two stories circulating about this door. The bench-ends of the nave seating are probably Elizabethan, and include some interesting profile busts of men, along with a curious shield device with the severed head of a dragon (or perhaps a serpent). Most interesting, however, are the adjacent bench-ends, one of which portrays a couple facing each other, the second of which portrays a couple looking away from each other. The myth-makers see the first as a symbol of a couple prior to marriage, the second as a symbol of that couple after marriage.

In the chancel stalls is a misericord which depicts a demon with a three-pronged hook; he has the lower parts of a goat and the upper parts of a monstrous human, with horns. There are two fine effigies in the St Thomas Chapel, the knight in chain mail being William Fitzwilliam, who was executed for his part in the Baron's Revolt at Boroughbridge in 1322. In the chancel floor there are some excellent brasses to a later William Fitzwilliam (died 1474) and his wife.

195 (facing, far left): Demon from a misericord (possibly 15th century) in Sprotbrough parish church.
196 (facing page): Bench-end with an heraldic device of the 16th century at Sprotbrough.

197: Bench-end with two human forms, in Sprotbrough parish church.

198: The stone seat (probably 14th century) said to be a mercy-seat used by those claiming asylum from the law, in St Mary's church, Sprotbrough.

STANHOPE, Durham C3

The fossilized tree stump at Stanhope (figure 199) is now on display in the churchyard and is claimed to be over 250 million years old. It was discovered in a local quarry in 1964.

STOKESLEY, North Yorkshire D3

The 'Wise Man of Stokesley', whose real name was Wrightson, died in the last century, but his reputation as a seer and healer lived on for many decades after his death. He himself attributed his gift to the fact that he was the seventh son of a seventh daughter. Most of the stories about his insights reveal him to have a detailed knowledge of events which had taken place a considerable distance from him, as well as a knowledge of futurity. In some cases he would heal with an inexplicable magic power. One story tells how a young bull became so ill that it was too weak to stand, so ropes were slung beneath its body to keep it upright. Wrightson was summoned by the farmer and asked if there was any way to save the creature. The Wise Man asked to be left alone and climbed into the bull-pen. When, a few minutes later, the farmer returned to find out how he was getting on, he was amazed to find the bull cured and enjoying its food. On another occasion a farmer bought some cows at Northallerton fair and had them driven to Stokesley by a drover, who penned them in a nearby field for the night, intending to deliver them first thing in the morning. However, at daybreak he discovered that two of the cows were missing. The suspicious owner, thinking that the drover might have stolen them, decided to consult Wrightson on the matter. He and his friend called upon the Wise Man, having decided to say that they were looking for missing horses rather than cows (this being to test the wizard). When they reached Wrightson's cottage, and before they had time to speak, the Wise Man shouted out that if they couldn't tell the difference between cows and horses they shouldn't bother him with their questions. Eventually they persuaded him to tell them the whereabouts of the missing cows, and he said that they were in the stream, where they had been since the previous night. Sure enough, the two bodies were found over a mile downstream; they had almost certainly missed the bridge while crossing it in the dark.

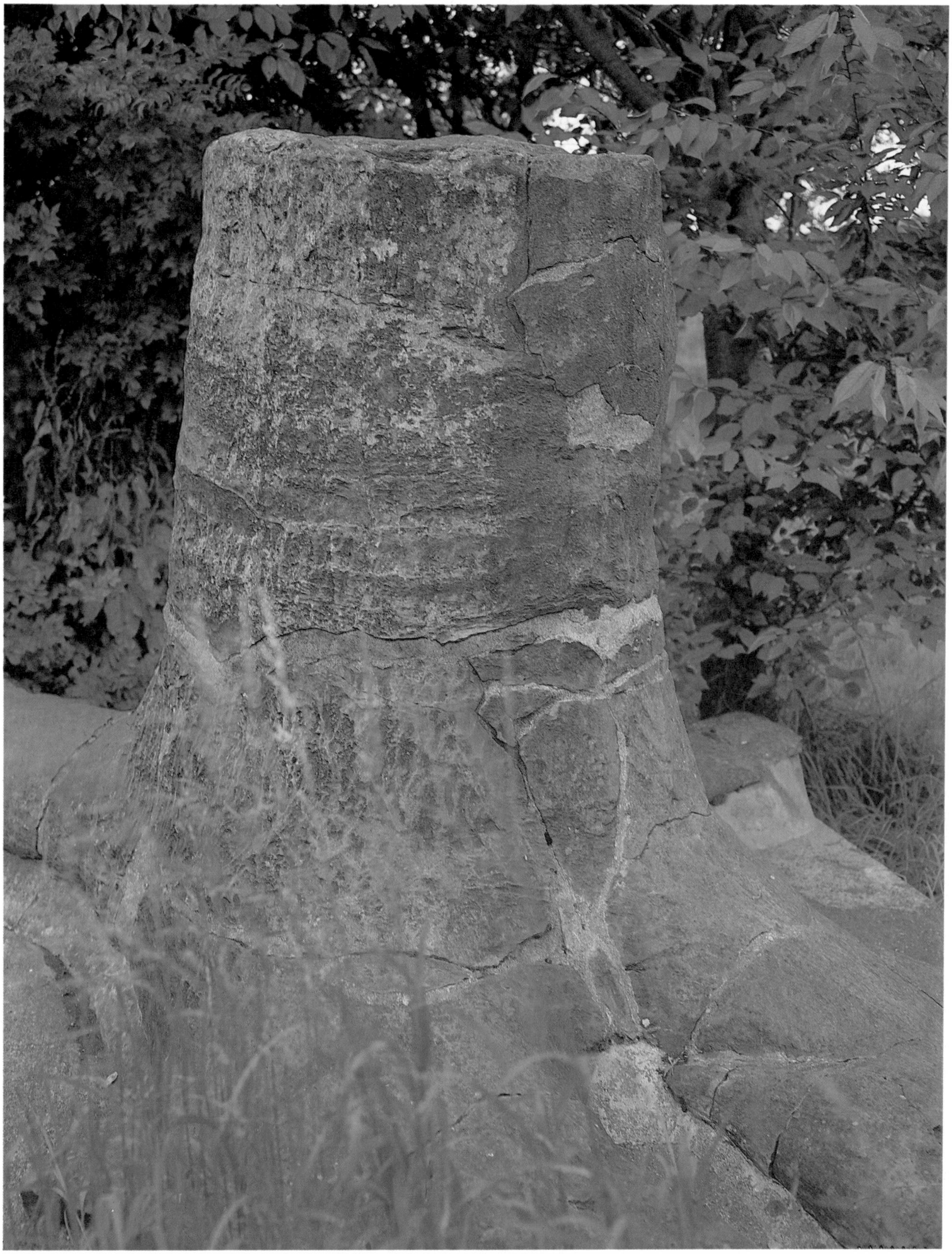

199: The fossilized tree stump which can be seen in the churchyard at Stanhope, Durham.

TEMPLE NEWSAM, West Yorkshire D5

200/201: Temple Newsam House, near Leeds. The site was originally owned by the Knights Templar, but the present building is the work of Thomas, Lord Darcy in 1521 and was modernized in the 18th century. The red brick maze in the courtyard is modern, but follows a traditional pattern.

As the name might suggest, Temple Newsam was once the site of an establishment owned by the Knights Templar. The manor of Newsam had been held by Anglo-Saxons from before the Conquest, but afterwards fell into the hands of the De Lacy family, one of whom (also the founder of Kirkstall Abbey in Leeds) made a gift of it to the Knights, who kept it until it was seized by Edward II after the Templars were disgraced by political chicanery. Records suggest that Temple Newsam was, and possibly still is, haunted, for frequent references are made to the ghosts of a lady in white, a lady in blue and a murderer.

It is said that the lady in white is Jane Dudley, who hanged herself when she learned of Lord Darnley's promise to marry Mary, Queen of Scots. The 'murderer ghost', who appears in the old-fashioned costume of his period, is said to be that of William Collinson who murdered his mistress Phoebe Gray in 1704. This man was eventually hanged for the deed in YORK.

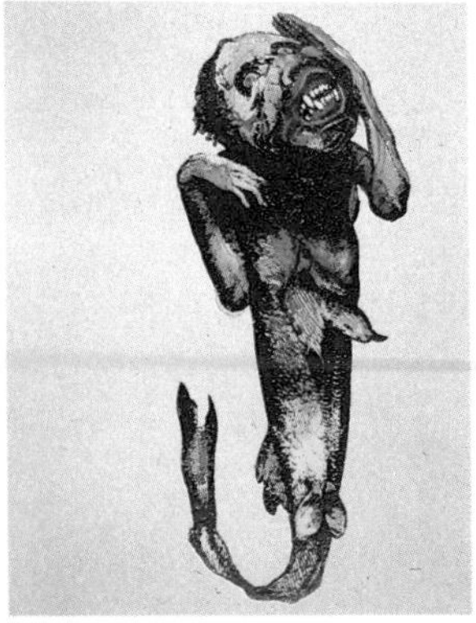

202: An illustration of Phineas T. Barnum's 'Feejee' mermaid, exhibited in the USA and England in the 19th century.
203 (right): The 'Nondescript' created by Charles Waterton, a wood engraving of the hoax fashioned from a howler monkey.

TODMORDEN, West Yorkshire C5

Henry Krabtree, curate of St Mary's at Todmorden, was an astrologer and unqualified doctor. He was the first of the local curates to keep a register of baptisms and burials in his church, and often added interesting astrological details to the entries. For example, in the entry for the birth of a son to James Taylor of Todmorden on 2 October, 1685, he reports that the child was born 'near sun setting and also near a full moon, which is a sure sign of a short life'. The astrological observation is far from true, yet Krabtree gained some fame with the publication of his almanack for that same year under the name 'Merlinus Rusticus'. He later acquired some notoriety in connexion with his attempted cure of a youth called Richard Dugdale, who lived near Whalley and was subject to epileptic fits. His first cure was successful, but a later attack was more severe, and some of the local religious folk announced that Richard was a demoniac in the grip of Satan — suggesting indeed that Henry Krabtree was really a wizard.

WAKEFIELD, West Yorkshire C5

In Wakefield City Museum is one of the most outlandish collections of the taxidermist's art in Britain, worked by the capable hands of the eccentric Charles Waterton of WALTON. Among the strange articles on display is the 'Nondescript' (figure 203), which Waterton created from the head of a howler monkey to fool his contemporaries

204: The 14th-century chantry on the bridge over the Calder at Wakefield has had a chequered history. Once used as a secondhand clothes shop, it has been restored in modern times and is now once again used as a church.

205: Stone griffin heads, once on the gates of the City of London, now decorate the lawn of Wallington House.

and to play a practical joke on a Customs officer, who charged Waterton duty on the specimens he brought back to Liverpool from his travels in 1820 — for some say that the Nondescript was an unsubtle portrait of the unfortunate Customs man. Strangest of all in the display cases of the Museum is the taxidermy model of 'John Bull and the National Debt', a composite creature weighed down by heavy bags representing a debt of £800,000,000, topped by the shell of a tortoise on which sits a 'dragon' made up from various parts of different lizards. This very strange 'Noctifer' reminds one of the demonic Lilith, who is said to be an owl-like night creature, and was described by Waterton as 'the Spirit of the Dark Ages, unknown in England before the Reformation'. This Noctifer reminds us that Waterton came from a long line of staunch Catholics, who had for centuries been persecuted for their religion.

WALLINGTON, Northumberland C2

Wallington Hall is said to be haunted, and there is even a 'ghost room', according to the records of the Victorian author Augustus Hare, who stayed at Wallington in 1862. Some believe that the house is haunted by a headless lady. The stone griffin heads on the huge lawn of the house (figure 205) were brought to the north of England as ship's ballast, after they had been dismantled from one of the old gates of the City of London.

WALLSEND, Tyne and Wear C2

It was the Roman Emperor Hadrian who commanded that a huge wall be built, stretching as a defensive line between Wallsend and Carlisle, the finest surviving section of which is to be found at Housesteads. When it was finished, he ordered his mint to strike coins which carried the image of a woman wearing a helmet and carrying an oval shield and a spear. Beneath the image was struck the word 'Britannia', which refers to the name of the Province (the larger part of what we now call Britain). The woman was not herself 'Britannia' but was intended to represent the Roman Goddess, the 'Roman State' as a personification, perhaps involved with the symbolism of the State keeping a 'watch on the wall', which marks the northernmost part of the Roman world. One wonders to what extent this design influenced the choice of the armed female figure who was later to appear on modern coinage under the name of 'Britannia', the first of which appears to be that struck on copper coinage in the reign of Charles II, in 1665. It is said that the model for this was Frances Stewart, who was later created Duchess of Richmond.

In Roman times, Wallsend was called Segedunum, and something of its Roman connexion is still preserved in the town's coat of arms, which shows the Roman Eagle with its wings outstretched, perching astride a wall, which is meant to represent the Roman wall.

WALTON, West Yorkshire D5

The eccentric Charles Waterton was born in the beautifully situated island-home of Walton Hall (figure 206) on 3 June, 1782. Waterton became one of the most extraordinary travellers and taxidermists of the nineteenth century, travelling through South American forests with only a handful of natives, usually bare-footed, and always prepared to capture his specimens alive by the most unconventional methods. His most daring capture was of a giant cayman, which was hooked rather like a fish and then ridden into the bank by Waterton as though it were an aquatic horse. In Stonyhurst College, where Waterton was a pupil, there is an oil painting by Captain E. Jones which shows Waterton riding the back of the cayman in a forest populated by the exotic birds which he later captured and stuffed. In some cases, Waterton would allow snakes to wrap themselves around his body and then throttle them to death, rather than spoil their skins by shooting them. On one famous occasion he came across a young Coulacanara snake (a boa constrictor) while travelling in Guyana in 1820: 'I let him come, hissing and open-mouthed, within two feet of my face, and then, with all the force I was master of, I drove my fist, shielded by my hat, full in his jaws. He was stunned and confounded by the blow and ere he could recover himself, I had seized his throat with both hands...I then allowed him to coil himself round my body, and marched off with him as my lawful prize.' Walton Hall is now used as a hotel, but many of the original fittings are still *in situ* , including the many-faced sundial marked with the corresponding times in the different parts of the world where he travelled (figure 207). There is a curious pair of facial door knockers, the left-hand face smiling, because originally the knocker was fixed and therefore could not be used to bang with, and the right-hand face grimacing in pain, presumably because it could be used as a knocker. For an account of some of Waterton's exploits as an eccentric taxidermist, see WAKEFIELD, where many of his specimens are preserved in the City Museum.

206: Walton Hall, the bemoated former home of the eccentric Charles Waterton, is now a private hotel.

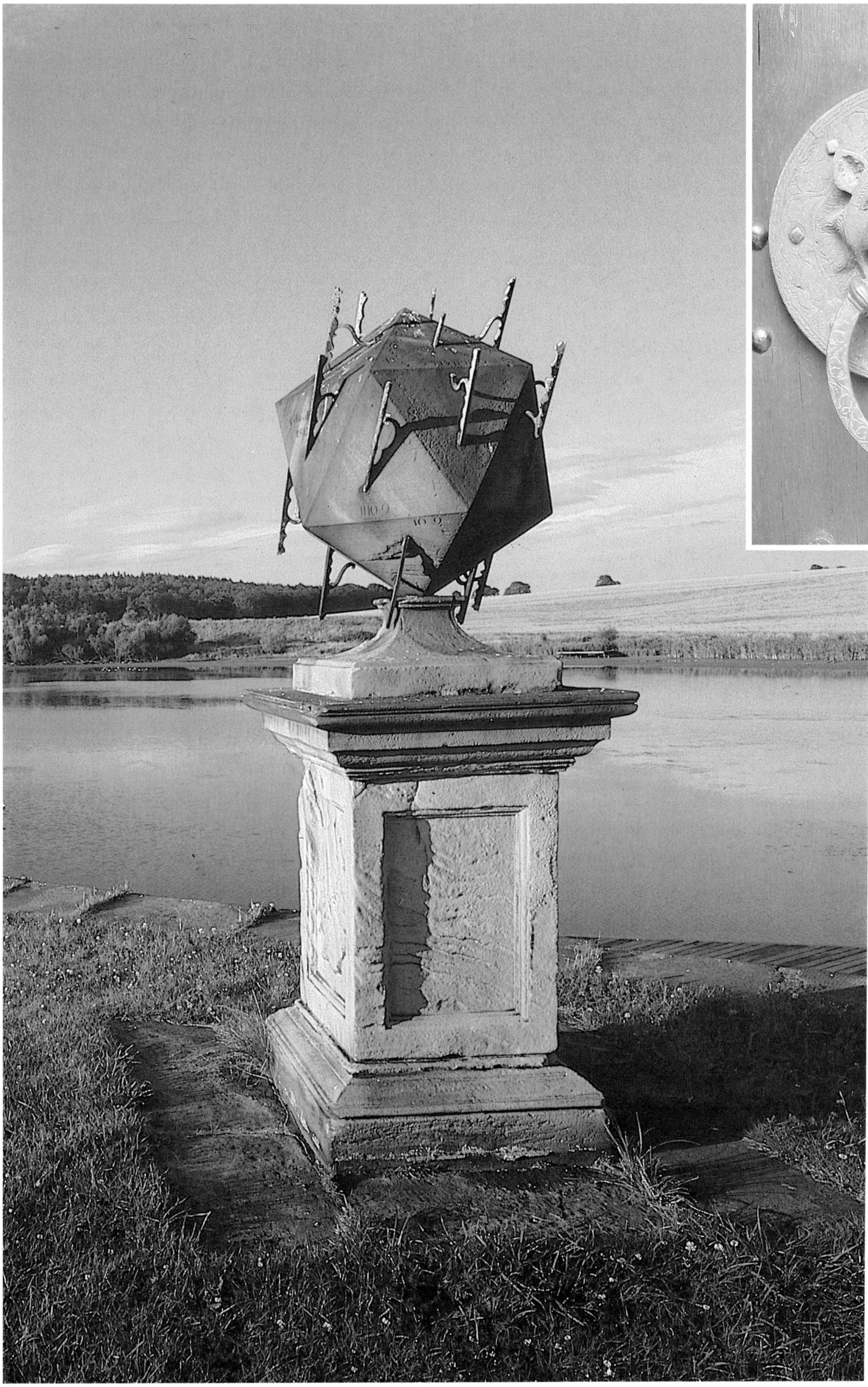

207 (left): The garden of Walton Hall contains this complex sundial, designed by Charles Waterton. The facets give a reading for time in different parts of the world.
208 (inset): Walton Hall is not the only building with a curious door knocker. This 13th-century sanctuary knocker with the head of a demon is on the south porch door of the parish church in Adel, West Yorkshire.

209: Wardley Hall, Greater Manchester, once known as the 'Skull House'.

WARDLEY HALL, Greater Manchester B5

For nearly 200 years Wardley Hall, Worsley, was known as the 'Skull House', and extraordinary tales circulated about the treasure it contained. This treasure was a skull which, according to popular belief, resisted all attempts to bury it. It is said that when it was thrown into the moat of the Hall it caused such storms that the water had to be drained so that the skull could be retrieved and placed in the Hall; if disrespect were shown the skull, then as one popular writer insisted, 'windows were blown in, cattle pined in the stall, and the things were bewitched'. In modern times, the Skull of Wardley Hall has been transformed by journalistic accounts into a screaming skull, which haunts those who live in this ancient house.

The skull is no haunted or haunting being. The story of how it happened to be kept in a staircase cupboard at Wardley Hall was told in 1910 by Dom Bede Camm, in his *Forgotten Shrines*. The skull was discovered in the Hall during the demolition of a room in 1745. Some time afterwards, a maidservant, thinking it was the head of an animal, threw it into the moat. It happened that on the same night there was a furious storm, and the owner of the Hall, 'having ascertained that the skull had been thrown into the moat, ascribed the storm to the indignity to which it had been subjected'. He therefore retrieved the skull and kept it in the house, without further trouble. From this single superficial belief arose many of the later stories told about the skull.

Even though the skull was preserved in the Hall ever afterwards, a popular tradition emerged which insisted that the skull was that of a rake called Roger Downes, who had lived in the Hall in the late seventeenth century and had been killed in a drunken brawl at Epsom Wells. Fortunately, it was possible to disprove this story. Roger Downes' coffin was opened in the family vault at Wigan and the skeleton was found to be complete, skull and all. Dom Bede Camm made a careful study of the Wardley skull and reproduced photographs of it in its glass case (figure 210), of the case itself in the stairway, and of Wardley Hall, and had no doubt whatsoever that the strange stories of a screaming, malicious skull were fabricated. Indeed, rather than being an evil skull, it appears to have belonged to an exceedingly good man. There may be no doubt that it had been preserved in the first place as a 'relic' of a brave Catholic priest, Father Ambrose Barlow, who was martyred for his faith in LANCASTER in 1641, by being hanged, dismembered, disembowelled, quartered and boiled in tar.

WENTWORTH WOODHOUSE, South Yorkshire D5

The folly called 'The Needle's Eye' at Wentworth Woodhouse was built by a gambler, whom many presume to have been the Marquis of Rockingham, who swore that he could drive his coach and horses at full speed through a needle's eye — and built the folly to prove it. The other follies in the park include a three-sided building, 'Hoober Strand', built to commemorate the Battle of Culloden, and the cigar-shaped Keppel's Column, about 150 feet high, started by the second Marquis of Rockingham and finished by Earl Fitzwilliam to record his indignation at the infamous court-martial of his friend Admiral Keppel. The fleet under Keppel's command had been soundly beaten at the Battle of Ushant in 1778, and in the court-hearing Keppel had pointed out that the ships in the fleet had been in a terrible state of disrepair due to the fact that Lord Sandwich had filched most of the money provided by the State for the upkeep of the Navy.

210: The skull is that of the Venerable Ambrose Barlow, martyred for his Catholic faith in 1641. It is still kept at Wardley Hall.

WHARNCLIFFE, South Yorkshire C5

The Dragon of Wantley is really the Dragon of Wharncliffe, which was slain by a local hero named More of More Hall, who knew that the one weak place in the dragon's armoury was its mouth. He dressed himself in spiked armour and then kicked the dragon in its mouth.

WHITBY, North Yorkshire D3

It is said that at a particular time in summer, between ten and eleven in the morning, sunbeams fall into the northern part of the choir of Whitby Abbey — falling in such a way that those who stand on the western side of the churchyard see, in one of the highest windows, the resemblance of a woman dressed in a shroud. This sun-made spectre is said to be a reappearance of the Abbess Hilda in her shroud. One local historian, George Franks, confirmed that he had in his possession a photograph taken by a Mr Stonehouse 'of the exterior portion of the east end of the chancel, in which, through the southern lancet of the top tier, the "ghost" is seen'. When the photograph is examined under a lens, this object gives the exact appearance of a human face peering out of the window.

211: Magical adder stone, a carved ammonite from the sea shore at Whitby.

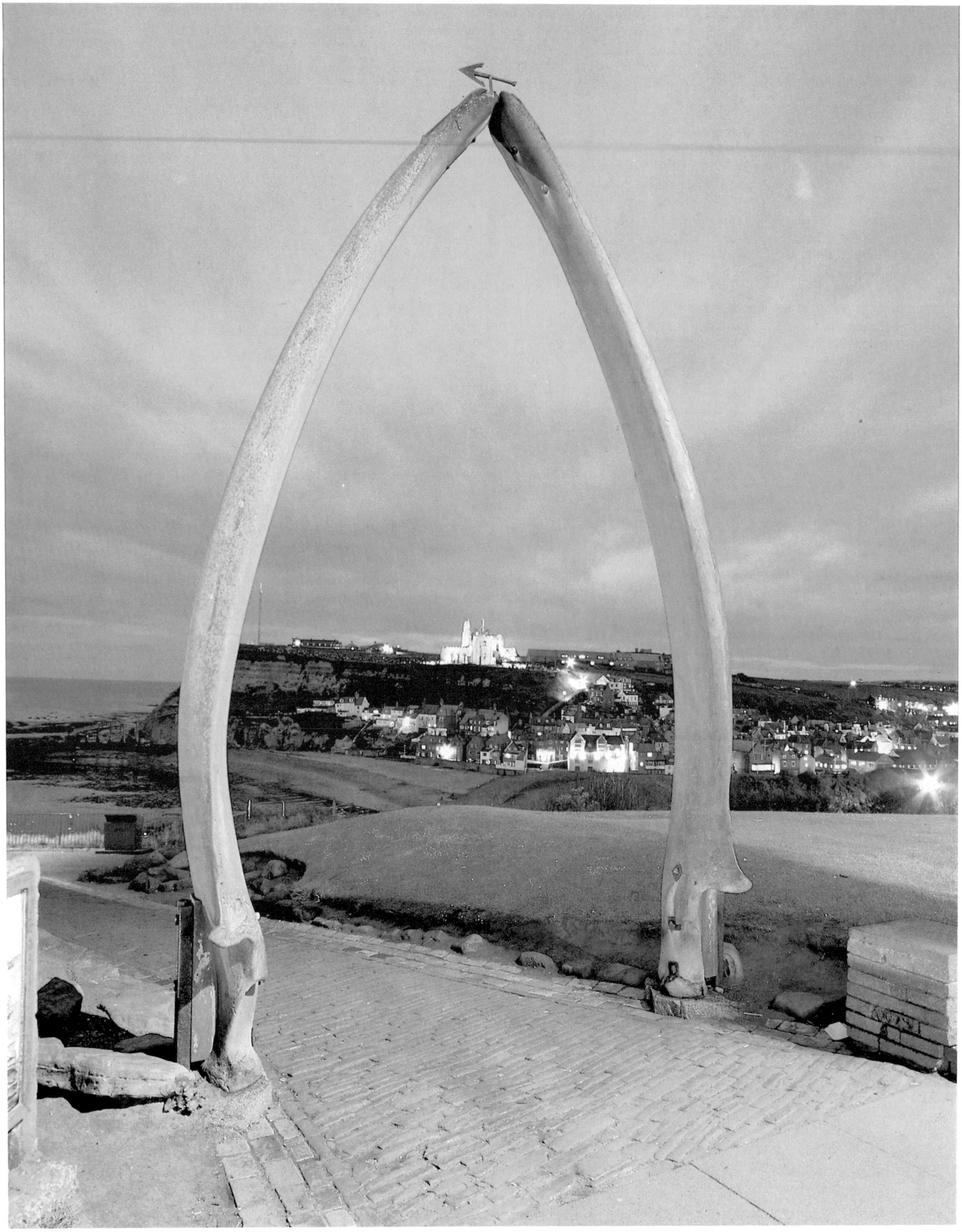

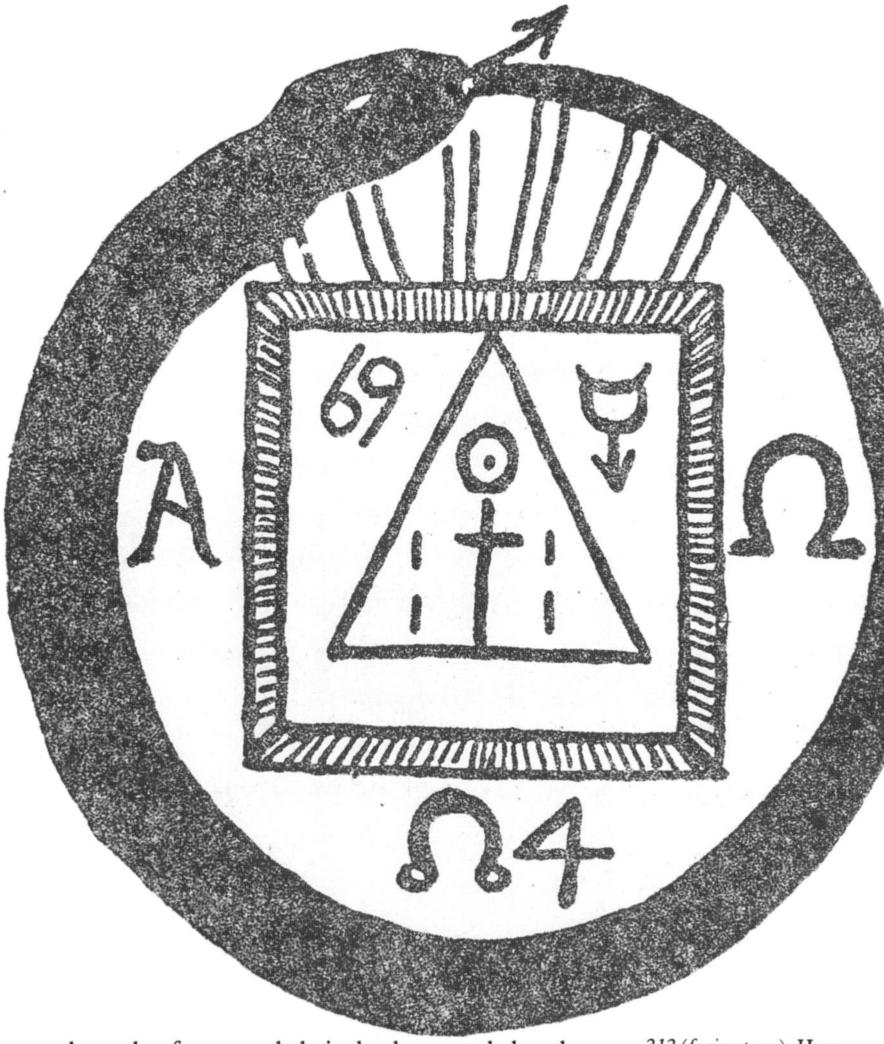

212 (facing page): Huge whalebones have been used to make a sort of triumphal arch on the northern promontory above Whitby harbour, from which point it is possible to see the remains of the castle and the Abbey of St Hilda.
213 (above): Magical design for an amulet intended for use against any sort of disease. From *Whitby Lore and Legend* by P.S. Jeffrey.

The God Thor may seem out of place in Whitby, yet he was a deity brought to Britain by the Vikings, and the fishermen of Whitby still carry as 'lucky charms' or 'lucky bones' what they call the 'Hammer of Thor', a T-shaped bone from a sheep's head. The local historian Percy Jeffrey also records that the fishermen are given to making a sort of sacrificial gesture prior to paying out their nets. They slice a piece of the cork floats attached to the nets and insert a coin, with the intention of informing the sea god that they are prepared to pay for the fish they catch. Jeffrey recorded in 1923 that there was hardly a 'pole cork' on the shores that had not a coin of some kind pushed into a slit made for it.

Whitby is said to have had its own family of legendary giants, made up of the giant himself, called Wade, his wife Bell, and their giant child and giant cow. The name Wade is near enough to the pagan god Woden, and reminds us that nearby there was a village called Thordisa, which stood at the head of the Eastrow Beck, while the name Bell is no remove at all from Bel, one of the most fearsome of the pagan gods. Many of the stones which litter the countryside around Whitby are said to have been thrown by these giants, but not all their activities were destructive. They are said to have built Pickering Castle and Mulgrave Castle at the same time, but having only one hammer they would throw it from one castle to the other, as it was needed. Wade's grave is said to be at Goldsborough, marked by two upright stones a hundred feet apart. 'Wade's Causey' is a Roman road which leads across the moors, and the ancient pagan tumuli which may still be seen from these old stones are said to have been placed there for the convenience of Bell when she went to milk her giant cow, which roamed loose upon the moors. It seems that for some years there was exhibited at Mulgrave Castle a whale's jawbone, which was said to be a rib from Bell's giant cow. It is not the only bone to pass as supposed bovine remains in Britain — see for example LONGRIDGE and WARWICK. The whale's jaw-bones mounted on the northern promontory at Whitby (figure 212) are a reminder of the whale fishing for which the town was famous in the nineteenth century. See also DANBY.

WINTER HILL, Lancashire B5

On Winter Hill, north of Bolton, there were once two fine examples of the many 'lads' which are found on hillsides. These were the 'Two Lads', cairns or stone piles which were originally placed in position as 'leads' or guide-posts. The same derivation, from 'lead' to 'lad', is found throughout the British countryside — the Lad o' Crow Hill (sometimes even 'Laddock Royal'), between Trawden and Haworth, was once such a 'lead-stone'. But men will make a myth from any upright stone, and a story was told how the upright, some five feet high, marked the place where a lost boy (a 'lad') perished in the Pennine snowdrifts. The 'Two Lads' were destroyed some years ago, yet before their demise they, too, left some interesting traditions. In one account, the two cairns were said to mark the burial place of two young princes of King Edgar's dynasty. Another legend stated that the top of Winter Hill was used by the spectral horseman in his career across Lancashire, some even dating his spectacular appearance to 'every twelfth return' of the feast of St Bartholomew.

Just as the 'leads' have proliferated legends of lost lads on the British landscape, so has the old word 'maen' (which meant nothing more than 'stone') turned out many legends of men and their deeds around the places where they are found. The most famous is the Coniston Old Man, whose 'Allt Maen' (High Stone), which appears to have been a shelter-chamber, gave its name to the entire peak. Is this the source of the belief that many of the ancient stones were nothing more than men, petrified for some unauthorized deed? The legends — and the names — attached to the ancient circles proliferate in their tales of men. Why, for example, is the isolated circle of Penmaenmawr so named?

WOLD NEWTON, Humberside E4

Just outside Wold Newton (on the Bridlington Road) is a large mound some 300 feet in circumference and 60 feet high, called Willy How. Like so many prehistoric mounds, it is said to be the habitation of fairies, and has several legends attached to it. One of the locals, after a drinking party, was passing Willy How late at night when, to his astonishment, he heard sounds of merriment within the mound. Drawn by the notion of yet more feasting, he approached the place and saw a door (previously hidden from human sight) in the side of the hill. Through the opening he saw a grand hall filled with magnificently dressed people engaged in a sumptuous meal. When he was observed by some of those inside, one of the canny fairies offered him a goblet of wine to drink. The rustic was conversant with fairy lore, however, and realized that if he drank, then he would lose consciousness and be transported for ever into the fairy realm. Wisely, he took the cup, poured out the wine, and galloped off on his horse, managing to reach his home in safety.

214: The cadaver from the double-effigy monument to Roger Rockley, dated 1535, in the church of St Mary, Worsbrough.

WORSBROUGH, South Yorkshire D5

In the church of St Mary at Worsbrough is a pair of the most impressive effigies in Yorkshire. The pair are set out on something resembling an oaken bunk-bed, with the upper image a representation of the knight Roger Rockley in full armour, looking upwards and in an attitude of prayer. The other image is that of his body a year or so after death, in the fulsome image of a grinning cadaver on the lower bunk (figure 214).

In the fourteenth-century vestry is a curious remnant of symbolism carved in stone, showing a centaur shooting with his bow and arrow at a bird. Both of these may be from the constellational symbolism which so influenced Norman art — but some authors suggest that the centaur was itself a symbol of Christ. The arms of the Worsbroughs consist of three centaurs, however, and these may be seen on the third shield from the bottom of the window in the Lady Chapel, the window designed to commemorate the ministry of Frederick Stock, who was vicar from 1893 to 1926. In descending order, the four arms represent York, Worsbrough, England and the Diocese of Sheffield. Those interested in medieval symbolism will be fascinated by the painted wooden image of Christ on the upper part of the chancel screen. This is probably of the early sixteenth century, and shows Christ emerging from a symbolic bank of clouds which in those times were used to denote the realm of the spiritual world beyond the physical earth. One wonders if it is an accident that the wrapping of the four 'tongues' forms the letter 'H', the first letter of the word Heaven?

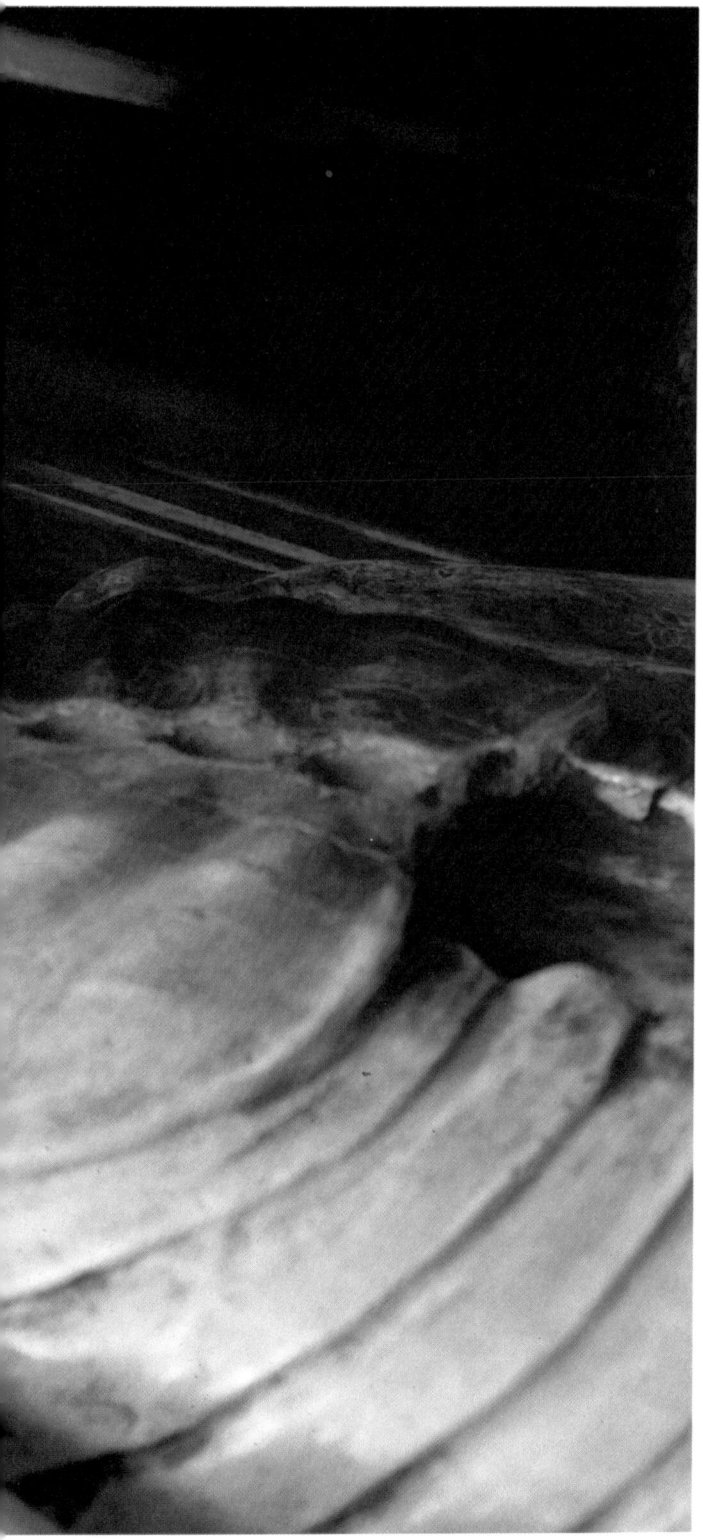

215: Unicorn from the Horn of Ulf (York). After Robert Brown, *The Unicorn – a Mythological Investigation*, 1881.

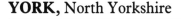

YORK, North Yorkshire D4

In the Minster at York are the 'Five Sisters' windows, each over 50 feet high, the story of which is woven into local legend. Tradition has it that the windows were given to the cathedral by five maiden sisters, who had each designed one in the embroidery at which they excelled. The story, true or false, was made famous when Charles Dickens introduced it into his novel *Nicholas Nickleby*, after he had visited Barnard Castle while researching the conditions of schools in the north of England. The almost abstract design of these windows is actually made up from the foliage of the herb bennet, often called the 'planta benedicta', linked with Saint Benedict. This plant was supposed in former times to have a magical efficacy and the power to repel demons, which is probably one reason why it is often found in church decorations, especially in stone relief work. The fact that it is worked into the north wall windows probably reflects the medieval belief that evil spirits could enter the church from the north side. The name 'Five Sisters' is not the original name, however, for it was originally called the 'Jewish Window', which would suggest that it might have been financed by loans from the Jewish community (then the great money-lenders) which suffered so much in later times at the hands of the locals.

This connexion between the Jewry of York and the building of the Minster is reflected in another set of windows, perhaps the most interesting in the entire building from a purely pictorial point of view. The glass images are in the Pilgrimage Window, which contains very many curious details from medieval art, especially from the realm of the bestiaries. In the first light is a fox reading from a lectern to a cock — a fairly typical image of the medieval view of priestcraft, and an interesting graphic sermon on the gullibility of people, especially as in another part of the window we see the fox with the goose safely in its mouth. Most of the remaining section of this window is taken up by the antics of monkeys, the theme being dominated by a monkey funeral in which four apes carry on their shoulders a bier, while a smaller one pushes up at the coffin. This curious detail would be unexplained were it not for an early literary tradition which was attached to the Life of the Virgin. In this tale it is told how the Apostles carrying the bier with Mary's coffin were attacked by a Jew, who tried to push the coffin over. The Virgin caused a miracle to happen, whereby the hands of the Jew remained fast to the coffin until he agreed to being converted to Christianity. The theme of monkeys persists, with monkeys in the guise of doctors, monkeys playing at falconing, and numerous other drolleries.

In the nineteenth century it was estimated that there is over half an acre of medieval glass in the Minster, 'at least twice as much as in any other English Cathedral', and 'unequalled by any other church in Christendom'.

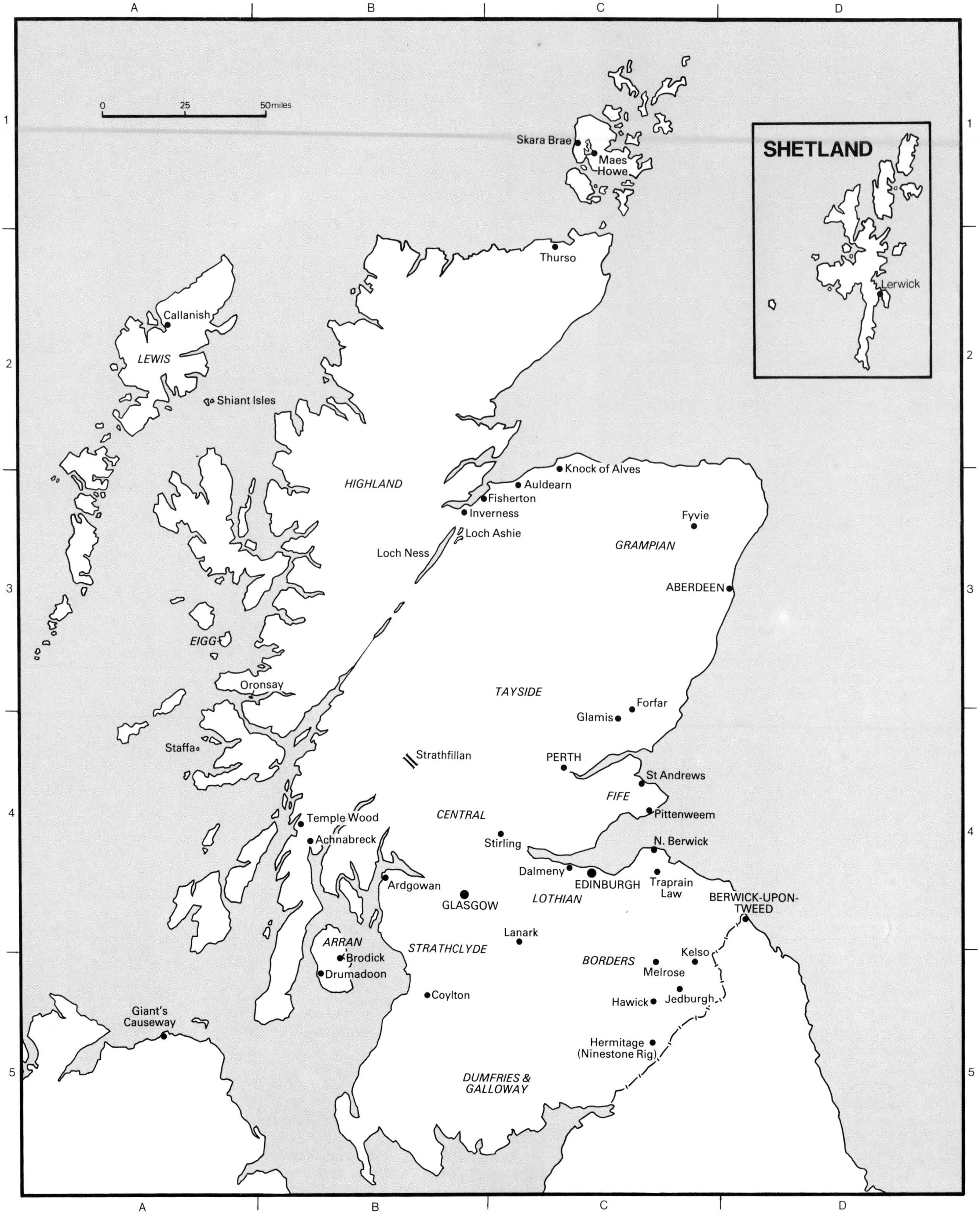
A
B
C
D
1
2
3
4
5
0
25
50miles
SHETLAND
Lerwick
Skara Brae
Maes Howe
Thurso
Callanish
LEWIS
Shiant Isles
HIGHLAND
Knock of Alves
Auldearn
Fisherton
Inverness
Loch Ashie
Loch Ness
Fyvie
GRAMPIAN
ABERDEEN
EIGG
Oronsay
TAYSIDE
Forfar
Glamis
Staffa
Strathfillan
PERTH
St Andrews
FIFE
Pittenweem
Temple Wood
CENTRAL
Achnabreck
Stirling
N. Berwick
Dalmeny
EDINBURGH
Traprain Law
Ardgowan
GLASGOW
LOTHIAN
BERWICK-UPON-TWEED
Lanark
ARRAN
Brodick
STRATHCLYDE
BORDERS
Kelso
Melrose
Drumadoon
Coylton
Hawick
Jedburgh
Giant's Causeway
Hermitage (Ninestone Rig)
DUMFRIES & GALLOWAY

Scotland

ABERDEEN, Grampian D3

In 1596 many of the witches of Aberdeen were accused of changing their forms in the likeness of cats and holding an orgy around the Fish Cross. One of the legal indictments against such a feline witch (one Bessie Thom) is more specific, for it claims that 'accompanied with ...devilish companions and faction, transformed in other likeness, some in hares, some in cats, and some in other similitudes...all danced about the Fish Cross'. In his fascinating study of cat lore, Oldfield Howey suggests that the Aberdeen witches merely wore costumes to represent the animals 'sacred to their cult', and quotes the dictum of Theodore, the seventh Archbishop of Canterbury, who objected to those who dress themselves as animals, 'putting on the heads of beasts' and the like, making such 'devilish' crimes punishable by three years penance.

ACHNABRECK, Strathclyde B4

Behind a farm at Achnabreck, on two groups of rock faces separated by enclosed areas just a little over 150 yards apart, are some of the most fascinating rock carvings in Britain, both surfaces being covered with a variety of ring-markings, grooves, straight lines, cup-and-rings and spiral forms (figure 216). As may be seen from the illustration, some of the concentrics are quite complex, with single lines reaching from the inner cup through the series of concentrics towards the outer circumference: one of the cups, which has seven concentrics, has a diameter of almost three feet — probably one of the largest in the British Isles. The purpose of these prehistoric markings is not known; suggestions include the notion that they are primitive calendars, sign-posts to religious centres or stone circles, maps of villages, genealogical trees, ancient forms of writing and so on, but perhaps the most frequently held view is that expressed by James Young Simpson, who wrote, 'these circles are similar to those used in astronomical plates for elucidating the revolution of the planets round the sun'. The most far-reaching interpretations have been offered by Ludovic MacLellan Mann in his *Archaic Sculpturings*, for he saw the various rock-surfaces as being far from an incoherent jumble of different symbols but rather an ordered system which pointed to a meaningful gearing of co-ordinates, probably linked with stellar or astronomical phenomena. Another Scottish site of cup-marked rocks (perhaps not so impressive, and certainly not so variable in design as at Achnabreck) is that at Cairnbaan.

216: Prehistoric rock carvings at Achnabreck. The cup and ring marks and spirals are dated to 2,000 B.C.

217: One of the outliers, marking the processional avenue towards the stone circle at Callanish, on the Isle of Lewis. The circle was used as a calendrical instrument some 4,500 years ago.
218: The stone circle at Callanish. The stones marked out important calendrical settings of the sun and moon.

ARDGOWAN, Strathclyde B4

One of the infamous witches of the Greenock area was Marie Lamont, who was brought to trial in 1662 and confessed that on one occasion she and her friends assembled in Ardgowan, where they met with the Devil. 'In the likeness of a black man, with cloven featt', he directed them to fetch white sand from the nearby shore and cast it about the gates of Ardgowan to achieve some mischief. But as they did his bidding, he raised his hands above his head and turned them all into cats. The group would be familiar with the feline shape, however, for Lamont had already given an account of how the Devil (this time in the shape of a brown dog) had organised a meeting in Inverkip to enable them to raise storms to hinder the fishing. Present at this meeting were Kettie Scot and Margaret Holm, both in the 'likeness of kats'.

AULDEARN, Highland C3

Historians of witchcraft have noted that according to the confessions of the 'Queen of Scottish witches', Isobel Gowdie, who swore her statement in April 1662, there were so many witches in the small village of Auldearn that they were divided into different groups (called 'covines'), each one commanded by two officials, one of whom was called 'The Maiden of the Coven', and the other of whom was an attractive young girl. Among the many extraordinary things which Gowdie confessed was that on Lammas Day in 1659 her own coven disguised themselves in the form of animals and birds, rambling through the countryside, destroying the goods of their neighbours. Among the 'diabolic' exploits of the Gowdie coven was their forced entry into a dye-works in Auldearn, where they changed the colours of the dyes so that the vat would dye only black, this being 'the colour of the Devil.'

BRODICK (Arran), Strathclyde

No fewer than 10 stone circles remain on the island of Arran (facing page), though it is clear that at one time there were many others which have not survived the ravages of men and time. Seven of the surviving circles are in the west, in the area around the Black and Machrie waters, and almost all of them have been linked with the legendary Fionn. Fionn, better known as Fingal, and linked with the music-making cave of STAFFA, would have found the construction of circles from gigantic stones as relatively light work, for in earlier times he was credited with the building of Fingal's cave from basaltic blocks, as well as the construction of the entire island of Staffa and the Giant's Causeway on the northern coast of Ireland.

Fionn of Celtic mythology was the son of a king who was apprenticed to a magician. In the Celtic legends we learn how when this magician had caught the wily old salmon of knowledge and had cooked it on his stove, the young Fionn touched it with his thumb, burned it badly and held it to his mouth in order to suck it. In this way Fionn became possessed of all knowledge, and became conversant with the magical lore. According to the old stories of Atlantis (of which the Northern Islands are said to be remnants), the stone circles were built by means of magic, for the ancient priests were supposed to have the secret of anti-gravitational forces. Precisely why Fionn constructed the circles remains a mystery: two of the smaller Arran circles (one on Machrie Moor, the other at Aucheleffan) have their stones orientated to the cardinal points, which has suggested that these circles, like those at Stonehenge, were designed with calendrical purposes in mind. A convenient centre from which to explore the ancient circles and cairns is Brodick, from where roads lead to within easy walking distance of the main centres. Seven miles west of Brodick, on the west side of the island, is the Auchagallon stone circle of 15 standing

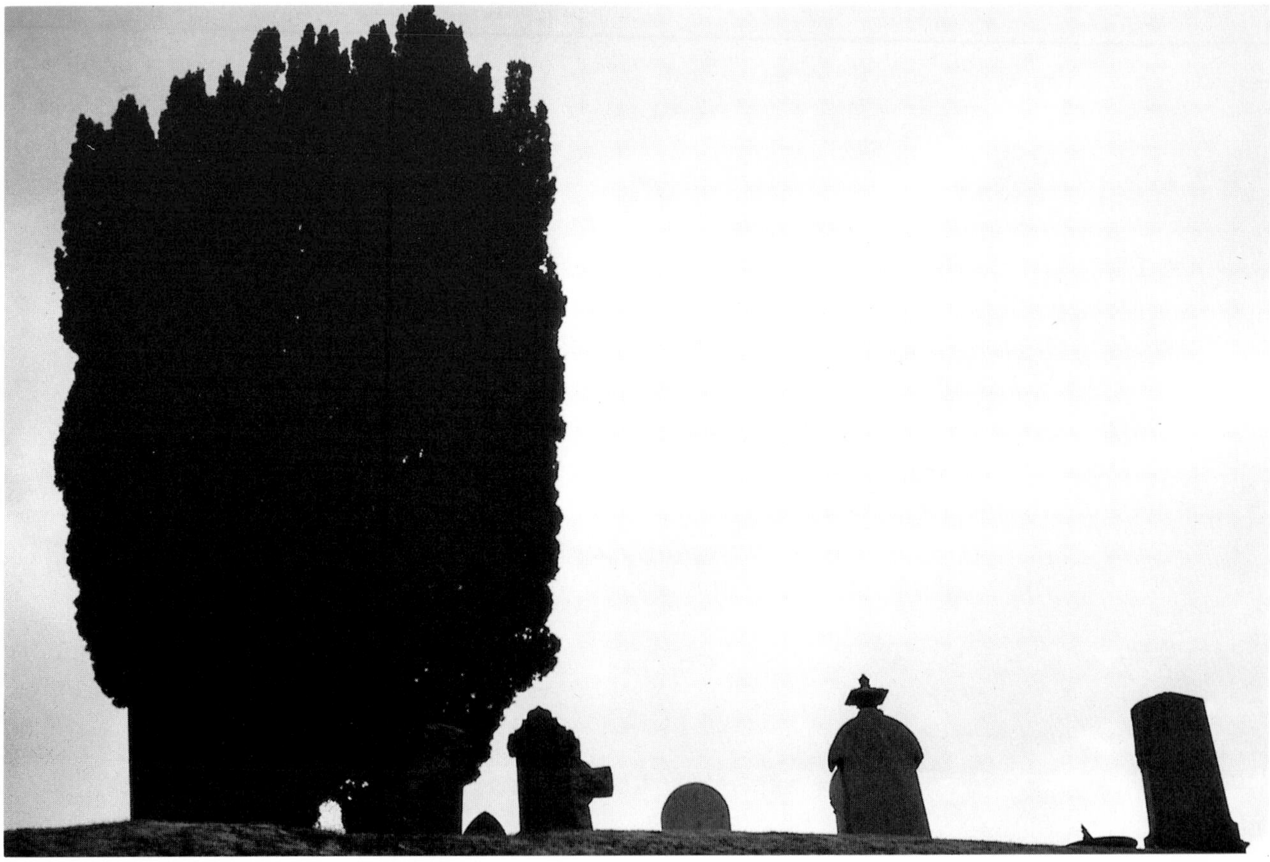

219: The graveyard at Auldearn, the site of a witches' meeting with the Devil.

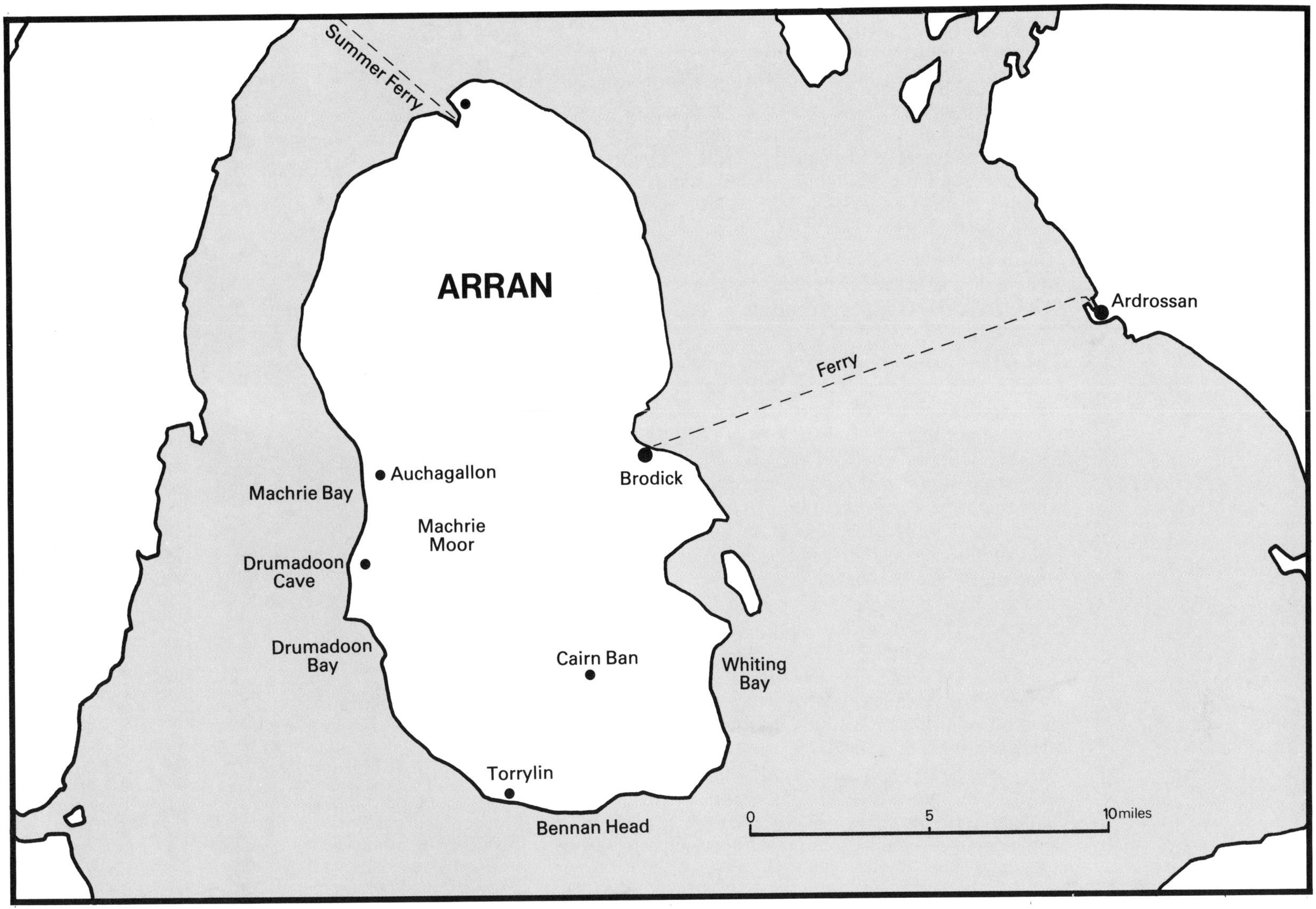

stones around a circular cairn. Six miles south-south-west of Brodick is the chambered Cairn Ban, some 900 feet above sea level, and consisting of a mound of stones 100 feet by 60 feet, with the facade and forecourt at the east end. The chamber within is divided into three compartments each of 15 feet length, with a slab roof set on corbelling at a height of about eight feet. Three miles further SSW from Brodick is the chambered cairn of Torrylin, in which were preserved the skeletal remains of six adults and a child, along with the remains of otters, birds and fish. Nine miles SW of Brodick at East Bennan, is a chambered cairn roofed with large flat slabs over the 20-foot gallery. Seven miles outside Brodick is the chambered cairn known locally as 'Giant's Grave'. A number of mysterious 'cup and ring' marks, consisting of double concentrics with gullies issuing downwards, as well as simple convex cups and triple concentrics, may be seen on the exposed rock face on the hill above the highest part of nearby Stronach Wood.

CALLANISH, Western Isles A2

One of the many stories told of the extraordinary circle at Callanish (figure 218) is that during a famine in Lewis a local woman was so much in despair that she waded into the sea in order to drown herself. As she walked into the waves, a white cow appeared, swimming towards her, and ordered her to take her milking pail to the centre of the largest of the Callanish circles, where the cow supplied as many pails of milk as were needed by the distressed community. However, as in the case of the white cow of Mitchell's Fold at LYDHAM, a witch soon put a stop to the magical cow by milking it into a sieve until it was dry. The cow disappeared and never returned to the circle, even though famine was known in the land several times afterwards. One wonders whether the story is some esoteric fable connected with the wisdom ('milk') which could be had from the ancient pagan lore for which the stone circles were the old lunar temples? The horns of the cow could symbolize the lunar crescents and the white milk could symbolize the pagan knowledge or power, in much the same way as the wolf milk represented the ancient knowledge which suckled Romulus and Remus, the ancient founders of Rome.

COYLTON, Strathclyde B5

It has long been believed that the name of this village is derived from the name of a fifth-century King Coilus, the original 'King Cole' of nursery-rhyme fame, the outline of whose story is give under COLCHESTER. Coilus was said to have been killed in a local battle and buried in the church at Coylton. Perhaps such a king was killed in this locality, for another burial place of Coilus is claimed by nearby Tarbolton 'within the grounds of Coilsfield House', where a number of large granite blocks are said to mark the burial place. The blocks are on top of a circular burial mound, which was excavated in 1837 and revealed cremation cist burials almost 2,000 years older than the period in which the historical King Coilus lived.

DALMENY, Lothian C4

The kirk at Dalmeny was built in the twelfth century, and the symbolism on its walls is both esoteric and profound. Many of the ornate burial stones and memorials are also extremely interesting. The eagle in figure 221 is almost certainly intended to denote resurrection, by pointing to the Gospel of St John, whose symbol is the flying eagle.

DRUMADOON, Strathclyde B5

The cave at Drumadoon, on Arran, which is now called 'the King's Cave' after Robert Bruce but in earlier times was identified with the legendary Fionn (as were the many stone circles on the island — see BRODICK), has several Viking carvings on the central pillar, the most interesting of which appears to represent a man holding what might be a bow over the top of his head; what the 'instrument' really represents is anybody's guess, however. Other carvings include the image of a horse, and what might be a two-handed sword or cross, suggesting that the cave might once have been used for religious purposes. The notion that Robert Bruce was associated with the cave appears to rest on the fourteenth-century Scottish-verse chronicle 'The Bruce', written by John Barbour, the Archdeacon of Aberdeen, which makes no mention of Bruce or his men even visiting the cave. It was during his stay in Arran, presumably at Whiting Bay, that Bruce met the Arran woman with 'second sight', who predicted that he would eventually free Scotland from the enemy. In order to show her own faith in the prophecy she had made, she sent her two sons in his service.

EIGG, Highland A3

On the island of Eigg is St Katherine's Well, famous for its healing properties and the object of the strange 'dessil'

220: Robert the Bruce, who is supposed to have sheltered at Drumadoon. The same claim is made for a cave on Rathlin Island, off the coast of Northern Island. This portrait is from an idealized 19th-century lithograph.

221 (far right): An eagle, the symbol of resurrection, on one of the 18th-century tombstones in Dalmeny Kirk burial ground. The kirk itself was built in the 12th century and is dedicated to St Cuthbert.

222: The witch Anne Bodenham invoking spirits into a magical circle in order to learn the future.

pilgrimage, which requires those approaching the island to do so sun-wise, or clock-wise. The original 'dessil' was involved with magical practices which involved walking, dancing or running around an object or place of devotion three times in a clockwise (sun-wise) direction to evoke the benefices of the solar element. The legends tell how the pagan sacred well of Eigg was consecrated for Christian use by a priest who encouraged those approaching the well to bring large stones, which were heaped around the well. After the holy ritual he handed to each a candle, with instructions that they should make the (pagan) sun-cult dessil around the well. From this simple Christian ritual of approaching the well grew the later practice of approaching the island. The Eigg ritual is practised at any time but is associated specifically with 15 April.

FISHERTON ANGER, Highland C3

Anne Bodenham was the servant of a notorious wizard named Dr Lamb, who, in the seventeenth century, was personal physician to the Duke of Buckingham. She claimed to have learned magic from Dr Lamb, and gained for herself a not unreasonable reputation as a witch (she wore a toad around her neck, in a green bag, at a time when toads were regarded as being nothing more than witch familiars). In his *Kingdom of Darkness* (1688), Nathaniel Crouch tells how Anne Bodenham had, in 1653, constructed a magical circle and then compelled demons or imps to appear in this 'in the likenes of ragged boys', in order to gain some knowledge about the future in regard to an impending court case. Anne was eventually tried as a witch at Salisbury, and, having been found guilty, was hanged, denying to the end all commerce with the Devil.

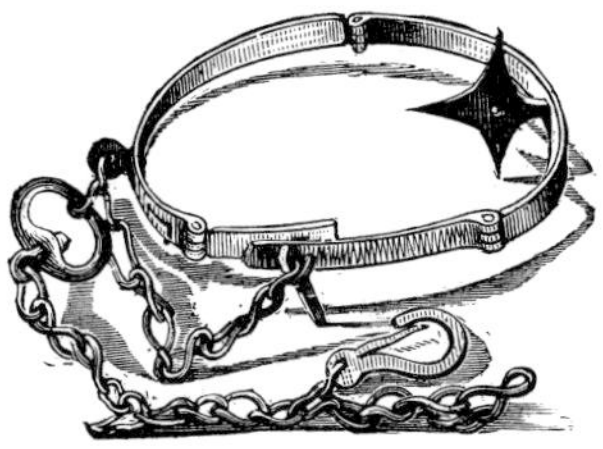

FORFAR, Tayside C3

In the Forfar Museum is a 'witch bridle', properly a branks, which consists of a metal frame designed to fit over the head of a person in such a way as to insert into the mouth a metal prong which prevents movement of the tongue, and hence ensures silence. Branks were often used in earlier times in both England and Scotland (see for example NOTTINGHAM), but the notorious Forfar branks was especially cruel as the metal insert which was pushed into the mouth was designed to cut the tongue and the roof of the mouth even when the person did not attempt to speak. Although supposedly designed to control gossips, scolds or rowdy people, it was apparently used to bridle witches when they were led to the place of execution. It was argued that this extra punishment (which was never sanctioned by law in either Scotland or England) was used not so much to hide the screams of the supposed witches as to prevent them from pronouncing the magical spells or formulas by means of which they could transform themselves into animal shapes, such as hares or cats, and thus escape their doom. The date 1661 is punched into the circlet of iron.

FYVIE, Grampian C3

The chateau-like castle at Fyvie was once famous for the ghost of a Green Lady which scared visitors by wandering its corridors and walking through the wooden panels of certain rooms. The ghost was reported several times in 1920, and it is said that one or two years prior to this a huge mass of fungus had unaccountably grown in the gun rooms, and the workmen sent to investigate discovered hidden in the walls a human skeleton. Only after these bones had been removed did the ghost begin to appear, and it was in order to assuage this spirit that Lord Beith (the owner of Fyvie) had the skeleton immured once again in the castle walls.

GLAMIS, Tayside C4

The fact that Glamis Castle has gained for itself the reputation of being the most haunted castle in Britain, if not in Europe, has tended to obscure other remarkable mythological and mysterious elements on the site. Among these, the most interesting is undoubtedly the Pictish Stone which stands in the garden of the Manse. Nearly nine feet high, one side is elaborately carved with a Celtic interlace cross, with a centaur armed with a couple of hammers, a dog (?), a pair of men fighting with cudgels, and what appears to be a doe-headed set of ring-handles. For all the Christian significance of the cross, none of these additional Pictish symbols appear to have anything to do with the religous symbols used in the south. On the back of the stone is another ring symbol, a fish and a snake. Such Pictish symbols have never been adequately explained.

JEDBURGH, Borders C5

The Candlemas Ba' played at Jedburgh is one of the last survivors of a game which was once widely played in the north of England and in Scotland, and which is presumed to be a survival of a pagan game introduced into the Christian calendar by way of Candlemas.

Candlemas is the name given to the day on which the blessing of the altar candles was made, during the celebration of the Purification of the Virgin, but there does not appear to be any obvious connexion between the Christian rituals and the spirited Candlemas Ba'. Those playing the match at Jedburgh are divided into the Uppies and the Doonies (though other divisions are also permitted, sometimes one parish being set against another). Play commences immediately after lunch, and continues for most of the day, the aim being to get a small football to various prescribed places. The casual observer will rapidly come to the conclusion that there are no rules to the game.

KELSO, Borders C5

In the eighteenth century there was a cruel sport (fortunately now long-banned) in which a cat was placed in a barrel of soot, and the barrel suspended from a cross-beam between two poles. Groups of 'whip-men' would then charge at the barrel on horseback and try to break it in with heavy blows from hammers and staves. Eventually, the metal hoops would be dislodged by this barrage and the cat would fall in a flurry of soot to the earth, where it was killed by the groups watching the spectacle. The game or ritual is almost certainly linked with witchcraft beliefs — perhaps the cat was visualized as a witch-familiar or imp which had to be punished like some scape-goat.

The fact is that one of the traditional ways of killing witches in Scotland involved putting the unfortunate victim in a barrel of tar, setting this alight, and then rolling it down a hill. Many of the witch-stones still to be found in such Scottish places as Forres (opposite the police station) or Spott, record where such burning barrels came to a stop in their downward career.

223: Fyvie Castle, Grampian, one of the many haunted castles of Scotland.

224: Glamis Castle, home of the Queen Mother, is said to be one of the most haunted castles in Europe. The Pictish stone in the gardens of the manse indicates that there has been a settlement here since very ancient times.

225: The desolate air of the Knock of Alves explains why it is popularly thought to be the meeting place of the witches in *Macbeth*.

KNOCK OF ALVES, Grampian C3

The 'Knock' or 'hill' of Alves, between Elgin and Burghead, is topped by a tower and a mausoleum, the former contained within the remains of an ancient fort enclosure. Although much mutilated by time and quarrying, the Knock still retains something of the feeling of desolation, which explains why popular imagination has proclaimed it as the place where the witches of Shakespeare's *Macbeth* met to weave their magical spells (figure 225). The York Tower braves the strong winds in the gorse and heather, and it requires little imagination for one to make the time-leap and see Macbeth standing upon the crenellated octagonal 'castle' — though such pictures would be going too far, as the tower appears to have been built in 1827 by Alexander Forteath in commemoration of the Duke of York. The three witches made famous by William Shakespeare had their origin in the *Chronicles* of Holinshed, as the 'weird sisters', or 'Goddesses of destinie', who could foresee the future of Macbeth, yet the Alves area had long been infamous for its witches and there are many varied accounts of how King Duffus (of the tenth century) had been ill to the point of death as a result of the activity of local witches. He would have died had not 'Donald, the Governor of Forres Castle, arrested a young wench who had been overheard to threaten the King, and she confessed that her mother, a notorious sorceress, and a whole coven of devil-worshippers were slowly taking the life of Duffus, who would expire in a few days.' A short while later a company of hags were surprised while roasting the King's image made of wax upon a long spit over a slow fire. The figure was destroyed, the witches burned at Forres, and the King recovered his health. Indeed, while the play was only loosely written around historical events, one of the most compelling of the characters — Siward — was part of medieval legend even before Shakespeare introduced him as 'the Earl of Northumberland'. Earl Siward was thoroughly Danish as a ruler, 'one of the last of his breed in England', as Charles Kightly reports. In truth he was a giant in build, yet mythology has made him even more gigantic, claiming that his grandfather had been a monstrous white bear and that he himself had hunted and killed dragons in the Orkneys, with the same fearlessness that other men might hunt rabbits. Rather than die in his bed, he is reported to have armed himself with sword and shield, that he might pass from life as a warrior. Near York there is a prehistoric barrow which is still called 'Siward's Howe', and taken to be his grave, but Siward was at least a thousand years later than this mound.

LANARK, Strathclyde C4

The Lanark Silver Bell Handicap is raced nominally for an ancient silver bell, said to be the oldest racing trophy in the West. Pursuit of the trophy is supported by a not insubstantial financial prize for the winner. It is claimed that the bell was originally made as gift from King William of Scotland in the late twelfth century, but the one now in use is probably not much older than the late sixteenth century, for it was made by a goldsmith from Edinburgh around that time. The winner of the race is not actually given this bell, but has his name inscribed upon a related shield.

LERWICK, Shetland D2

The crest on the arms of Lerwick, capital of the Shetlands, is a black raven, a reminder of the ancestry of the islanders, who sprang from the Vikings. The Danish raven came across the sea in the monster-headed raiding ships of the Vikings, and was said to represent the two birds named Huginn (Mind) and Muninn (Memory) who acted as spies and newsgatherers for the many-named pagan Odin, the hero-god of the warriors. Odin was the god of the dead, and the chief of the Raven clan, which is probably why so many of the tales of ravens as evil creatures, familiars of the dark witches, survive in British lore. Whatever their origin, ravens were birds of omen even in distant times, and legend survives that if the ravens in the Tower of London ever leave their post then the city will be destroyed.

LEWIS, Western Isles A2

The historian-cleric, the Venerable Bede, tells us how until the eighth century the Island of Lewis was not only destitute of men, fruit, trees and plants, but was the meeting place of evil spirits, who regaled themelves with their awful ceremonies until the monk Cudbrecht exorcised them. However, the exorcism does not appear to have been completely successful, for there are several witchcraft stories attached to the stone circles to the north-west of the island (see CALLANISH), and there are records that until as late as 1750 there was a diabolical cat sacrifice practised on the island, which rite went under the name of Taigheirm.

This connexion between the ritual and the notion of second-sight is expressed in the reason given by some for the practice of the cat sacrifice in the Western Isles, for after the Taigheirm the magicians were able to demand of the demons the gift of second-sight in return for their sacrifice. The terrible ritual lasted for a period of four days and nights, commencing at midnight on the Friday.

LOCH ASHIE, Highland B3

To the north-western end of Loch Ashie (north-east of Dores) is a large boulder called by the locals 'Fingal's Seat'. It is said that in ancient times the legendary Fingal (see STAFFA) led his Fianna into battle at this spot against the Norsemen (the men of Lochlann) under their leader Ashie. According to local tradition, this battle is re-enacted as a silent phantom-play soon after dawn on the first of May. When the ghostly battle was observed in 1870, the curious happening was 'explained' in terms of its being a long-distance 'mirage reflection' of men who were even at that time fighting in the Franco-Prussian war. The same phantom battle was also seen during the First World War.

An equally 'phantom' battle was said to have been seen near a small well on the road from Uig to Portree in Skye, on 15 April 1746, with the ghost of a young man watching the battle and lamenting. On the following day the battle of Culloden was fought, and the Scots defeated. A few days later, the fleeing Prince Charles drank at the same small well, and the locals immediately took the earlier vision as a presage of the disaster which occurred at Culloden.

LOCH NESS, Highland B3

The 25-mile strip of Loch Ness, which is in places over 750 feet deep, is famous for 'Nessy', as its sea monster is affectionately called. There are many old references to the idea of the Loch being 'haunted' by a monstrous creature, but the truth is that there is scarcely an extensive lake in Britain which is not believed to have its resident creature. The difference between the other mythological monsters and the one believed to be in Loch Ness is that this one has been photographed several times, in each case the pictures revealing a long-necked creature which many have taken to be a surviving prehistoric monster. The first photograph to gain any notoriety was taken in November 1933 by Hugh Gray, very much an out-of-focus amateur picture showing a serpentine creature throwing up spray on an otherwise calm lake. Perhaps the finest photograph of 'Nessy' was that taken in the April of the following year by R.K.

226: Although the fame of the Loch Ness Monster is comparatively recent, such monsters have featured in mythology for thousands of years.

Wilson. That was a good year for Nessy, as a letter from Sir E.M. Mountain in *The Times* of 6 June 1938 indicates. He engaged a force of 20 men, each equipped with a camera, and placed them at strategic points along the shore of the Loch. During the first fortnight, these watchers managed to secure 21 photographs of the creature, five of which were good enough for reproduction in newspapers. A moving film of the monster was also made at this time, and shown to the Press in London on 28 August. In July of the same year a Mr Spicer saw the monster leave the water and cross the road some distance in front of his car; he later wrote that the creature was 'horrible, an abomination...It looked like a huge snail with a long neck'. Another photograph, taken by Mr L. Stuart in July, 1952, records the monster 'travelling towards Dores from Urquhart Castle'. Stuart estimated Nessy to be about 40 feet long, with a body some three feet in diameter, and its head about the size and shape of a sheep's head.

MAES HOWE, Orkney C1

Maes Howe is a chambered cairn some 36 feet high, 92 feet in diameter, with a 300-foot circumference, and is therefore the largest of the many chambered cairns in the West, though its inner chamber is only some 15 feet square. It has been shown by the specialist historian Magnus Spence to be part of an enormous complex of ancient measuring stones incorporating monoliths, stone circles and other siting points relating to the calendrical system used by the ancient peoples who inhabited this part of the world. For a long time it has been recognized that the entrance chamber (which is over 50 feet long) is directed along a line which points to a standing stone marking the position of sunset ten days before the Winter Solstice, indicating that the complex is a sophisticated observational instrument. Spence argued that this sighting would herald the the Yule Feast (circa 12 December), which was a 'period of fasting and sacrifice', the object of which was to persuade the Sun-God not to desert the world, but to retrace his heavenly journey. For a very long time it had been believed that Maes Howe was nothing more than a burial chamber, but as Spence himself wrote, Maes Howe should 'take its legitimate place as the Observatory of the Prince of Light (Sun) and the heavenly hosts, instead of being the ghastly receptacle and charnel house of the dead; to be the palace of the Arch-Priest instead of the prison of death'.

Spence, who as headmaster of the nearby Stenness Public School had ample opportunity to study Maes Howe and the complex of standing stones and circles in the vicinity, has shown that there is even a ratio-relationship between the different points used for the Maes Howe cosmic measurements, which depend essentially on the places of sunrise throughout the year. For example, he showed that the distance between Maes Howe and the Winter Solstice Stone (at Barnhouse) is exactly the same as from that stone to the Equinoxial 'Watch Stone' and that there is a sighting line directed by the Winter Solstice Stone and Watch Stone which enabled precise sunset positions at the festival of Beltane, and another line, joined by marking stones, which indicates precisely the sunrise at the festival which we now call Hallowe'en. The eccentric Cotsworth (see ACOMB) suggests quite sensibly that there was probably another monolith (now removed) which indicated the direction of sunrise at the Summer Solstice. One wonders if the man-made hill of Maes Howe was one of the 'beaconed hills' used by the ancient priests for their fire festivals? It was

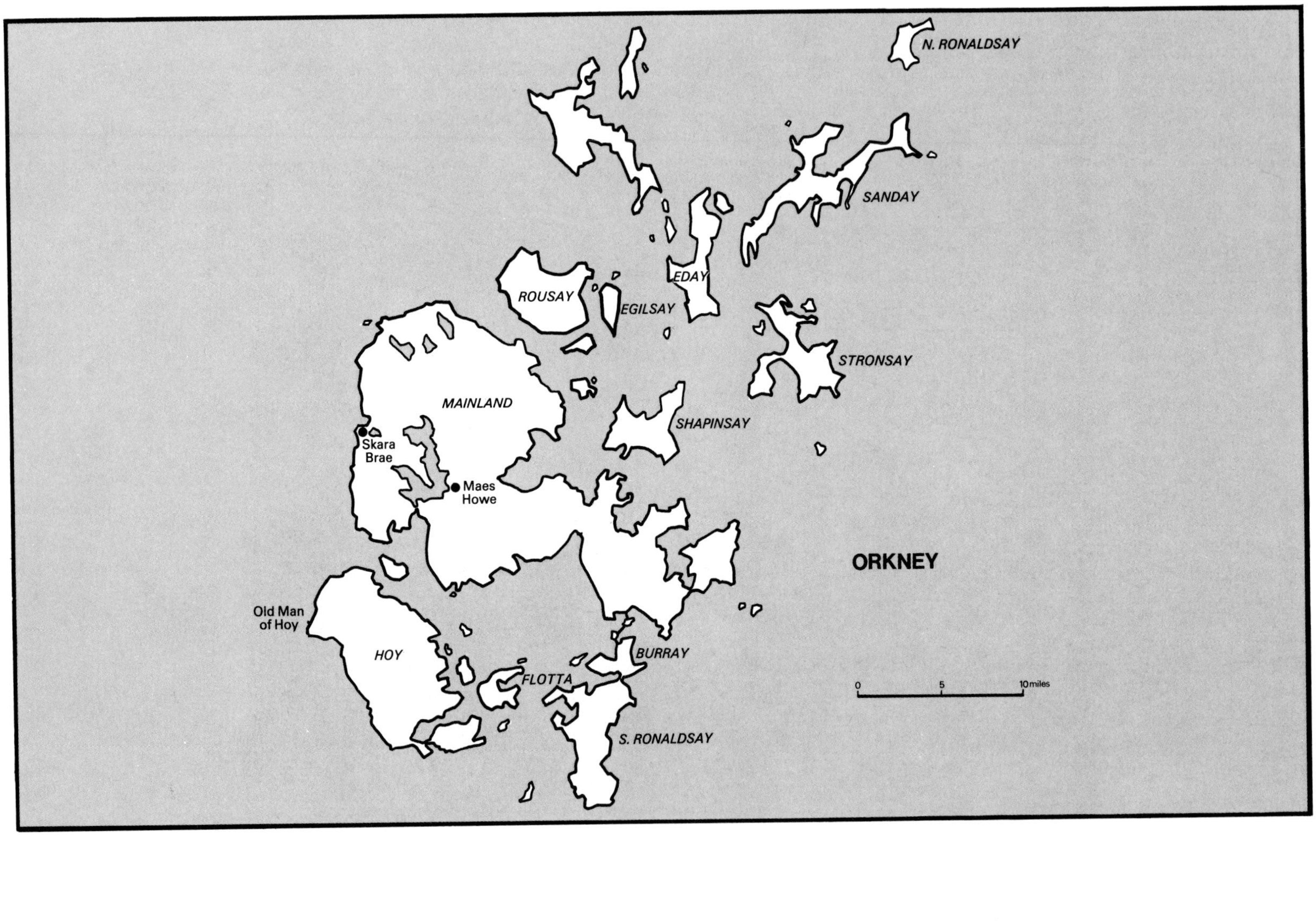

227: Temple Old Kirk gravestone, dated 1742, depicting a farmer, John Craig of Outerston, in a long coat and knotted scarf with his two sons.

228: Hermitage Castle, linked with the legends of Ninestone Rig, is said to be haunted by the soul of Lord Soulis.

recorded that at midsummer a wheel covered with twisted straw was taken up such hills, set on fire, and then rolled down to symbolize the Sun in its receding course.

The nearby circle which was once called the 'Moon Circle' has a diameter of 116 feet, which means that it has a circumference of 365 feet, which is the exact circumference of the nearby Sun Circle. Cotsworth mentions that at the beginning of the nineteenth century there was an upright called the 'Stone of Odin' which had bored through it an observation hole, similar to the portholes found in such stones as the Men-an-Tol near Morvah in Cornwall, the Holestone near Doagh in County Antrim, and the so-called 'Stone of Constantine' in Cornwall.

MELROSE, Borders C5

When Robert the Bruce died, he left a will ordering that his heart be taken to Jerusalem for separate burial in the Holy Land. This dying wish was recorded also on a specially engraved sword (still in the possession of the Douglas-Home family) which instructs Sir James Douglas (the legendary Black Douglas), 'I wil ye charge efter yat I depart/To Holy Gravfe and thair bury my hart'. The crude pictures on the blade show two hands reaching out for a heart, while further along the metal are a number of unexplained magical symbols. The request was fulfilled in part, for the cask containing his heart was

indeed entrusted to Sir James Douglas, who unfortunately died on the long journey, with the result that it was returned to Scotland and buried in Melrose Abbey. Legends tell how Black Douglas helped the King of Castile in his fight against the Moors in Spain and, when it became clear to him that he had no chance of survival, threw Bruce's heart into the fray and then charged in after it to die; somehow, the cask containing the heart was found and returned to Melrose, its journey uncompleted. Notable among the ruins of Melrose Abbey are the gargoyle figures high on the exterior — a mason with his mallet, a cook with his ladle, a fat monk and a pig playing a bagpipe: is the animal playing a dirge to the Scottish hopes which died with Robert Bruce, one wonders? This strange double burial was not the end of the Bruce saga, for in 1819 the tomb of Robert the Bruce at Dunfermline was opened to reveal his skeleton wrapped in leaden sheets. The skull was removed for sufficient time to enable technicians to make a cast of it, and is now preserved in the National Portrait Gallery of Scotland, EDINBURGH.

NINESTONE RIG, Borders C5

This remote stone circle, which is on the moorland some 10 miles south of Hawick, and above the squat castle of Hermitage, consists of eight upright stones on an oval of which the greatest axial length is 23 feet. The tallest stone is about six feet high. By the standard of Scottish circles, such as one finds on Harris or Skye, Ninestone Rig is not very impressive; its fame rests more upon its mythological associations than upon size or quality, for the stones are linked with the awful destiny of the evil Lord Soulis, one of the most renowned of Scottish devil-men. The stories tell how Soulis could summon the Devil whenever he rapped three times on an iron chest; the Devil would appear, and would do him no harm provided that Soulis did not look at him. One day, on calling the Great Beast, Soulis did happen to glance at the terrible figure, and his fate was sealed. He had been protected by special charms to prevent injury or enclosure from rope or steel, so he could not be bound in the ordinary way. However, cognizant of this secret strength, his enemies wrapped him in sheets of lead, and boiled him to death at the 'Nine-Stane Rig' which was near to his castle of Hermitage.

> On a circle of stones they placed the pot,
> On a circle of stones but barely nine;
> ...
> They plunged him into the cauldron red,
> And melted him body, lead, bones and all.

Montague Summers, who tells the story as though it were history rather than mythology, records that once every seven years, 'the old wives tell', the tormented ghost of Soulis still keeps tryst with the Devil in the chambers of Hermitage, the scene of his earlier demonic orgies.

NORTH BERWICK, Lothian C4

The strange trials of the North Berwick witches in 1590-92 appear to have been derived mainly from the imagination of King James IV of Scotland, who took an interest in the fact that some of these witches were supposed to have raised a storm in order to destroy a ship in which he was sailing from Denmark. To modern ears, the stories drawn from the coven of witches are quite incredulous, and savour of the ravings of unfortunates caught in the horror of torture. According to the accounts drawn from the men and women under torture, Satan preached to them from the Old Kirk at North Berwick while also instructing them how to raise a violent storm by means of black magic, involving the sacrifice of a cat. The unfortunate John Fian of Saltpans (now the Prestonpans of Lothian) who 'confessed' under the most horrible torture to following this feline baptism for storm-raising, claimed that he had done it under the compulsion of the Devil, who had appeared to him at night 'appareled all in blacke, withe a white wande in his hande.'

ORKNEY

On Mainland, Orkney, is the Ring of Brogar (figure 229), the most cryptic of all the strange ancient relics of the past and one of the finest stone circles in Britain. Set between the small lochs of Stenness and Harray, it consists of 27 uprights (the tallest almost 16 feet above the ground), though it has been calculated that originally there must have been as many as 60. A number of stones are fallen, while the broken bases of others may still be seen. The diameter of the circle is 340 feet, which means that it was probably constructed according to the measurement now called the 'megalithic yard' (2.722 feet), to a length of 125. One of the stones in the northern section is inscribed with Norse tree runes — no doubt scratched by Viking invaders over 1,000 years ago. It is reasonably certain that the Ring of Brogar, like many other stone circles throughout Britain (see for example STONEHENGE), was designed to act as a solar-lunar observatory, by which the times for rituals and festivals could be determined.

ORONSAY, Strathclyde A3

In the Prior's House in the ruined Oronsay Priory, itself on the tidal island of that name on the island of Colonsay, are a number of fascinating medieval graveslabs in a variety of designs ranging from somewhat formal and stiff recumbent knights, to slabs carved with the image of a galley in full sail, down to virtually abstract curvilinear designs alive with animals and human figures, of a nature so often linked with Celtic art forms. Immediately to the west of the priory church is situated a raised medieval cross which is almost certainly the most impressive in Scotland, consisting of interlaced foliage and ribbon-work, with a raised figure of Christ crucified at the juncture of the cross. The Latin inscription near the foot of the west face reads, 'This is the cross of Colinus, the son of Cristinus MacDuffie'. The Augustinian priory was founded by the Lord of the Isles, John I, in the fourteenth century, but much of the most important carving was done in the following century.

PERTH, Tayside C4

The murder of King James I at Perth on 21 February, 1437, by Robert Graham merges into Scottish mythology, for a long story is told of how the death was foreseen by a prophetess or witch. On leaving Edinburgh to cross the Firth of Forth by boat, the woman called out that if he crossed those waters he would never return alive. Having reached Perth, and while playing a game of chess with the Duke of Atholl, the old woman called upon him once again but, it being late, he commanded her to return the following day, when he would speak with her. She went away, muttering, 'hit shall repent yow all that ye wil not let me speke nowe with the kyng.' During the night, the King was murdered. The chief conspirator had been the Duke of Atholl, and the

229: The Ring of Brogar on Mainland. The circle originally consisted of 60 large stones, of which 27 still stand.

230: The 'image' of a face in the stonework of St Salvator's College, St Andrews.

historian Buchanan tells how, because certain witches 'for whom the county of Athole was always infamous' had told Atholl that he would be 'crowned a king in sight of all the people', prior to his execution his tormentors placed upon his head a diadem of red-hot iron for all to see.

PITTENWEEM, Fife C4

Among the colourful houses which jostle down the hillside towards the lovely fishing-boat harbour of Pittenweem in Fife is Cove Wynd, one side of which is a cliff-face into which has been built an iron grille gateway, leading into a number of caverns. This cave-system was said to be the cell of Saint Fillan and has been preserved as a shrine for many centuries, being rededicated in 1935. Besides its famous saint, Pittenweem has had its famous witch. Beatrix Laing was accused by the local minister, Patrick Cowper, of having cast a spell over the 16-year-old son of the blacksmith, Patrick Morton. Under torture, Beatrix confessed to diabolical forms of witchcraft and included in her recital of dark deeds the names of several other Pittenweem ladies. These were rounded up and tortured until they all confessed to terrible crimes of dark magic. After months of cruel imprisonment, Beatrix Laing was fined and released, and managed to escape to St Andrews, where she died as a result of her ill-treatment. One of her so-called 'accomplices', Janet Cornfoot, was tortured for a second time and flogged by Patrick Cowper, but somehow managed to escape. Caught once more by a search party, she had her hands and feet tied together and was swung from a ship beneath the waves until she almost died. Finally she was put out of her misery by being pressed to death beneath a pile of boulders. Patrick Morton eventually confessed that the original accusations against Beatrix Laing had been false.

ST ANDREWS, Fife C4

In the tower of St Salvator's College, inset into the stonework of the facade, is a distorted 'image' of a face (figure 230). This is said to have been magically formed during the burning of Patrick Hamilton, one of the Protestant martyrs, in front of the College in 1527/28.

SHIANT ISLES, Western Isles A2

The remote Shiant Isles in the Minch were the site of one of the strangest of all 'tragic histories' which have become part of Scottish mythology, and has been turned into the Gaelic song *Ailean Duinn*. Allan Morrison, a sea captain, was betrothed to Annie Campbell, who lived on the island of Scalpay. On the day he sailed to marry her, his ship was sunk by an unexpected storm and, along with all his crew, he was lost. On hearing the terrible news, Annie herself died of grief. Her body was coffined, and taken by ship for burial on the south of Harris. This ship also fell victim to a violent storm, and the coffin was swept overboard. Shortly afterwards, Allan's body was washed up among the puffins on one of the lonely beaches of the Shiant Isles, and a few days later Annie's body was found in exactly the same place.

SKARA BRAE, Orkney C1

The early neolithic monument at Skara Brae, on the Mainland Orkneys, was covered for centuries by sand and was only recently completely excavated. The numerous rooms discovered, which would once have been covered in skins or thatch, have built-in furniture in stone — such as box-beds, shelves and cupboards.

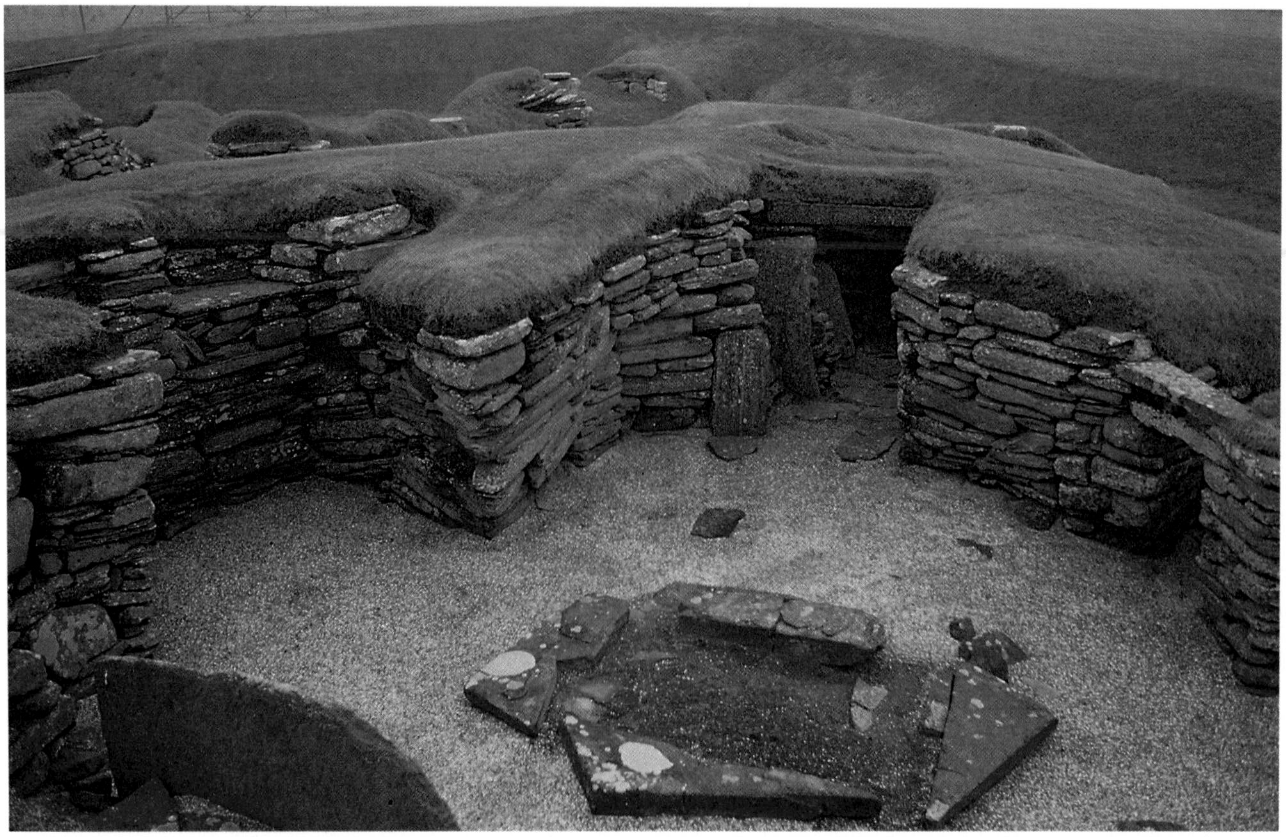

231: The settlement recently excavated at Skara Brae was covered by sand for centuries. It is early neolithic.

STAFFA, Strathclyde A4

Although the island of Staffa was regarded as one of the great natural wonders of the ancient world, and interwoven into the mythology of both Scotland and Ireland, it was 'discovered' in modern times as late as August 1772 by Sir Joseph Banks. It was this same Sir Joseph who had been the companion of Captain Cook on his first voyage round the world, and who encouraged Cook to name Botany Bay in Australia on the grounds that all the plants there were new to science. Thus, as Donald MacCulloch points out, Sir Joseph has left his name with the northern Hebrides (by way of Staffa) and with the southern Hebrides (the 'New Hebrides'), among which is a group of islands called 'Banks Islands'. In his first report of the discovery of Staffa he remarks that it 'is reckoned one of the greatest natural curiosities in the world: it is surrounded by many pillars of different shapes, such as pentagons, octagons, etc. They are about 55 feet high, and near five feet in diameter, supporting a solid rock of a mile in length, and about 60 feet above the pillars. There is a cave in this island which the natives call the Cave of Fingal: its length is 371 feet, about 115 feet in height, and 51 feet wide... The Giant's Causeway in Ireland, or Stonehenge in England, are but trifles when compared to this island...' Who was this Fingal after whom the remarkable cave had been named? For an answer to this question we must turn to Irish mythology, which seems to have given birth to this semi-legendary leader of men who not only had the Staffa cave named after him, but was even said to have constructed with his own hands the entire magical island itself. Finn MacCumhaill (sometimes, Fin MacCoul) is the earliest name of Fingal, who was so renowned as a 'builder' that he is said to have erected many of the stone circles in Scotland. Finn was more than a mythological king — he was also a magician, who learned the power of magic-making almost by accident (see BRODICK). Perhaps this is one reason why a natural break in the wall of basaltic columns above the Causeway of Staffa is called 'Fingal's Wishing Chair', and why it is said that anyone who sits in this cavity and makes a wish will have this wish come true. Fingal is the central hero of the Ossianic cycle, the mythical ruler of a race of giants called the Fianna, a sort of Celtic equivalent of the British Arthurian knights.

Those who claim Fingal to have been a living leader of men, rather than a product of mythologizing, say that he died towards the end of the third century AD. The original epic of Fingal was said to be written by the third-century Ossian, whom many claim to have been the son of Fingal, but there was much dispute about the authorship of this fragmentary verse. James Macpherson's *Fingal* , published in 1761, and supposedly adapted from the 'original version' by Ossian, was challenged by Dr Johnson. It is certain that one of the reasons why Dr Johnson made his famous tour of the Hebrides was in order to accumulate proof that there was no poetry by anyone named Ossian. For further exploits of Fingal, see LOCH ASHIE.

STIRLING, Central Scotland C4

Sir William Wallace was a Scottish patriot whose life has been almost completely submerged in a derring-do mythology which makes all attempts at an assessment of his actual contribution to Scottish nationalism extremely difficult. Almost nothing is known about him prior to 1297, at which point he emerges as a leader of the Scottish resistance against the destructive policies of Edward I. He was thus a supportive precursor of Robert Bruce, that other mythologized historical cult figure (see MELROSE). Revolt throughout Scotland was encouraged by Wallace's successful attack on the garrison at Lanark, and the killing of Hazelrigg, the English King's sheriff. Wallace marched south and defeated the English army at Stirling, more by cunning strategy than

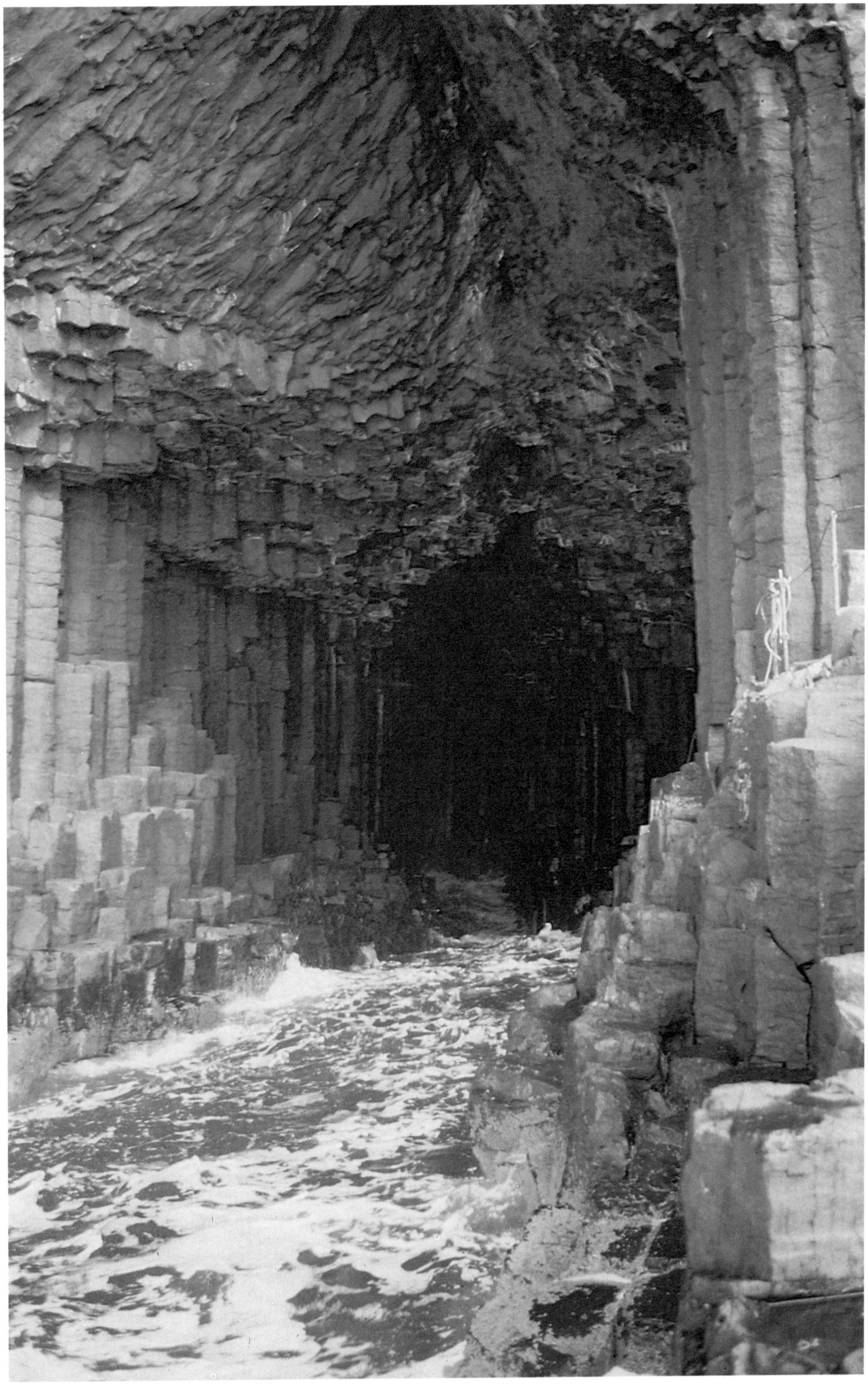

232: The entrance to Fingal's Cave on the island of Staffa in the Hebrides. This natural cave, which has all the appearance of being designed by man (or by giants, as the myths insist) was the inspiration in the 19th century for *Fingal's Cave* by Mendelssohn.

233: Stirling Castle, on a headland above the Forth Valley, was once the most important of Scottish defensive castles. Robert the Bruce took it after Bannockburn in 1314 and Mary Queen of Scots was crowned here in 1543.

force of arms, below the place where the distinctive Wallace Monument still stands on Abbey Crag. Alerted as to the seriousness of the revolt, the next army was led from England by Edward I himself, whose seasoned troops inflicted a terrible defeat on the Scottish at Falkirk in 1298. Wallace fled to the continent, but was back in Scotland by 1303, still adamant in refusing to abjure his Scottish independence to Edward I. When at length the patriot was betrayed by Sir John Monteith in 1305, he was taken to London and cruelly and slowly put to death as a traitor, his quartered body displayed publicly on the gibbets of Newcastle, Berwick, Stirling and Perth, his severed head displayed on London Bridge. The mythology built around this remarkable man is of an even more fantastical nature than the historical facts. None of the mythological account of his exploits may be traced beyond 1363, almost sixty years after his death, until the Aberdeen priest John of Fordun gave him considerable praise at length in his own chronicles of the time. In 1468 Wallace emerged as a true mythological superman in Blind Hary's lengthy poetic novel *Wallace*, which appears to have formed the basis of much 'history' until the last century, even though Hary had collected together the daring deeds of many Scottish heroes and attributed them to Wallace. Wallace's encounter with a ghost in a deserted hall; his being thrown into the dungeons of Percy's castle at Ayr (merely for killing three of Percy's soldiers single-handed), where he was starved, only to be revived by his old nurse who fed him with milk from her daughter's breast; the execution of his mistress or 'lawful wife' Marion Braidfute at Lanark for saving Wallace from the English — an execution watched by lace in secret, and then avenged the same night in less secret — all this is scarcely history, but makes excellent mythology and was supportive of the Scottish cause at a time when many Scots had good reason to lament. No wonder that the monks who witnessed his horrific death reported that they saw visions of their hero's glorious reception into Heaven immediately afterwards.

STRATHFILLAN, Central Scotland B4

The Holy Pool at Strathfillan was once a centre for the healing of the insane. On specific days, between sunset and sunrise, lunatics were immersed in its waters and then persuaded to pick up three stones from the bottom of the well and walk three times around its circumference, three times around the cairns on the bank, and then to throw a stone on each cairn. They were then carried to the remains of St Fillan's Chapel and left on a bed for the rest of the night, in the expectation that by morning they would be cured. It is said that Robert Bruce prayed at the Holy Pool on the night before the battle of Bannockburn.

TRAPRAIN LAW, Lothian C4

The 500-foot high natural hill, sometimes called the 'hog-back', sometimes the 'harpooned whale', is striking when seen against the flat landscape of East Lothian north of the Lammermuir massif, its north-eastern part now gashed by modern quarry works. Still visible, as a stone-faced turf rampart some 3,500 feet in length and 12 feet thick, is the ancient line of fortification which is probably almost 2,000 years old — though 'finds' such as bronze axes and cremation urns point to occupation of the site as early as 1,500 BC, and mark it as by far the most important prehistoric place in Scotland. Mythology insists that this hill was once the camp of King Loth (from whom we are supposed to have derived the regional name Lothian), though it was almost certainly the capital or principal fort of the Votadini, a tribe which appears to have been unique in its ability to live without much conflict alongside the invading Romans. Those in support of the King Loth theory point to the standing stone called the Loth Stone (or the Cairndinnis Stone), some eight feet high, about 330 yards south-west of the hill. For all its fame and historical importance, this stone has been moved in modern times to enable the landowner to cultivate his fields more efficiently. Nearby is another stone which, in contrast, has given its name to the locality, being situated in Standingstone Farm. There are said to be about 35 upright stones in Lothian, of which a good many are found between the Traprain Law and Dunbar. The stone at Easter Broomhouse is a red sandstone monolith 2.7 feet high, on the summit of the broad ridge overlooking the coast around Dunbar. The three cup-marks on its western side are probably connected with religious practices (perhaps with sun-worship), but the deep grooves near the base are relatively modern, being made by the wire cable of a steam plough which appears to have been harnessed to it for leverage. The ancient upright on Kirklandhill is assumed to be a marker-stone, for it is obviously aligned to the peak of the North Berwick Law over which the sun would set at the summer solstice.

TEMPLE WOOD, Strathclyde B4

The circle of 13 stones at Temple Wood once consisted of 20 stones set in a 40-ft diameter ring centred on a cist, which had been rifled (no doubt for buried treasure) in the distant past and then excavated and reconstructed in modern times. Radiocarbon dating has suggested that this is one of the earliest circles in Scotland, even if it is far from being the most impressive. The most unusual element in the Temple Wood circle is a pecked-line carving on one of the stones, the design being that of a double spiral which continues over two adjacent sides of the single stone. Carvings on stones within ancient circles are very rare, though some indication of surface carving has been noted at Stonehenge. In Scotland, the later Pictish standing stones are often covered in strange symbols, including spiral-forms, as for example may be seen at Aberlemno, while many prehistoric rock carvings also illustrate simple and complex spirals, such as those at ACHNABRECK. Perhaps, therefore, this strange Temple Wood spiral was not contemporaneous with the building of the circle?

THURSO, Highland C2

What the historian Howey described as 'the classic Scotch story of repercussion' took place in Thurso in December 1718. Repercussion belongs to the occult tradition and maintains that wounds received by someone who has changed shape will manifest also in the body of the original shape when they return to it. Put briefly, this means that if a witch changes into the form of a cat, which then has its ear damaged in a fight, then when the witch returns to her female shape she will find her ear also damaged in a similar way. The 'Thurso witches' story related by Howey was about a merchant called Montgomerie, who lived in Scrabster and had petitioned the sheriff to rid his house of an infestation of cats. These were no ordinary cats, however, for they 'spoke among themselves'. Witchcraft was suspected, but the sheriff appears to have done nothing about the feline plague and so Montgomerie armed himself with a variety of sharp instruments and killed two of the cats, striking off the leg of a third. Shortly afterwards, a suspected witch called Helen Andrew died suddenly, while another drowned herself; a third old woman, Margaret Nin-Gilbert, was seen to have a leg missing. Inevitably, the three ladies were identified as part of the Thurso coven. Margaret's putrefied leg was taken as grisly evidence to the sheriff, who (not before time) ordered that she be imprisoned. A few days later she confessed, only to die in prison, no doubt of gangrene.

Index

All pictures in this book have been supplied by Images Colour Library (Leeds and London)

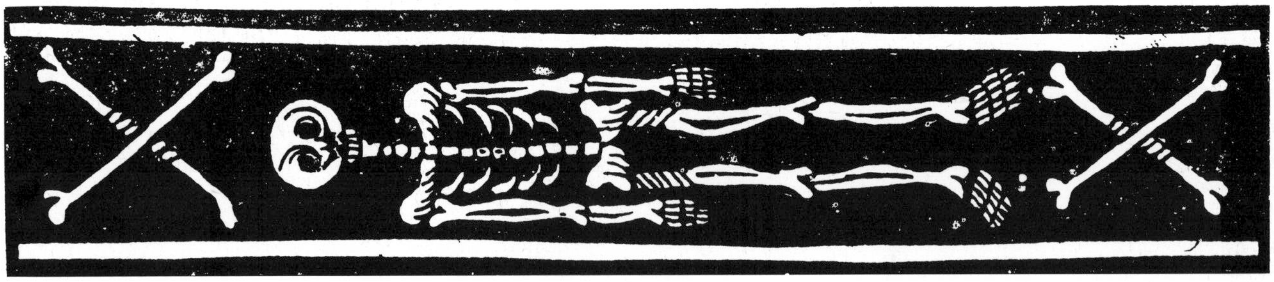